WHITETAIL

*Fundamentals
and Fine Points
for the Hunter*

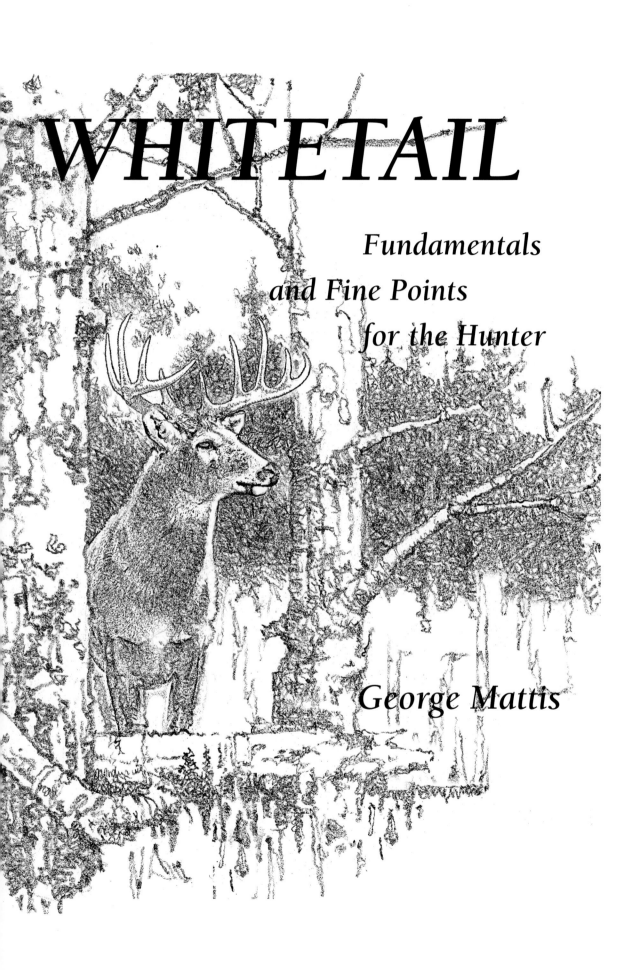

WHITETAIL

Fundamentals
and Fine Points
for the Hunter

George Mattis

Illustrations by Ron Finger
Cover photo by Rick Rupert

Published by

krause publications

700 East State Street • Iola, WI 54990-0001

Please call or write for a free catalog of publications. The toll-free number to place an order or request a free catalog is (800) 258-0929, or use our regular business number: (715) 445-2214.

Library of Congress Catalog Number: 2002105100

ISBN: 0-87341-919-7

Printed in the United States of America.

To THE HUNTER *whose heart hungers for the sight of a bounding buck, the first snowfall to cover the sere woodland floor, or the somberness of a November woods, I dedicate this book.*

Contents

	Introduction	9
	Preface	16
1.	The Still-Hunter	21
2.	The Small Hunting Group	43
3.	Gang Hunting	49
4.	Trail Watching	59
5.	Running Down Your Deer	87
6.	Snow Tracking	93
7.	Unusual Hunting Methods	102
8.	Lucky Breaks	115
9.	Hitting Them on the Run	124
10.	Hunting in Milder Climates	132
11.	Whitetails in the Arid States	139
12.	Wounded Deer	146
13.	After Your Deer is Down	155
14.	Buck Fever	161
15.	The Buck	167
16.	The Rut	176
17.	Wintering Whitetails	182
18.	Spring and Summer Whitetails	199
19.	Deer Guns and Sights	210
20.	Clothing and Equipment	219
21.	The Trend	225
22.	The Future	234

Whitetail – *Fundamentals and Fine Points for the Hunter*

Introduction

George Mattis was more than a hunter. He was a naturalist who studied deer to hunt them and hunted deer to study them. Mattis' lifestyle reflected the essence of the white-tailed deer: independence, self-sufficiency and simplicity, all underscored with a constant yearning for the solitude of the November deer forest.

Mattis observed, photographed and wrote about deer behavior for more than 67 years.

Born in Streator, Ill., in 1905, Mattis moved with his family to Sawyer County in northern Wisconsin in 1918. Growing up on a small farm in the middle of a logged-over wilderness, Mattis' earliest impressions of whitetails must have been scant because the deer population was low compared with today. In 1920, when Mattis killed his first deer, 69,479 Wisconsin hunters tagged 20,025 bucks.

In a February 1982 interview, just months before he died, Mattis told me about his early fascination with whitetails.

"As children we saw them on our way to and from grade school," said Mattis. "To me they appeared like overgrown cottontail rabbits with their supple bodies and continuous nibbling on browse as they filtered through the brush."

"Most every able-bodied man or youth was a deer hunter during the '20s. But my interest in whitetails went a bit beyond merely hunting them during the deer season. My interest in them during the off-season was just as intense."

Mattis recalled how he'd take evening walks along a railroad track to observe deer that browsed along the right-of-way. He studied them in their winter deer-yards and at cattle salt licks in early spring. He remembered learning that deer were easiest to spot during summer, when their reddish coats contrasted sharply with green foliage.

Mattis earned his earliest hunting knowledge while attending a deer stand with his older brother.

"I learned to sit quietly, be patient and endure the weather. I felt I played a part in any kill he made," said Mattis. "Later I made short drives for him, and when I was successful in driving a deer onto him, I felt some measure of elation. I soon became a responsible member of our deer-hunting group."

Mattis called his first buck "somewhat of a fluke." An older brother had put Mattis on a stand with directions to remain quiet until he returned.

"It was a chilly morning and I soon became a bit cold, so I moved about in an attempt to keep warm," said Mattis. "I saw a buck come along, and he likewise spotted me. Suddenly I remembered I was to remain quiet. The buck was determined to cross the dirt road where I was stationed, so he ran parallel to it in order to avoid me. I likewise ran parallel to the buck. He decided to cross the road, and did so just a matter of a few yards ahead of me."

"I shot, undoubtedly from my hip, and down he went on the frozen road where he knocked himself out. The bullet just grazed his shoulders and stunned him momentarily, but the hard fall put him down. When my brother came through, the buck was on his feet and ready to go. My brother finished him off. I learned two early lessons here: one, to remain still at a stand, and two, to be sure your game is down to stay."

The deer population changed dramatically for the better after the early 1920s, and Mattis went on to kill many Wisconsin bucks. Although the deer population changed, Mattis did not. He lived a simple bachelor's existence in a one-story brick home near Birchwood.

"I just married the great outdoors," he frequently said.

In a letter, Mattis' friend, outdoor writer Joel Vance, reflected on the quiet deer man:

"I met him through my aunt, who retired to a home on Birch Lake and entertained an endless string of visitors, among whom was George. We hit it off and went fishing back on Thirty Three Creek, a brook trout stream. George was a tireless, stocky little guy who … knew his country better than anyone."

"A lifelong bachelor, he lived in a tidy little house, drove a tidy little car. His gear was as well-worn as he was — but just as tidy. He took care of things."

"George had just heard that Outdoor Life Books would publish his deer-hunting book when I first met him. It would go on to be the best-selling book they ever published, and he'd later do a revision."

"But he always remained the same, in the same little house, prowling the backwoods the way he'd done for 60 years or more. You couldn't change George by making him wealthy — he'd been wealthy his whole life, incomparably rich from the treasures that the woods and waters gave him."

In an article in the Eau Claire Leader-Telegram, Dave Carlson described the working space in Mattis' home:

"Furniture? Why he's got a folding card table and two chairs, an old couch, an easy chair, lamp, and a modest collection of books and magazines stacked on shelves and the floor. In the corner behind the door is a typewriter on a stand."

"Through another open door, though, there is a huge set of white-tailed deer antlers hanging on a wall … If you are hung up on material things, you would never believe you are in the home and working place of a man whose first book, *Whitetail*, has become a classic that went through eight printings. … "

Like the whitetail, Mattis rose early each day. But unlike the whitetail, he spent only half the day amidst wildlife and plants. But that's half a day more than most of us accomplish.

Also enviable was that he looked about 20 years younger than his age. I have a feeling that good tracking snow, the sight of leaping bucks and prime venison roast greatly contributed to his youthfulness.

Mattis made a living out of deer hunting and trout fishing — a dream most of us never accomplish. From his northwoods retreat he wrote his regular column on outdoor recreation for *Sports & Recreation* magazine. At the time of his death, he was writing a new book, *Excursions in Nature*, which remains unpublished.

For more than a half-century, Mattis never missed a deer-hunting season except for the years he spent studying journalism at the University of Wisconsin and for his military term serving with the Third Armored Division in Europe during World War II, during which he received the Purple Heart. When Mattis returned to America, it seemed he became as much a part of deer season as the deer themselves. You will find *Whitetail: Fundamentals and Fine Points for the Hunter* in more than a half-million homes, resorts, cottages and deer shacks.

The original edition was written over a two-year period. At first, national book publishers were not interested, because it didn't read like the common how-to books of the time. Mattis received a break when Alfred A. Knopf Inc., recommended the book to John Sill, publisher and editor of Outdoor Life Books. Sill contacted Mattis, and the relationship produced one of the 20th century's classic deer books.

When the first edition of *Whitetail* appeared in Fall 1969, it went through eight printings and sold more than 200,000 copies. Like many outdoorsmen in the 1960s, Mattis read Thoreau and Leopold, and placed the whitetail and its hunting in a broad ecological context for the first time. Consequently, many nonhunters contributed to the dramatic sales. The revised, 1980 edition received enthusiastic praise from outdoor columnists in more than 100 reviews across the United States and Canada.

Although Mattis loved the camaraderie of deer camp, he preferred to hunt solo or still-hunt with his best friend and deer-hunting partner, Dr. Noland Eidsmoe, of Rice Lake. One of Mattis' greatest contributions to the literature on deer and deer hunting revolves around his emphasis on the virtues of solo hunting:

"The science of still-hunting is being somewhat neglected today because of the trend of sociability in all our outdoor recreations. But the camaraderie of gang hunting is often maintained at the cost of the success of the individual; and the hunting pattern of the group becomes something of a standard ritual from which no single member must depart. Consequently, the routine hunt goes on day after day with little regard to weather conditions or any other situations that might suggest a needed change in hunting plans."

"In contrast is the flexibility of the solo hunter who plans his hunt from day to day and even from hour to hour to take advantage of weather change, deer movement or hunter concentration on his hunting grounds."

"If the solo hunter scores better, it is because he hunts better."

Mattis always believed that the solo hunter made quicker and cleaner kills of deer not running scared with high levels of adrenaline. Why do these solo deer hunters score every year? Because they catch whitetails completely off guard. As Mattis observed, they are in "full possession of their senses."

In a classic article, he wrote, "Whoever is idle or resting, the hunter or deer, is the one that has full possession of his senses. It is the moving hunter or deer that is readily seen or heard by the other. If the hunter remembers this basic fact, he can expect to see more whitetails, especially bucks, for the good, clean shots that count."

Mattis also noted that, by being unattached to any group, solo hunters can be extremely versatile in their hunting practices. They can enter small timber patches overlooked by the group hunters. They can change their hunting methods and grounds whenever conditions or the spirit warrant. They can appraise situations quickly and make the best of them — without a lot of needless opinions.

Solo hunting meshed well with Mattis' naturalist-observer role. He never entered the forest just to get a buck. During his lonely trail-watching vigil, he took great delight in watching weasels, "the Lilliputian gangsters of the forest," prowl the snowshoe trail. With his back against an aspen tree, he witnessed ruffed grouse burst forth from dense foliage. Young porcupines clinging to small sagging saplings provided the lone Mattis with a pleasant break in the early morning hours. Foxes frequently came down the deer trails Mattis watched, as did brush wolves on rare occasions. Mattis fondly recalls the day he saw a mink wrestling with a large walleyed pike "in a mad fury of spray, fur, and fins." While on his stand, playful chickadees popped out of nowhere and amused the solitary Mattis as he patiently waited for a whitetail to appear. The solitary deer hunter, Mattis tells us, not only becomes a keen observer of wildlife, but takes a grandstand seat where he can observe the foibles of many deer hunters who pass by in an endless parade, pounding the forest floor and unfortunately remaining detached from everything wild.

Mattis enjoyed the utter silence of the autumn woods, the cherished hush of forested terrain. In the eerie silence of the deer forest, his senses became attuned to the muted activity of wildlife. Unlike the pseudo-outdoorsmen loaded with all manner of accoutrements from the sports shop, Mattis traveled alone in silence with the bare essentials.

The lone still-hunter, Mattis explained, "gets as much satisfaction from the hunt itself as he does from bagging his quarry. He is actually more than just a huntsman out to get a deer; he is a man with more than an ordinary love for the solitude of autumn woods. So content is he with his lot that he is unwilling to share it with others … It's a great sport whether or not you get a deer … Enjoying the outdoors, having a safe experience and cooperating in a friendly manner with landowners is the important thing."

Above all, he urged an aesthetic appreciation of our remaining wilderness, and to study nature from an ecological point of view. He rightly insisted that "we have spent the youthful energy of our pioneer past in striving to subdue the raw outdoors; and in our anxiety to do so, we overlooked the fact that we could do much better by learning to live with our natural heritage instead of subjugating it to short-sighted, selfish ends. Where ecology was once understood by only a few, today it is the concern of all of us."

Mattis clung to the traditions of the outdoor clan with a certain reverence, and like T. S. Van Dyke and Larry Koller, he passed them along for future generations of deer hunters to nurse and perpetuate. He read with great delight Larry Koller's *Shots at Whitetails* and Jack O'Connor's books on big-game hunting, appreciating their practical lessons. He admired the classic deer prints of Bob Kuhn, Ned Smith and Carl Rungius. Leaning toward the naturalist's love of deer, he preferred the books of Leonard Lee Rue III. It's not surprising that in deer rifle preference, Mattis chose perhaps the most traditional of all deer rifles: the Winchester lever-action in .30-30.

He hastened to add, however, "My attachment to the .30-30 is not without some sentiment. The gun is the right weight for me, especially for still-hunting, but I am aware of — and willing to accept — its limitations."

Mattis knew well the bend of many trout streams and the fork of many deer trails. He knew the deer forests of our Eastern and Western states. He sampled the trout streams and deer forests of England, Scotland and Germany as well. After 50 years of deer hunting and trout fishing, George Mattis brilliantly emphasized one basic fact of life: "There are more tensions released, anguishes soothed, and racking decisions realized on our fishing waters and in our deer forests than in the offices of psychiatrists or family consultants, or in the offices of all the other trouble shooters for our ailing humanity."

Mattis described one particular whitetail he shot while it reached high for sumac on its back legs. At the Winchester's report, the whitetail slowly slumped to its back haunches. It then fell slowly forward with its front legs folding peacefully beneath its body.

"Never before or after have I seen any animal yield to death so easily," he wrote.

On Aug. 13, 1982, at 77, Mattis yielded peacefully to death. He died while playing cribbage with his brother in his hometown. In a eulogy, Vance wrote, "He died the way he had lived — quietly and without fuss. ... Only in the woods and in the legacy of his heartfelt writing was he a giant."

Indeed, George Mattis was a giant among deer hunters. Like the sudden crack of a .30-30 Winchester on a crisp November day, his words echo loudly and clearly among American deer hunters.

Robert Wegner
Deer Valley

REFERENCES

Carlson, Dave. "Widely-Read Birchwood Writer is 'Married' to The Outdoors." **Eau Claire Leader – Telegram**. 12-13-1980

Henry, Steve. "Eulogy for George Mattis / He Loved to Hunt and Fish." Incomplete newspaper clipping.

Leys, Ron. "Here's a Book for Wisconsin Deer Hunters." **Milwaukee Journal**. 10-26-80.

Mattis, George. **Whitetail: Fundamentals and Fine Points for the Hunter**. Illustrated by William Reusswig. New York. Popular Science/Outdoor Life Book Division, 1969. 273 pp.

_____. **Whitetail: Fundamental and Fine Points for the Hunter**. Illustrated by William Reusswig. New York: Van Nostrand Reinhold Company, 1980. 248 pp. Revised Second Edition.

_____. "Whitetail! Lucky Breaks." **Georgia Sportsman**. November, 1979. pp. 14-15, 59-62.

_____. "Solo Hunting The Whitetail." **In Deer Hunting Across North America**. edited by Nick Sisley. New York: Freshnet Press, 1975. pp. 55-69.

_____. "The Persevering Solo Hunter." **Deer & Deer Hunting**. March/April, 1982. 5(4): 22-25

_____. "A Prime Buck and the Lay Naturalist." **Deer & Deer Hunting**. March/April, 1982. 5(4): 24-25.

_____. "My Phantom Buck." In **Excursions in Nature**. Unpublished manuscript.

Riis, Dick. "Whitetail Deer Book A Must!" **Outdoor Outlines**. St. Cloud, Minnesota.

Vance, Joel M. "George Mattis – Through the Eyes of a Friend." **OWAA Outdoors Unlimited**. October 1982. p. 13.

_____. Unpublished letter to Rob Wegner. 11 October 2001.

Wegner, Robert. "A Solo Deer Hunter." **Deer & Deer Hunting: Book 1**. Harrisburg: Stackpole Books, 1984. pp. 19-28.

_____. George Mattis: "A Solo Deer Hunter." **Deer & Deer Hunting**. March/April, 1982. 5(4): 14-20.

_____. **Wegner's Bibliography on Deer & Deer Hunting**. Wisconsin: St. Hubert's Press, 1990. 328 pp.

"Whitetail Author George Mattis Dies." **The Spooner Advocate**. 8-19-1982. p. 6.

"Woodlands and Trout Streams Have Lost a Companion." **The Rice Lake Chronotype**. Incomplete newspaper clipping. 1982.

Preface

*T*HERE was a time when the American hunter lived closer to the environment of his quarry than he now does. Because the hunt served him some practical and obvious end, he looked upon woods lore as the tool of his profession. Such a man was ever conscious of the simple phenomena in his outdoor living. He was quick to observe a change in wind direction, was aware of the moon's phases, could interpret tomorrow's weather by today's sunset. He sensed when his game was flighty and when it was restful and calm, and he knew how the weather affected the movement of wildlife.

The serious hunter willingly footed a backwoods trail during inclement weather, or kept a lonely surveillance over a deer runway till dusk because he knew here were his best chances for seeing a deer. In short, his success as a provider of game for the table depended upon knowledge gained from his personal experiences in the wilderness.

Because wild game for food no longer plays a great role in our economy, much acquired outdoor lore has been lost to the modern hunter. The hunt now takes on a totally new significance in our urbanized society; it has become primarily a much needed recreation for a large sector of our outdoor-minded population.

Skyscrapers and asphalt are not the answer to the man seeking final contentment. He yearns for a plot of green, an untrammeled scenic view, or a mere glimpse of wildlife. Who does not dream that he will someday own a wilderness cabin to which he can retreat when the pressure of civilization becomes unendurable? We are still properly creatures of the outdoors, but we have become enmeshed in the intricate machinery of modern economics, and we find it difficult to escape its demands upon us.

What we need now, more than ever before, is a closer involvement with the outdoors. It is not sufficient for good recreation merely to take a hunting trip if we do not submit to it completely. We get from the hunt no more than we put into it, and the man who has troubled to learn something about his quarry is not only more successful in his role of hunter, but he also participates more eagerly in the chase for a more enjoyable recreation.

When a man makes a studied effort for a favorable still-hunt, trains his eyes on a distant moving twig, or strains his ears to catch a faint sound far down the runway, he is a complete hunter for the time, whatever his occupation otherwise. And this is good for him.

The American hunter is, indeed, fortunate in having such an adaptable big-game animal as the whitetail deer. It has developed those characteristics in its nature which are most important for its survival. Unlike other of our large game animals, it does not languish in a changing environment, but rather seeks to move into an area to fill a void. The whitetail is represented on our continent by some thirty subspecies, and its distribution throughout the United States is pretty general except for parts of the West.

It is at home in heavy forests, brushy marginal lands, most any available cover found in agricultural areas, swamplands of the South, and the arid country of the West and Southwest. Its behavior is much the same in all this diverse habitat, though methods for hunting it necessarily vary because of cover and terrain differences.

The whitetail appeals to every type of outdoorsman from the rugged still-hunter of the back country to the occasional gunner in the densely peopled areas. And the followers include inveterate riflemen as well as devoted shotgun men. Whether you pursue the sport alone or are a member of a congenial group that prefers a sociable hunt, the whitetail fills your requirements.

Your quarry can be a most difficult adversary at times so that even the experienced hunter's patience is tested to the limit; then, on rarer occasions, it might be intercepted in a less spirited mood by the beginner hunter who feels elated over his easy success. As no hunter can be certain of filling his bag, so also no participant, however untried, need feel himself inadequate in the chase. Success is generously distributed among all who share in the sport to make the whitetail America's favorite game animal.

It is my desire to make the reader of this book more intimately acquainted with the whitetail, to extend to him a knowledge of his quarry a little beyond what it might take to get his deer. But regardless of his success, the man totally involved in the pursuit will have a good hunt.

WHITETAIL

Fundamentals
and Fine Points
for the Hunter

The Still-Hunter

*H*UNTING is one of man's oldest professions and, though the modern hunter relies little on the subsistence furnished him from the wilderness, there still remains in each of us a desire for elementary self-sufficiency, which begs expression. What man does not satisfy a hidden ego when he plunks down fish or game on the kitchen table to elicit admiring gasps from the household? Time was when the only good man was the good provider of game for the larder, and this sentiment has not been entirely lost to our civilization. This wholesome desire for independence and self-sufficiency is best expressed in those individuals who prefer to hunt alone.

Solo hunters are becoming the minority in the woods these days, for the modern trend is toward group hunting with its regimentation, fellowship, and varying degrees of fanfare. There was a time when a large portion of the men afield was unattached to any closely knit hunting group. Many of these men camped in the same deer country year after year, or else they stayed with friends or relatives who resided there.

Only a few years ago one such dedicated veteran of this vintage stopped in the neighborhood of his old hunting grounds and visited with my father, who also did much hunting in this area. The eighty-odd years with which this man was now burdened did not lessen his interest in the country he saw grow up from fire-ridden barrens to a respectable stand of young timber. He covered those ridges and scanned those swamps for about thirty consecutive deer seasons. My father hunted with him only once, back in the twenties, but like all men who are more than passingly familiar with a specific deer country, they had a world in common. It is this familiarity and love of the land that determines the still-hunter.

In those earlier days, the individualist hunted his country in his own way season after season, and he had little desire to enter strange grounds. Undoubtedly, the opening up of roads in the backcountry and the common use of automobiles have done much to broaden the hunting grounds for all sportsmen. At any rate, the automobile encourages hunting in new territory each season, and strange grounds are not especially conducive to good still-hunting. In time, the mass of redcoats became extremely mobile, changing its hunting grounds daily, or even several times a day. Group hunting, in one form or another, was the natural consequence.

For the most part, those relatively few men who take to the field alone today are the remnants of earlier days. They are usually old-timers whose sole pleasure comes from hunting rather than from any conviviality associated with the sport. Many of these oldsters I know are in their seventies, and they are usually passed off as being much too aged to gain acceptance in the society of the younger and more energetic hunters. Still, these veterans carry on, getting the utmost from their hunts, and they are happily unmindful of the stepped-up tempo about them. Occasionally, a newcomer, who for some reason or other breaks rank from his group, joins and perpetuates the small clan of lone hunters.

The unattached whitetail hunter has very definite advantages over the gang hunter, for he usually confines his efforts to deer territory with which he is thoroughly acquainted. Since any hunter's success comes in direct ratio to the amount of time he spends under ideal conditions in good deer area, the lone still-hunter has the better odds, for unlike the organized party hunter, he puts in full time from the moment he enters the woods until the time he unloads his gun at the close of the day. This is in considerable contrast to the time-consuming procedure usually involved in group hunting, and especially in deer driving.

The individual who goes it alone is unfettered by any time limits, appointments, or any of a dozen things that can come up when he is part of a group. Being strictly on his own, he is free to change his tactics or direction of travel to suit the occasion anytime he desires, and he suffers no loss of hunting time in making these changes. Whenever he feels a bit tired, he can rest on some vantage point, and even when he lunches on his cold sandwich he is exposed to deer country under the most favorable hunting conditions.

The still-hunter learns to become self-reliant, observing, and somewhat of a lay naturalist, and, as a consequence, he develops a keen appreciation for the outdoors. This is not always true of all members of large hunting groups, some of whom are attracted to the chase because of the camaraderie it affords rather than for the love of the outdoors or the sheer sport of hunting.

There is no doubt that the solo hunter fares better bagwise through the years than do the individuals of any gang, although this fact is not always recognized. If any group of eight or ten men comes up with a full bag after the season's hunt, the story is bruited about with considerable acclamation. Yet, if the lone still-hunter kills his deer the first or second day out to fill his bag, his success is not heralded in equal manner.

It might truthfully be said that the inveterate still-hunter gets as much satisfaction from the hunt itself as he does from bagging his quarry. He is actually more than just a huntsman out to get his deer, and he is a man with more than ordinary love for the solitude of autumn woods. So content is he with his lot that he is unwilling to share it with others.

In group hunting, whether it be a drive or just a concentration of men in a given area each hunting on his own, the hunters strive to keep the whitetails on the move so that all participants have shooting opportunities. These are mostly running shots and, all too often, at great distances. This is in opposition to the still-hunter, who strives to contain the undisturbed game in the area he slowly and carefully probes. Under these ideal conditions, his single, well-placed shot at his unsuspecting quarry proves more effective than the results of those staccato reports he hears in the distance surrounding him.

Still-hunting differs as terrain and habitat vary. One can be proficient in his own bailiwick but something less when he leaves his home grounds. Not every man has the same patience required for slowly covering a limited area for the duration of a full day, and you will find differences in method even among confirmed still-hunters in an equal situation. Regardless of their individual peculiarities, they all have one thing in common when they take to the field with their guns: They tax their eyes more than they do their legs.

The solo hunter must plan his tactics according to weather conditions prevailing, type of terrain he encounters, and the information he gathers from any deer sign observed. In addition to this, he will seek to confine his efforts to such areas that have not been heavily driven or overhunted in recent days. Ordinarily, he will have no difficulty in finding such spots, either in the more remote country not conveniently accessible for group hunting, or else in the many available small pockets so often bypassed by big gangs.

The Whitetail's Senses

The man attempting to surprise a whitetail in range for a good shot depends largely on his sense of vision. Ears help the hunter little except when he himself is standing and the deer is moving. And a man's sense of smell is of no use to him whatever in the chase, unless a buck brushes his musky-smelling metatarsal glands against the hunter's nose.

The sense of smell is most developed in the whitetail, with hearing and sight following in close order. Yet, this is not always the order of their importance to the still-hunter. The deer's sense of sight is extremely keen in picking up a

moving object at a great distance on a normally clear day, and this is what creates a problem for the hunter. At close range, however, say about fifty feet, the animal is unable to identify a man not in motion, especially if the man's outline is broken by a tree trunk or any cover. Such a man when seen in the open arouses curiosity and suspicion in the deer, and while the strange object is under scrutiny, the whitetail might get a whiff of the man's scent or else catch a slight movement in him to complete a picture of danger. This weakness in a deer's eyesight at close range is of little benefit to the hunter if his quarry has detected him from a great range and already fled the scene. Slow movements of the still-hunter are most essential for an approach to his game.

I have many times come very close to whitetails that were bedded down under windfallen trees where they had little vision for any great distance. Their gifted noses and ears failed them because of some or all such factors as very damp weather, adverse wind, or my noiseless walking.

The sense of smell in deer, practically nil in the hunter, is at least equally important for the hunter to surmount. It can detect danger when neither its eyes nor ears have sensed it. Sometimes a scent alone puts the animal into flight, and it is a clincher when either sight or hearing has already alerted the deer. Here, the hunter's only recourse is to walk into any wind so that none of his scent will be carried ahead of his progress.

The deer's hearing power, though far keener than man's, might be classed last in importance to the deer for its effectiveness against the still-hunter. Here, the man has some leeway in selecting a route for a noise-less stalk, the aid of a favorable breeze, or the quiet footing of soft snow or damp ground. Or if he is trail-watching, then the problem of noise is completely licked. The hunter cannot cope as effectively with the other two senses in his game. There is little he can do about the erratic air currents in the woods which so often betray his presence to the game even in a well-planned stalk. Nor is there much he can do to keep himself from being seen while in the field, especially if his quarry is not preoccupied with browsing or loafing.

It is not often that the use of any single one of these senses is sufficient to satisfy the deer of an immediate presence of danger. A whitetail likes to see what its nose or ears have detected, and it also likes to smell or hear what it sees. And this delay in escape, slight as it might be, caused by the animal's curiosity is advantageous to the huntsman.

It is interesting to observe just how the whitetail uses these senses in appraising the danger element in any situation. In many instances, I have been able to come upon a loitering or browsing group where I could watch them at close range. Starting from a point where the animals were completely unaware of my presence, I had the opportunity to study their reactions as I slowly and carefully projected myself into the scene.

The snap of a twig alerts the deer instantly, and they nervously search about for the source of the noise. It takes but a little time before they settle back to their former composure, however. Another snap of a twig and their heads are brought up sharply, and now they mill about definitely alerted to some obtrusion. If I expose even part of myself here, they dash off with no restraint.

In like situations, I have often exposed myself to deer without making any noise. Now they appear just as alert as though they had heard a warning sound, but they seem more curious than startled. Here, the snap of a twig is all they need to complete the image of danger.

The whitetail's nose has caused many still-hunters to shake clenched fists in vengeance in the direction of a whistling snort. Here, the quarry is well alerted even when danger is not seen or heard. The huntsman is defeated, for he knows his stamping buck is waiting for any slight movement or sound from the intruder. And the animal is willing to expose his general location in exchange for any supplementary information the stalker might give. The whitetail usually wins out in the waiting contest, for he has the patience to wait and the advantage to see, while the hunter gains nothing by waiting; and he brings the situation to the usual end if he attempts to get himself in position to see his deer.

There are times when, due to terrain, footing, or weather conditions, some, or even all, of the whitetail's senses prove less than efficient in detecting the approach of an enemy. And again there are times, especially during cold, crisp, quiet days, when the animals are in top spirits and all their senses readily respond to the slightest stimuli. But by and large the normal situation lies somewhere in between, where the hunter and the hunted are somewhat on acceptable terms. It is on these grounds that the still-hunter parries with the three senses of the elusive whitetail deer, hoping to profit by some strategy to gain the better odds.

The slower the hunter travels, the more advantageous it is for him to move into any wind, however slight it might be. Scent accumulates about a man if he lingers for long in one spot, and if there is no breeze to carry it away or dissipate it, he will soon be surrounded by the scent for a considerable circumference. The effect of this concentration of man odor, when it is wafted to a deer's nostrils by some slight erratic air current, is experienced by most hunters. Such is the case when a man pauses on a vantage point for a few minutes. He hears and sees nothing and is about to move on. Then comes the loud snort of an alarmed deer that has just intercepted the spreading scent.

This scent problem holds true, too, in an area containing numerous hunters where the animals are pretty well alerted by human odor pervading the woods. The deer have learned to tolerate this threat to their safety, and they might even accept it with surprising calm. Nevertheless, they are aware of its presence, and the huntsman will find it most difficult to surprise his game for a good shot under these conditions. Even those animals bedded down or resting, seemingly relaxed, are a bit jumpy. The addition of any slight disturbance the still-hunter might make in their proximity is enough to trigger a hasty exit. This is why still-hunting in heavily driven areas is not too effective.

It is not always practical nor necessary for the hunter to move directly into the wind. Quartering into the wind in zigzag fashion gives one more favorable coverage of a given area. If the hunter travels directly into the breeze he might reach the end of his territory in an hour or so, and then he must return downwind to another starting point. A full half-day's stalking could be had here in one trip if the man made long quartering thrusts to the right and left of wind direction.

Hunting With Your Eyes

The still-hunter works over the grounds with his eyes. He uses his legs only to carry him over the terrain he has carefully scrutinized. Each time he comes upon a change of grounds he must pause to scan the area about him. It is best to adopt a systematic procedure in searching the terrain effectively. A quick search from left to right will suffice to detect any movement of game within shooting distance, and a standing or browsing whitetail at close range should be spotted at once. Now a thorough study of the thicket should be made, beginning with the foreground, sweeping back and forth in a wide arc and extending the search further into the background with each sweep of the head. Such an examination is best made from any convenient elevation, however slight.

After the survey is completed, and this could take several minutes, the hunter moves on at a slow pace, picking his way carefully in order to avoid snapping any twigs underfoot or brushing against overhanging branches. His movements, like those of a bird watcher, must be smooth and slow, for these are less likely to attract attention to any wildlife about him.

It must be remembered that the still-hunter is looking for standing, browsing, or bedded-down deer. If he is just looking for any whitetails, chances are he will see them more easily — but they will be mostly out of range and running. There will be a difference in your mode of walking and searching if you make up your mind you are seeking the standing target only.

It is hardly possible for any man walking through the woods to refrain from making a disturbing noise sometime or other. The experienced still-hunter will pause for several minutes after such an incident, for he knows the whitetail, if within hearing distance, is now awaiting further evidence of an intruder. A deer's memory is somewhat short, and if there is no follow-up of disturbance, the animal will soon dismiss its anxiety. It is the series of man-made noises that is the bane of the huntsman.

In canvassing deer country, the hunter should avail himself of any high ground along his general course of travel. Those slight depressions on either side of him are worth some investigation even though they take him a bit off course. It is in these depressions, sometimes hemmed in by small ridges, where the whitetail can best be surprised. These shallow basins, especially if located on high, flat ground, are ideal sanctums for the unmolested animals. Such spots are pretty well insulated against outside noises and odors. On many occasions, during a buck season, I have spent considerable time studying a group of antlerless deer in such seclusion.

A big advantage for the solo hunter is his ability to follow successfully in the wake of heavy group hunting. Deer driving can become very noticeably ineffective after the hunting season has progressed for some time. About the middle of the season, gang hunters start scurrying about, searching for fresh areas to infiltrate. After one unsuccessful group leaves a tract of deer country, another gang moves in with great anticipation, but often with equally poor results.

The fact is that after the whitetails have been shunted about day after day in any territory, many of them gradually enter secluded pockets where they might remain for the duration of the season if not molested. These odd spots could be the thickets in a small triangle of only several acres bounded by roads, lakes, or farmland. They could be points of land projecting into lakes or wet swamps, the thickets along a fence line adjacent to a pasture, or the wooded pasture itself now devoid of livestock.

I remember finding many such hideouts, some of them practically in my backyard, after I had spent the season scouring the remote hinterlands. Once an old buck had taken refuge for the entire season in a portion of the pasture scarcely 400 yards from the house. At night he fed on a dense clump of sumac in full view of the farmstead. During the day he withdrew to a thicket just outside the fence line. There was nothing here to disrupt his simple routine, and like a true slacker, he let the season go by, sitting it out smugly on the sidelines.

The last day of one hunting season, I cut across a four-acre wedge formed by the intersection of a highway and a railroad. As I skirted a small swamp that formed the other boundary of this triangle, I started a veritable explosion of shaking brush and bobbing flags. Seven deer bounded out from this small retreat. There were no tracks leading in, and the snow was two days old, so it appeared the animals had hoped to see the season through in the safety of this confinement. This withdrawal to odd recesses is common with whitetails, especially the wily old bucks, when the large deer areas are heavily and continually hunted. The animals seem to recognize a pattern in the hunters' routine, and they find respite from disturbance by retiring to the edges. Most hunters, meanwhile, hopefully probe the depths of the big country, thinking that somewhere in the deep hinterlands they will find the whitetails concentrated in happy numbers.

The small, often neglected pockets are most ideal for the lone hunter. Because of their size and success possibilities, the man can well afford to appraise each nook carefully for the most effective approach. Usually, too, the deer in such small confinements are reluctant to leave their retreats unless they are roused into flight by rash intrusion.

Some of the older still-hunters I know spend their entire efforts carefully probing these lesser grounds. This is especially productive when the legal bag is bucks only, for any animal with a noticeable rack soon learns his hide is a prime target. The seasoned patriarchs long past their physical peak are often taken here. After a buck has attained a respectable age and becomes aware that he is a marked animal, he is willing to forsake his species and lead the life of a recluse. He has, perhaps, attained the age where he is less interested in does than he is in his own safety. He becomes fat and lazy from inactivity, his reflexes might be on the decline, but from his years of hazardous living he has acquired the simple knack of self-preservation with a minimum of exertion.

Sometimes, if these refuges are partly open like pasture lands, a buck will bed down on a hillside under some scraggly growth or alongside short shrubbery. From his elevated couch he might occupy his time watching highway traffic or studying the movements of hunters as they gather in groups to plan an attack on the big deer area across the road. All of the activity outside the sphere of the buck's limited domain causes him little concern. The white-tail becomes uneasy only when his immediate grounds are invaded. Even then, if the trespasser seems unaware of the deer's presence, or makes no overt attempt to approach, it is likely the animal will trust the security of his bed.

When a number of men scour any deer territory it does not matter greatly where the animals might be so long as some individual is able to jump them. Once they are spooked, most members of the party have equal shooting possibilities. The lone stalker must find his own game without spooking it, and he must know where to confine his efforts in accordance with the animal's habits. The whitetail is strictly a creature of habit, and when he is not often disturbed, his living routine does not vary greatly from day to day. And his normal behavior, too, is somewhat different from that of the deer subjected to intense hunting pressure.

When Whitetails Feed

It is generally accepted that whitetails stir about and feed mostly during the evenings, early mornings, and sometimes during the night, while during the daylight hours they confine themselves to inactivity and seclusion. Actually, it is the security factor that largely governs their feeding, and this would quite normally exclude the broad-daylight hours.

The whitetail's response to security when feeding is easily observed on fields where the animals habitually come to graze on young, tender grasses. They usually venture on fields adjacent to busy highways after sundown, or if the fields are large they might start to feed on the distant margins long before sunset. On isolated farmlands where there is little to disrupt their daily routine, the animals are sometimes not averse to feeding in the open hay lands in the light of high noon.

In the backwoods country away from farmlands with their tender grass growth, the deer's feeding hours are also largely confined to early mornings and late evenings, but the hunter cannot hope to find a concentration of feeding animals in any one area. The feeding grounds are any relatively sunny spots conducive to young growth suitable for browse — the margins of swamps, the flats along streams, edges of old logging camp clearings, logging slashings, or any glen where young growth is not hampered by dense timber.

The browsing hours are by all odds the best time for the hunter to find his game for most favorable shooting. The fact that the animal is on its feet and not in its bed is a big advantage for the hunter. And the shaking of twigs or any slow movement of the browsing deer itself is sure to catch the eye of the alert hunter.

The feeding animal is preoccupied and, although he constantly interrupts his rapid nibbling with furtive glances and ever-twitching ears, he is still unable to detect any approaching danger as readily as when he is bedded down or idling along a trail. The strong factor favoring the man still-hunting in remote or neglected areas is that here he might hope to find his game relaxed to the point where daytime browsing is not unusual for the species.

A group of whitetails feeding in a thicket is not too difficult to approach if the hunter keeps his eyes on them while he slowly advances under any available cover. Each animal seems to depend upon the others for detecting any signs of danger, for they constantly glance about to check on each others' movements. When they do raise their heads to survey the outer area, this attempt at vigilance appears somewhat mechanical and routine. For the moment he is reaching for browse the whitetail is completely off guard, and the hunter can now advance a few steps. It is probable that the deer does not hear well when chewing his browse, for often he will stop short with his mouth bristling with protruding twigs. Now he listens intently, but only briefly if all seems well. It is only when he fidgets about without chewing his mouthful of browse that he is aware of some infringement on his privacy. This caution in the one animal becomes contagious for the group. Now they mill about nervously, desperately searching a cause for alarm. Any slight movement the hunter makes at this point sends the animals bounding off in unison.

Weather and Whitetails

Weather conditions are an all-important agent in influencing temperament of all game, and the whitetail deer is especially susceptible to behavior moods brought on by the elements. The hunter learns from experience that on certain days he finds more than usual temerity in his quarry, while at other times the white flicker of a tail over a distant rise marks the nearest approach he can make to his nervous game.

One of the best opportunities the still-hunter has for coming upon a walking or browsing deer is during a heavy mist or gently falling rain in the absence of any wind. The whitetail is farsighted, and any obstruction, however slight, moving through the air greatly impairs his vision. His sense of smell becomes considerably incapacitated in heavy atmosphere, and the moisture-laden air muffles the subdued sounds the hunter makes in the soft, wet leaves. The animal seems to accept all this as a cloak for his own protection, and he leaves his bed to move about freely with little restraint or fear. If the precipitation is something more than a mere drizzle, the hunter might catch his deer flat-footed at very close range, and the once high-spirited buck can become as gentle and mild-mannered as a farm deer.

Most hunters prefer to clear the woods during a rain, but the avid still-hunter properly attired for the occasion is willing to suffer some discomforts in return for the better odds of success. Here, the hunter seeks the animal's likely feeding grounds, or if he prefers to avoid the moisture-laden brush, he can walk the side roads, logging trails, or the rail-roads traversing the deer country. The

animals are on the move now, and they leave the dense thickets for the browse of the open country. In their stirring they spend as much time walking as they do feeding. This is the high tide of whitetail movement.

The reverse of this situation, however, is true if there is a heavy rain, especially one accompanied by strong winds. The animals now retire to the backcountry where they bed down or just stand under what cover is available to them, often seeking shelter under the protective branches of evergreens. Here they await the passing of the storm with a very minimum of activity.

Most redcoats believe they have it made when the season opens with a blanket of snow on the ground. The association of snow with hunting is natural with the mass of men invading the north woods. Many of the men participating in the annual chase have little or no experience with whitetails except during the open season on them, a time when there usually is snow on the ground. And, somehow, from the association of "tracking snow" with the whitetails comes the common impression that a deer season without snow is something akin to a deer season without deer.

Undoubtedly, the model hunting situation would call for about three to four inches of soft snow occasionally freshened with an added light cover as the season progresses. This, frankly, is more idealistic than realistic. Sometimes the season opens with a deluge of knee-deep snow, perhaps followed soon by an additional blanket of the white stuff. Then there could be the other extreme of only several inches of fluffy snow followed by a thaw, a heavy freeze, and the subsequent noisy crust. In between, sometimes, you get that tracking snow — that critical depth that does not hamper your hunting stride one whit, yet is substantial enough so that it does not evaporate before your hunting shakes are fully subsided late in the afternoon of your deer season opener.

Snow, generally, is not the magic factor that always works for the hunter's success. It is a definite advantage in aiding one to spot his quarry if it is within range of vision. It enables the hunter to observe deer signs and to follow the tracks of a particular animal. But most important of all, it mercifully reduces the loss of wounded animals. Aside from these benefits of snow cover, the task of approaching game can still remain a problem for the still-hunter The snow can be his every wish or it can be his very defeat. It

does give the lone hunter a wider spread of stalking conditions, both better and worse than does bare-ground hunting.

Too often, in the aftermath of a snowfall, the weather turns abruptly colder. The deer have been feeding heavily before and during the snowing period so they now bed down, and like a mink after the first snow of the trapping season, they lay tracks with great reluctance. They might hole up for two days, and the hunter strongly suspects his game has left the country. This could be termed the low tide in their activity. Then, as hunger urges them to their feet again, the whitetails emerge from nowhere during the night to track up the once barren-looking snow country.

The best snow conditions the still-hunter can hope for — in fact, the best conditions he can ever find in any weather situation — is a quiet falling snow with a thin white blanket already underfoot. This is it, and the man leaving the woods at this time simply admits his love for comfort is greater than his love for the hunt.

There is something both lonely and fascinating in probing the woods during a steady falling snow, the kind you hear gently grating on bare tree branches and ticking endlessly until your ears buzz from hearing these scarcely audible sounds.

The layer of soft snow almost completely absorbs all walking sounds made by even the careless stalker, and the white blanket gives him the needed contrasting background for sighting his game under the prevailing poor light conditions. There is also the tremendous advantage of being able to ascertain when deer are in the immediate area. Tracks age rapidly during a snowfall, and relatively fresh signs should put the hunter on the alert.

Now the whitetail is in no great hurry to cover ground. He feeds along an irregular course of travel, led to the left or right by tempting browse, ever sampling but never deciding which shrubbery yields the most satisfying mouthfuls. Occasionally, he pauses to look about, but his jaws continue working with the same rapidity as those of a nibbling rabbit. The whitetail is now thoroughly engrossed in his feeding. If ever he lets down his guard to the still-hunter, this is the time. His response to an intruder on his domain is one of surprise rather than of fear. His eyes seem no longer able to register the crisp image of danger.

I have seen deer so absorbed in feeding during falling snow that they appeared completely devoid of any traces of fear. Heavy atmosphere and fuzzy vision brought on by precipitation induces a state of indifference or else a sense of security in all wildlife. At any rate, the whitetail is now completely relaxed, and any attempts at self-preservation seem only overt but empty habitual expressions of caution, such as the constantly moving ears or the occasional quick glances over the shoulder.

A browsing deer, or any feeding animal for that matter, readily succumbs to even a fair-placed rifle shot, and the well-placed hit will most probably bring it down in its tracks. Once, during a snowfall, I chanced upon a six-point buck feeding on the maroon fruit clusters of staghorn sumac. The buck raised himself on his hind legs and, with neck outstretched, he nipped at the topmost velvety clusters of the fruit. Then he dropped down gracefully on all fours while he disposed of his mouthful. I took him at the base of his neck near the shoulder as he strained for a tidbit at the very top of the sumac. At the sound of the shot he very slowly crumbled to his haunches and retracted his long neck to his body. His squatting hulk tottered forward to complete the collapse, and he lay in an inert heap with his legs carefully folded under his body as though he expired peacefully in his bed. Never before or after have I seen any animal yield to death so easily.

An animal alerted to danger, or one that has been harried or slightly wounded, does not often die without considerable struggle even when hit with a well-placed shot. On one occasion, I shot a running buck through the heart, and he continued his dash for over 200 yards before he fell dead. One especially nervous buck, started by drivers, was coming toward my stand. He stopped abruptly when he spotted me, hesitated a bit and turned in the direction of the drivers. Again he stopped, turned broadside and stood in indecision with his tail twitching. Meanwhile, his adrenal glands must have been operating at top output. I got in a quick shot at about 120 yards with the .30/30 carbine, aiming for the shoulder. My buck pulled out in full flight, but his trail was well marked with blood spray. He traveled about 300 yards after the bullet shattered the lower half of his heart.

Often a wounded or hounded animal displays almost unbelievable stamina in bearing up under successive and well-placed shots. The still-hunter taking a deer by complete surprise is most likely to make a clean, quick kill, and very frequently with his first shot. No true sportsman takes even the slightest satisfaction in telling of leaving a wounded deer in the woods. A crippled animal is not a consolation prize for the unsuccessful hunter.

Even after the snowfall has ceased sometime during the night, if the temperature remains mild, deer will often browse throughout the next day when they have not been harassed. Fresh, fluffy snow and heavy air on a mild day always make for good still-hunting. One pleasant afternoon, warm enough for trout fishing, I came upon a spruce swamp where a concentration of deer had apparently not as yet been disturbed that season. The sun shone brightly on the sparkling new snow, and the dark coats of the animals along the swamp's margin showed up in sharp contrast, like a winter weasel against bare ground. Yet, the deer I encountered scattered about this veritable oasis were as docile as sheep.

It was a buck season only that fall, and the does and fawns were feeding singly as though none were related to the other. They merely walked or slowly trotted off my course of travel as I approached.

Then they would stand watching me, and after having been bored with my presence they would nonchalantly resume their feeding. One big doe, in particular, behaved like a bovine when I met her in a narrow neck between a spruce swamp and a deep pothole. She was feeding toward me and seemed concerned at the blockage of her passage. When she stood no more than forty feet off, I accommodated her by sidling to the edge of the pothole. This bit of backwoods courtesy was not unappreciated, for the gentle doe civilly moved to the edge of the spruce swamp. We brushed by each other at about ten gun lengths, and a carbine at that.

Such behavior in game is, of course, exceptional, but only because the weather conditions are exceptional. However, as the snow settles down and the air becomes crisp, the whitetail becomes his alert self again, and his daytime browsing now is certainly more restrained. The hunter will now have to search out his game much as he would on bare ground, but with the added advantage of being able to readily discern sign left by his quarry. Now he will save much time by passing more quickly over grounds barren of tracks, or where fresh sign is lacking. Old tracks, after all, indicate only where the animals have been. They are, in themselves, no proof that the deer are now in the immediate vicinity.

Often country well dotted with old slots proves disappointing to hunters, while an adjacent area just a mile off with less deer sign contains a concentration of the animals. The still-hunter learns to appraise his grounds, and is not carried away by abundant sign if there is not a fair sprinkling of fresh tracks mixed with the older slots. Once a man comes upon fresh sign, made no earlier than the past night, he should proceed with all stealth. Meandering tracks indicate the deer were feeding on the move. A good sprinkling of fresh sign in a thicket means they have paused here for some time to fill up on browse.

At this moment comes the test of the hunter's patience and skill. The odds are that the whitetails are close by, either feeding or else bedded down. The stalker can do no better than pause for at least a few minutes before making another move. This is the ideal time for a brief rest, preferably with one's back steadied against a tree trunk while the area is thoroughly surveyed. Often, moving twigs in the distance are a clue to the presence of deer. Maybe the click of brush against antlers, or the sounds of a deer pushing through shrubbery growth can be heard in the quiet of the woods. Whitetails can sometimes be surprisingly careless and noisy when they are in an unrestrained feeding mood.

After the hunter is satisfied that the animals are not in the scope of his vision, he slowly moves on, keeping in mind the fact that they might be bedded down. Even a bedded deer can be approached at reasonable range when the stalker uses utmost care. If the animals become uneasy in their beds, they will rise to their feet and stand for a second or two to look about for the source of disturbance, and then they decide on a route of hasty exit. The conscientious hunter might have a quick but easy shot in such a situation.

Where there is a fair and even distribution of fresh deer sign in the territory the man can simply hunt throughout the area without paying too much attention to the tracks. There is no advantage here in following a particular set of slots. This additional chore, in fact, diverts the purpose of the hunter who is already in good whitetail habitat. Too often a novice hunter becomes so possessed with tracks that his eyes unwittingly look for little else. He is the chap who complains of seeing a waving flag, but always from the corner of his eye.

Such a young man trudged right by me as I sat on a stump to watch an alder swamp. The lad was hot on a two-day old track, bent over it like a question mark, and from his big parka his scope of vision did not extend beyond a couple of arm lengths. It was as though he were tracking a dozy bear to its winter quarters. Yet, I hesitate to criticize anyone's mode of hunting, for even this simple lad might have stumbled upon a deer with equal faculties.

High winds affect the temperament of all game, and animal life now becomes nervous and retiring. Strangely enough, the whitetail often leaves his bed to forage or lounge about in the dense thickets during the days of extremely high winds. Some men prefer such days, with or without snow, to all others for stalking their game. The woods are noisy with falling branches and vibrating twigs, and both deer and hunter are somewhat handicapped in the game of hide and seek.

There is this strong point in favor of the man, however. He knows that his quarry is confined to the thickets, and he need not be greatly concerned with any normal walking noises he makes. Likewise, he cannot be expected to be warned of any commotion a flushed animal makes. During a heavy blow it is surprising how even a big, wide-racked buck can crash through a dense growth and not raise a sound above the atmospheric disturbance.

The hunter, moving even any slight angle into the wind, needs only to search the lowland thickets. Tracking is not especially favorable now, for the whitetail does not travel a great distance across the country. The game depends mostly on its vision for protection, and the hunter likewise depends on his eyes for finding his quarry. The man can ill afford to divert much attention to following tracks or seeking a stealthy approach.

Though the hunter can come within good shooting range of his target, the animals are now extremely fidgety, and they do not hesitate to scamper off at the sight of an intruder. If snow is absent, there is little contrast in the woods, and each swaying clump of reeds, nodding ferns, or rustling, persistent leaves of scrub oak growth stops the hunter's searching eyes. He will have some difficulty in discerning his game now, especially on a cloudy day, and by evening his strained eyes will need more rest than his legs.

Heavy snowfalls come pretty often in the deer country of some of our northern states — much too often to pass them off as unseasonal

or unusual. The resourceful individual had best learn to cope with this condition. This situation calls for a brand of hunting that is not easily accepted by any but the more avid redcoats.

A deep blanket of white stuff is definitely a handicap to the movements of the hunter. But any handicap knee-deep snow makes for the man is often more than offset by the limited movements the same situation forces upon deer. In short, the huntsman works harder than usual, but in a vastly smaller area.

An early, deep snowfall changes the habits of the whitetail overnight. He no longer makes those long treks from his bedding grounds to distant feeding spots. The rigors of oncoming winter are impressed upon him, and he expends energy rather niggardly. In fact, he will now most likely refuse to stir from his bed for a day or two after the big fall, as though he were unwilling to face his new, harsh world. Even before the snow has ceased falling, he has abandoned the open country and receded to the environs of his winter quarters. As the animal becomes uneasy with hunger, and the snow becomes more acceptable to him, he moves about more freely. But the open field and edge country are largely neglected and the deer crossings along the roads are now virtually abandoned.

Only the stout-hearted and stout-legged man accepts the challenge of deep-snow hunting. Yet, it can prove very effective for the man acquainted with the country. The whitetails are in the backcountry but not necessarily a great distance off the road. The local lads who get around a bit know where the animals set up their winter quarters — the areas of swamps fringed with young evergreen growth, a mixture of thicket and evergreens, or any dense thicket usually along a flat or creek bottom. These are not the big deer "yards" given so much prominence, but they are the winter quarters of most of the animals in the North country. Often such spots are just off a road with little or no sign to indicate that a small band of animals is there.

For once, even the normally fast and careless walker is soon forced to a very slow stride in the deep snow. He becomes a good still-hunter in spite of himself, for as he expends his excess energy he pauses often to catch his breath. And he is only too happy to take longer breathers when he comes upon any tracks, especially fresh sign. This combination of slow movement, noiseless walking, and frequent rests are the

cardinal rules of the good solo hunter. And when you know the whitetails are likely to be somewhere in the immediate area, you cannot ask for a better deal.

It is likely the deer have not been shunted about lately, as few men are in the field, and the animals feel somewhat secure in their new snowy habitat. Most sere, short growth, so often mistaken for deer, is now covered, and the hunter can easily pick out the outline of his game. The whitetail is not all agog for leaving his recently established home at the appearance of a hunter, and his glassy stare at the intruder of his sanctum seems to reflect a measure of defeat in the animal. Even when roused from his bed, he hesitates a bit before plunging into deep snow, and after a short spurt he prefers to stop and glance over his shoulder to reappraise his plight. The man willing and able to take deep-snow hunting in stride can put in some pretty good licks while the fair-weather boys are shaking their heads at the roadside drifts, or else watering down their disappointment at some crossroads bar.

The still-hunter can adjust his strategy for most weather conditions prevailing as well as for the type of terrain he will hunt. There is, however, the extremely difficult situation of stalking the elusive whitetail on a relatively quiet day when the air is crisp and the snow is crusty, or if there is no snow and the forest floor is sere and the leaves underfoot crunch noisily with each step. Now big game is as alert and spirited as it has ever been, and the still-hunter is pretty much licked. If ever he wants to take a day off from the chase for a breather, this is the most opportune time.

The undaunted and confirmed solo hunter will still play the lesser odds, for after all, he feels pledged to his lone role, and he takes the days as they come. There is always the happy thought that he might chance upon a careless buck with his mind completely absorbed in romance, and this could be the day for such anomaly in whitetail behavior.

Deer reduce their daytime activity to a bare minimum now, and they have a distinct advantage over the hunter by virtue of their roused senses of vision, hearing, and smell. An old buck, especially, likes to bed down just below the crest of a hilltop to command the view of a valley before him, with any light breeze coming from above to his back. Resting on this strategic point, he is as secure from his stalker as he will ever be, yet his seemingly quiet repose could belie his feeling of security. Every movement within his scope of vision is quickly picked up by his farsighted eyes. His ears constantly bend to catch any sound, and his nostrils are now quick to detect the faintest scent. It seems that much of the whitetail's response to possible danger stems from the animal's peculiar temperament rather than from any real existing situation. The weather affects his moods, and his moods rule his fears.

The crunching noises of his arch-enemy, man, made with a measured tread over crusty snow, is readily recognized over all other sounds. And when the pursuer comes upon the bed, the vigilant whitetail has long ago slinked away. He seeks to keep the inevitable noisy clues to his departure from reaching the hunter's ears. If, by some quirk, the deer has been taken abash by the hunter's close approach, the animal will very often choose to remain put rather than hazard a noisy escape. But the second he feels the hunter's eyes have discovered him, he will explode into flight with complete disregard for a cautious exit.

A sage old buck, which has taxed all his wiles in order to escape the fate of the meat pole year after year, is ever conscious of the noise he makes on crusty snow. When started from his bed, he dashes off to leave the immediate grounds, but he soon slows down to a stop. He throws his head back to evaluate his situation, then slowly moves on. Each step is taken with reluctance, and unless he is hard pressed, he will pause often in order to follow the progress of his pursuer. He prefers not to make a rash and complete escape, but strives only to keep a safe distance from his enemy.

The hopeful hunter trying for a whitetail under these unfavorable conditions must walk into any wind and scan the more distant terrain. His shots will most likely be at a running target at long range. If a buck only is the man's choice, he will be hard put. About the only other alternative he has is to take a stand and hope some other individual, as intrepid as he, is stirring about the woods to keep the inactive animals on the move.

Hunting the Jackpines

There is some deer country that is utterly different from the more open lands of popples and hardwoods and not easily accepted by the still-hunter. These are the jackpine thickets of the sandy, high grounds and the cedar growths of the wet lowlands. Both are veritable evergreen jungles, but the jackpine country offers much better underfooting and is, therefore, more suitable for the still-hunter.

My first experience in hunting the jackpine country was a new and pleasant adventure. The group of us who had forsaken the aspen country for a fling at the pinery saw many deer, or parts of them, but there was no sag in our meat pole in this first attempt at jungle hunting. Yet, we return here on occasion for a few days of hunting, for there is something about the desolate evergreen woods and the softness of its floor which appeals to the still-hunter.

For one thing, the heavy pine cover often shelters a pretty fair concentration of deer, and the still-hunter can well afford to be on his best mettle when he knows the animals are there. Walking over the lush bed of pine needles is most ideal for stalking your game. If there is snow on the ground, chances are that being heavily shaded it will not be encrusted from normal warm temperatures and subsequent freezes.

Your one possibility of making a noise is by snapping off or whipping the lower dried branches of the trees. Since your stalk must be carried on at a slow pace, you will work around such situations or else stoop under the branches. And while you are in a stooped position you can get a surprising view of the woods terrain about you from under the level of the lower pine branches. If one gets into the habit of dropping to one knee at regular intervals to search the grounds about him, he can locate his deer before it is flushed. What appear to be small tree trunks in the distance may well be the legs of a whitetail. The hunter continually walking with his body erect poses a distinct advantage to the animal which has learned to sense danger from beneath the growth. The hunter with his eyes at foliage level might not see the deer which easily sees the man's moving legs.

Because of the density of jackpine growth the deer usually use well-defined trails in traversing their bailiwick. This is in direct contrast to the open-country whitetails which now choose to abandon the summer trails. Frequent pauses, especially at the crossroads of two good runways, are essential here. Any deer surprised in these gloomy depths can be taken at close range for a quick but close shot. Deer flushed by the slow-moving hunter quietly leave the immediate area of disturbance; and, because they regain their composure quickly in the dense growth, the still-hunter can hope to intercept them later.

Most men prefer a fairly unobstructed view of at least a few hundred feet. Not many care to push through the sunless, cramped quarters of the scrub pine forest. When a hunter says he likes the "wide open spaces" that is just about what he means. And that is what excludes a lot of redcoats from the jackpines. The hunter is either completely sold on these hunting grounds, or else a half day's hunt here cures him of any desire to try it again.

The Small Hunting Group

THE clamor these days seems to be for joining forces with larger groups of deer hunters. The supposition is that by doing so the individual is bolstering his own chances for success. It is, in a way, an admission that the individual hunter feels himself inadequate. When a large assemblage hunts as a group, it can be expected that not all of the men are adept huntsmen; but when a very small group hunts as a unit, it is more probable that each member is an experienced hunter and woodsman.

The best combination for a whitetail hunt is the two- or three-man team, and of these the two-man unit is most ideal. It is merely a case of each man using the tactics of the solo hunter, but getting together for the hunt so that each man's efforts might aid the other. Such combinations are generally made up of father and son, two brothers, or any two men who have hunted much in the same deer country.

Two men can do a very good job of still-hunting as a team in any situation and, the more the men hunt together, the more efficient they become. Much of the success of the pair is due to the fact that the men get to know how the other hunts and what to expect of him in any situation. They can travel abreast, spaced just to be within sight of each other, they can skirt opposite sides of a marsh, or they can take two parallel ridges to watch the broad valley in between. After the two men have hunted a territory for some time, they learn to know where the whitetails are most likely to be and which way they might go after being spooked.

A good method to pursue when something is known of the habits of the animals in a given area is for the two men to stagger their probes into the woods. They space themselves as in hunting abreast, but one man starts first on his stalk while the other remains at his standing point. After the first man hunts his way for about 200 yards, or to a point of advantage, he pauses to watch. The second man starts his slow thrust into the area and hunts his way past his confederate and continues to the next suitable watching point. And so they alternately still-hunt and watch. The progress need not be in a straight line but preferably along a course that offers the best opportunities, keeping in mind a favorable wind direction. I first used to hunt this way with an older brother when our knowledge of the vast deer country was limited to but a few small areas. We followed each other's progress in the hunt by whistling on a rifle shell when either of us selected his stand. This was a signal for the other to leave his watch to continue onward.

The two-man team is so flexible that there is no end to the ways in which it can be applied for most any hunting situation. Shortly after World War II, an army buddy joined me for a whitetail hunt in country that was totally new to him. He was, however, an experienced woodsman, and we worked out a system that was most suitable under the circumstances. I planted him on a high stand in good country, while I still-hunted in a large circle to one side.

After rejoining him at the stand, I sent him on a short similar circuit in another direction.

This proved fruitful for both of us, for on one of my circuits I came upon a small forked buck feeding at leisure and dispatched him with an easy shot. The next day we carried out the same routine and I started an unusually big buck toward the stand. Just as I picked up the running tracks, I heard two spaced shots ring out like a knell proclaiming the demise of another buck. Such an arrangement for two men is most practical, for about the time the hunter returns to the stand, the watcher is anxious to flex the muscles of his stiffening legs.

The trail-watching and still-hunting combine can also be used by a father and his eager but untried sons. I know one considerate father who introduced both his lads to whitetail hunting by placing them on appropriate stands, helping them with their fires, and instructing them in all details of gun safety and trail watching. He then hunted the environs, reporting at intervals to each boy at his post. This system worked so well that the trio, with the sons grown to strapping young men, still pursues this mode of hunting.

The two-man team is practical for those many small nooks that require only one man for driving. These little drives can be made even in the wake of a big gang of hunters, for deer like to retreat to such spots after being harried in the bigger country. Two men can specialize in working over these many small hideouts, especially as the season wanes and hunting becomes progressively unproductive in the big deer areas.

If the lone driver takes the time, he can serve the purpose of several men and in this way a bigger area can be covered. My youngest brother, Francis, and I tried such a stunt while we were hunting strange country. As we stood on a tall hill, we noticed two swamps in the distance separated by a narrow ridge. This appeared to be a good spot for a stand if the country to either side were driven. There were no hunters in the region so we decided to see what we could do with a one-man drive. My brother went to the distant stand, and I waited until he was near his post. Then I swung to the big country to the east of the two swamps and worked rather rapidly back and forth, covering much ground and always closing in toward the direction of the stand. When I heard the single shot, I was just on the runway that led to the ridge that separated the two swamps.

The lone deer was a six-point buck, and after dressing him out, there was still time for a like drive from the opposite side to this same point. Over an hour and a half had elapsed before anything happened on this second attempt. Then two does trailed by and another six-point buck came trotting to the natural crossing. Whitetails have little apprehension of such crossings when past experience gives them little reason for fear. The buck was killed from less than a hundred-foot distance. It is very probable that the two animals were twins, for they were as alike as two bucks could be.

Two men who know their country can be masters in snow tracking. When a man hunts the same grounds season after season, he not only learns the lay of the land, but he also observes the general route of any whitetails moving over this terrain. This is especially so if the animals have entered the area sometime during the night or early morning, traveling undisturbed along a normal route, perhaps stopping to browse and finally bedding down later in the forenoon. When such tracks are picked up early in the morning, whether the snow be soft or a bit noisy, here is a good chance to intercept the animals. One man stations himself at a likely crossing and the other slowly follows through.

My biggest buck was taken this way. I was hunting with my brother, John. We found a large track, and he suggested a stand for me on a broad flat where deer often crossed. He followed the tracks for a full mile and a half. A heavy mist hung in the air, and the snow was melting rapidly. The old buck lumbered toward me like a well-fed steer moving about the feedlot. As soon as I brought him down, my brother also loomed upon the scene through the heavy fog. The buck was either unaware of being followed so closely or else he felt secure in the shroud of fog.

The mere thought of having someone in the woods with them gives moral and physical support to those men who like to still-hunt but prefer not to be entirely alone. One is naturally more alert if he knows there is someone else in the area; then he will hunt slower, watch closer, and make frequent stops. He will do a better job of still-hunting even though his partner flushes no game his way.

Some situations crop up suddenly during the hunting season that best require a change of hunting tactics, if not a change in hunting grounds, and the small group of two or three men can meet this requirement without much ado. One of these needs for a quick change in hunting method comes the day after a particularly rough night of winds and storm. Deer will even stop their habitual nightly feeding on alfalfa fields during such nights of inclement weather. If the next day is normally agreeable, one can be sure the deer will be afoot and feeding. This is a good time to follow tote roads, logging trails, and hilltops in the vicinity of good browse. With two or three men in the area, there is an excellent chance of someone finding the animals feeding, and if the game is flushed by one man, another hunter of the group might be in line for favorable shooting.

The hunt should be pursued slowly, for if you are in good game habitat with ample feed available, there is no point in passing through quickly only to enter less suitable country. In any still-hunting, one should keep his pace down below the point where he might perspire, for the odor of human perspiration wafted about by uncertain air currents of the woods registers strongly to a deer's sensitive nostrils. If one is dressed for the chill of the morning and then finds himself too warmly attired for the afternoon, he is better off to adjust his pace to his comfort rather than shed some of his clothing. The still-hunter had best dress on the heavy side, as any slight chill of the body encourages restlessness and a quickened step.

Whitetails will concentrate on good browsing when they are seriously bent on daytime feeding. I remember one particular calm day after a stormy night when I found eight whitetails, singly or in pairs, scattered about the edge of a several-acre swamp, all of them nipping shoots of the short shrubbery surrounding this wet marsh. To the distant sides in all directions were tall, slender red oaks and other young hardwoods, and in this thick growth, underbrush was naturally scant. This one day the hungry animals from the surrounding area chose to converge on the abundant food growing around the swamp opening.

I can recall other such instances of numerous deer feeding in a small area, but this was years ago and I sought no explanation for this grouping of animals, perhaps taking for granted that this was where they always stayed, and that I had just discovered their quarters. This is much like the situation of today when hunters happen onto a number of deer late in the afternoon. When they return the next day to this Utopia, they find it no better than the hunting grounds they had left behind.

Slashings make good cover for deer, and the hunted bucks like to bed down under such tops of fallen trees where they have a good view to their front. If they are spooked out from the rear they are pretty sure to run straight ahead, keeping the obstruction between them and the hunter. Any man to either side might have an easy shot here, but the lone man has little chance. Bucks feel just as secure in the protection of treetops alongside a logging trail as they would further back, so the solo hunter is better off here where he has easy going.

Hunting in heavy slashings is always difficult, and usually such spots are driven to standers posted at what advantageous shooting points they can find, or more likely, the hunters stay entirely clear of this obstacle hunt. Yet, such downed treetop jungles have two appealing points to offer this small group of still-hunters: the possibility of a very close approach to game; and a convenient logging trail for one of the men to follow through the debris-strewn deer habitat.

Three men make this the ideal hunt; one man moves slowly and silently along the trail and the other two flank him at a short distance to the sides. All men still-hunt as though each were alone, for it is better here to jump a deer at close range than to have it filter out of the area unseen. Deer started by the men on either side of the logging road tend to cross the road for safety, and the unhampered man in the middle can expect the more favorable shooting. There is great advantage in being able to jump deer within a hundred feet of you, for if the animal is seen to rise to its feet, the gunner might find time to get in a quick shot before his game is in high gear. As the distance between the gun and the target increases, the shot must be taken more deliberately, and this becomes difficult when greater distance also means increased obstruction of the target.

Deer tend to drift toward the more rugged backwoods country as cold weather and deep snows set in, and this normal trend is greatly augmented by heavy hunting in the open country of short growth and the environs of abandoned farm fields. Toward the end of a wintry deer season, the hilly, heavily timbered country, not so conducive to summer deer, will be gradually invaded by the animals seeking protection from the weather. This is the start of the movement to winter quarters, though it can vary considerably according to weather conditions.

Hunters from outside a territory often have little or no knowledge of any deer movements that take place after the season progresses or after the weather turns sharply colder. These men might continue to hunt those accessible roadside tracts that were the whitetail grounds earlier in the season, but which are now less populated with the animals. The small, resourceful hunting group can follow the drift of the whitetails with no great conclave for making plans. On many occasions, a partner and I made sample jaunts into the remote, rough country just a mile or so back to learn if the whitetails started gathering for their winter stay. At times, especially toward the end of the season, we found the animals were here in good numbers.

Whatever the movements of whitetails or the change in weather, the small group of hunters is best able to meet the new situation as it arises. This closely bound hunting unit is, in reality, composed of individual still-hunters and trail watchers pooling their efforts and knowledge for the group, yet none sacrificing his own love for solo hunting in the practical, sociable arrangement.

3

Gang Hunting

THE big drive is as ancient as man's long struggle for food and survival. It was used by the Indians in one form or another as a practical means for getting up the winter's supply of meat for the village. White settlers, too, banded up frequently for such big hunts solely for the purpose of obtaining venison. Even as late as the early 1930s there was ample evidence of the local folk gathering forces for such occasions. Since venison was the big objective, these hunts took place when it was most convenient or when meat was needed. The affair was accepted as a matter-of-fact practice, something akin to the sociable but purposeful wood-cutting bees of the time. It was a democratic hunt; the experienced riflemen on the stands sharing the spoils with the less adept, the brush beaters.

Even today the big deer drive appeals to many redcoats because of its get-togetherness and practicabil-

ity. Hunting does not have precisely the same connotation for every man packing his duffel for the yearly trip to his hunting grounds. It is the man himself who decides what he wants in a hunting trip, and the individual's tastes can vary from the desire for a serious and sober hunt by himself, to the other extreme of joining a convivial group of men who take their hunt less seriously. There is room for both these extremes, as well as for the mass in between.

There is good, practical argument favoring group hunting. It gives every man a chance to participate actively in the game, regardless of his own capabilities; and the beginner's odds for a kill are brought closer to those expected of the veteran in the party. Were it not for gang hunting, there would be fewer new men joining the redcoats each fall, for the novice not native to the deer country most likely would find still-hunting or trail watching not exactly enthralling for his initial experience in whitetail hunting.

Great care in gun handling must be exercised by gang hunters, since this type of hunting brings together a large group of men, some quite inexperienced, to a limited area that might already contain other hunters. Making a big drive in country infiltrated with hunters is certainly not to be recommended, not only from a hunter's safety viewpoint, but also because such a drive is not very effective.

Generally speaking, gang hunting falls into three methods of pursuit, and the particular type of hunt selected for any situation will depend upon many factors, including physical stamina of the participants, knowledge they have of the country and its terrain, weather conditions, and the type of habitat to be hunted.

If the weather is a bit chilly and the country to be hunted is bounded on two sides by roads a half mile to two miles apart, the hunters merely line up on one road and leave at a given signal to proceed to their destination on the other parallel road. A knowledge of the country here helps but is not essential, for even on a cloudy day, with the aid of a compass, the hunter should have no difficulty in following his proper course.

Each man hunts on his own but he also has the advantage of seeing game spooked onto him by the men to his sides. There is necessarily some lost time in this hunt since not all men walk at the same pace or are able to keep their proper course for any length of time. Yet, despite some mix-ups and delays in reassembling the men at the end of the hunt, many an inexperienced redcoat comes upon and bags his first deer on such a hunt. It is probable, too, that more whitetails are seen by the entire gang hunting abreast than by any other method of deer pursuit.

The second common type of hunt for a large group is the popular big drive. This is most often used early in the day before the deer have been spooked by hunters, although it can be used most anytime. Here, some knowledge of the country is essential, at least by a few of the men who can plan the direction of the drive and select good stands where the flushed whitetails are most likely to pass. The better rifle shots are naturally picked for the stands, and the drivers are instructed in the direction they must go, the distance they will travel, and the approximate time it will take them to complete the drive.

The group hunter must be time-conscious, and the members of a driving gang, especially, must plan to execute their hunt within a limited space of time. The watch becomes as important as the compass, for the men must be on their stands at a specified time, the drivers must start their push at a given time, and the drive is expected to be completed in a limited time. The driver knows the approximate time he is to be at the line of standers. If he filters through the standers unnoticed, he will continue on into the country beyond to cause considerable delay in regrouping the band for the next hunt.

There are times when the standers can be lined up on a small backwoods road or a mere tote road. When such an arrangement can be made there is little suffered in lost time and inconvenience by the gang. Here, the drivers merely spread out from a starting point, usually a road. They space themselves to cover the width of the area they will drive, and all proceed toward the men on the stands. They hunt as they walk and all try to keep a fairly straight course with frequent use of a compass, if need be, so they will not converge on one another and thus leave big breaches in the driving line through which the animals might escape to the rear.

The third method of gang hunting is simply a combination of hunting abreast and driving, although no definite plans are made for an organized, tactical hunt. It is often resorted to when the men are a bit tired from a hard morning of driving, or it can be used merely as a change of pace in hunting, especially if the afternoon becomes a bit warm. No one has the zest for any elaborate hunt and most are quite willing to laze about the deer area for the balance of the day, each in his own way with no attachment to the gang.

The hunters are spaced as in hunting abreast, and each will alternately still-hunt and pause as he feels inclined. After a bit all the men are widely dispersed, some move slowly, others more rapidly, and some few might be content to sit at some strategic point most of the time. Then there are the younger and more exuberant who might crisscross the hunting grounds several times in their impatience to find game.

With this diversified hunting in a limited area where whitetails are known to be, chances are very good that someone in the group will get good shooting. Those men moving most of the time might see more deer, but the relaxed, easygoing hunters poised on stands or slowly edging along a ridge will more likely get in the shots that count.

Whether the gang hunts abreast in a given direction, the members alternately move and stand, or they make drives, the idea is to keep the whitetails moving so that somebody gets shooting. Very often the successful man is some newcomer taken under the wing of a more seasoned hunter. I remember such a situation, ironic in the extreme, when a lad of fifteen years was somewhat reluctantly accepted in the membership of an established hunting party. The new charge, who was somebody's nephew, was civilly but promptly relegated to a stand for the season, while the much relieved Nimrods went on to pursue their big plans. And, of course, it was the simple, neglected lad who got the only deer in the party — a fine ten-point buck.

Often hunting groups are loosely organized or else composed of too many inexperienced men. Even in such a situation, as long as the hunters mill about in deer country, each individual is better off than if he strikes out for himself. It is only when a very large gang without direction or understanding strives to hunt as a unit that hunting efficiency greatly suffers. I hunted only once in such a group of sixteen men composed of odd individuals gathered at random. Only two futile drives were made that day, while hours were wasted in assembling the straggling members. That cured me of ever again being mustered into a hastily organized army of raw and undisciplined recruits.

The very large, unwieldy gangs are effective only in driving such large areas as are confined by roads, farmlands, or other definite boundaries. There is necessarily much time lost in regrouping, seeking new suitable grounds and planning for the next big push to the standers. It is too often true that mere additional numbers do not always add to the effectiveness of a drive.

Yet, despite the many inducements for lost motion in big-group hunting, this type of tactic cannot be frowned upon. There are times and places entirely fitting for big drives, in fact, occasions when little else will avail. The jackpine and cedar strongholds, as well as any very brushy country, might best be driven if the hunters are to get even fair shooting. And where the growth is extremely dense, a large number of men are needed to start the animals. In ordinary deer country, too, when the underfooting is noisy, as on frozen leaves or crunchy snow, a well-planned drive can be very effective and, perhaps, the hunter's only recourse.

One of the big oversights in making drives is the failure of getting the men on the stands far enough in advance of the actual push. Great care should be taken by the men in walking to their posts, the same caution used as when stalking deer. If a group of standers carries on a conversation as they walk along to their posts, they have given away their position to the deer. Even with a careful approach, the men should be situated at their positions about fifteen minutes before the drive starts. After a lapse of this time, the whitetail forgets or ignores any noises he has heard in that direction.

The whitetail is not frightened by a man's voice, or at least not nearly as much as he is at hearing a snapped twig, but he simply avoids going in the direction of the voice. I was on a stand during a drive when I heard two men conversing as they walked along a tote road to the back of me. A buck came over the hill toward me, stopped short, pricked up his ears, and looked in the direction of the chattering men. The animal stood for several minutes, turning his head to follow the progress of the men. And when they were gone and their voices were lost far to my left, the deer tossed a hasty glance in the direction of the drivers and continued down the runway toward me, thoroughly convinced any danger had disappeared with the voices.

The initial drive of the day should be the best, for the animals have had the night in which to settle down. Therefore, this first effort should be executed with more than ordinary care. If the flushed whitetails are ever inclined to follow the natural runways at all, this would be the time. The men should be at their stands even before the drivers are assembled. Once the group gathers for the push, especially if the morning is quiet and walking is noisy, the whitetails will be alerted and edgy; and if all has been quiet at the stands for some time, the animals will turn their attention to the drivers.

Often there is considerable delay in getting off the drive. The men on the stands need not feel their time is wasted, for they are putting in the best hours for trail watching. Also, if other hunters filter into the area before the planned drive gets under way, the standers are at their posts to cover the vantage points and runways. There is much to be gained in getting to your stand early with all possible caution.

My brother, John, once sent me to a stand at daybreak. He was to make a drive to me while enroute to his trapline, and I was to be on the spot without fail when he came through. Sure enough, an eight-point buck came browsing down the trail toward me just as the sun rose up to sparkle the frosted twigs. About two hours after I dispatched the deer and dressed him out, John came rapidly down the trail to make up for the lost time. For some reason, he had never left the house until after I had bagged the deer. I was at my post a couple of hours too soon for the drive, yet my time there was not without purpose.

There is common belief among many hunters that the standers alone are all important and that the driving should naturally fall to the less experienced men in the crew. Unfortunately, the drive can suffer at either end for lack of able men. There certainly is a very distinct advantage in having good drivers — men who know the country and who take time to penetrate the thickets, follow the fringe growth along swamps, and, in general, walk through the spots where whitetails are likely to be. Such men do a more thorough job than a driver who follows the line of least resistance in walking through the area. Often

there are pockets to the side that warrant the expenditure of the extra time and effort it takes to cover them. After all, the point of driving is to get the deer on the move, and any halfhearted attempts to do so are reflected in mediocre results.

I have never been partial to any but the slow, quiet drive where each man moves at a steady pace and is able to watch the terrain about him. The hurried, noisy drives offer the least shooting opportunities, for the deer, once accustomed to such tactics, learn to locate the drivers by the noises made and, consequently, the animals filter back between the men. What deer are pushed past the drivers go by at such speed that running shots are inevitable.

The slow-moving drive, where each man is somewhat of a still-hunter, will more often simply alert the animals so that they merely move ahead at a slow pace. Whether they stay to the front or turn back to get past the drivers, the deer are not overly alarmed, and fair shooting can be expected. The whitetail, especially a shrewd buck, if gently fore-warned of danger, will leave the area quietly. At such a time, he is less averse to following natural runways. When he completely succumbs to fear, as when noisy drivers close in on him, he chances

dir
ens
the
dri
con
wh
trei
squ
clai
mic
we

I h
hov
vig
dis
hal
the
to
the
wo
the
tro
dir
car
res
los

the
sce
sid
de
rap
thi
by
bec

an immediate escape, often between the drivers; for he has a great dread of being surrounded on all sides. The whitetail's escape is now reckless, through unpredictable routes, and with all possible haste; and the hunter, whether on the stand or driving, is likely to be caught off guard. The point in any type of hunting is to realize an advantage for favorable shooting.

It is good to have the flanking men in the column of drivers keep well ahead of the moving line; or better still, have a man on each end of the driving column cover a vantage point about midway between the drivers and the standers. Where the area driven is bounded by side roads, the men can cover the roads, moving along well ahead of the rest of the driving column.

It is the nature of the whitetail deer, after a few experiences with gang hunters, to sense a squeeze play in the making. The deer are afraid to remain in the area, and they are equally afraid to try an escape. Whatever they do seems not to follow any particular pattern of behavior, and the hunter knows not what to expect of them.

Time was, only a few decades ago, when the whitetails were far more cooperative than they are today. They retreated from the drivers in orderly fashion, and they were naive enough to take to the established runway for escape. But that is in the past, and that is why so many hastily made drives are of little avail today. Yet, the fact that the whitetails refuse to be driven out does not indicate they remain complacent and unruffled. Long after the drive is completed and all of the hunters have departed, the deer still are apprehensive, and after all is quiet again they commonly take the courage to leave the scene and enter neighboring country. It is not the hunter alone that they fear; they also fear the environs where they experienced their peril. And they quickly regain composure on grounds not associated with threats to their safety.

The more an area is driven in the same fashion, the more difficult it is to get the whitetails to move in the direction of the stands, and after a while the animals simply refuse to be taken by the same routine. While driving with the wind is the common method, and certainly commendable in country where the deer have seen little hunting pressure, this practice is becoming increasingly less effective in coping with the modern whitetail. This seems no longer an artifice but rather a giveaway, for when the animals sense a drive in progress

fifteen years have we put a buck through this bottleneck, and only rarely has a doe or fawn been forced down the well-defined trail. Yet, we have taken our share of bucks in this area, but always the fortune fell to one of the drivers. This story is pretty much the same with all drives. The brush beater has turned hunter, for he is seeing more deer than does the hopeful man on the stand.

Whether a man can fare better, bag-wise, by hunting with a group or hunting alone depends mostly on the individual; and whether a man enjoys hunting alone or prefers the companionship and association of others is a matter of the individual's makeup.

The trend today is toward a generous sprinkling of sociability in both hunting and fishing. Not all anglers enjoy fishing alone, and, therefore, not all anglers readily take to trout fishing. Partridge hunting in the backcountry is best done by the solo hunters, but these men are in the minority; most find it preferable to be with a companion and slowly prowl the side roads in the comforts of a car.

Whitetail hunting is yielding to this modern trend. Indeed, many hunters are lured into an area because of the number of cars parked along the road in that vicinity.

Trail Watching

*E*VERY redcoat is a trail watcher of sorts. It seems such a simple matter to plunk one's self comfortably on a good runway and merely wait for a deer to come ambling by. Maybe every hunter, sometime or other, has vowed he will watch a particular trail or wait it out on some strategic point the first day of the season. But, perhaps, the barrage of shots he hears in the distance from most every direction works havoc with his plans. After a brief hour or less at his stand he begins to believe that in this apparent oasis of deer country, he alone is unfortunate to have selected the desert.

Consequently, he moves on to a new territory and, of course, the shots ring out all around him as before, and he falls victim to chasing the will-o'-the wisp. After a time, he roams about rather freely in his unquiet search for better deer country; then he becomes neither a trail watcher nor a still-hunter.

Trail watching requires patience, something that is somewhat lacking in the hurry and spectacle of modern hunting. And it seems more acceptable to the older, experienced man than it does to the anxious beginner with quick beating pulse and restless legs. There are not many inveterate trail watchers these days, especially of the old type where the lone hunter seeks to intercept whitetails in their normal daily treks. The numerous hunters in the woods today hamper the natural movements of the animals, and most trail watchers now depend considerably on other hunters to put game past their stands.

My brother John, who even in his younger days back in the late twenties had a special aversion to any form of group hunting, did about as much trail watching as anyone I ever knew. And, for the time expended on his efforts, he fared far better than the rest of us brothers or anyone else in the neighborhood who toted a gun. Even in those days of fewer hunters, he preferred the untrammeled hinterlands to the runways near at hand. He would stick stubbornly to a stand for days, if necessary, and, eventually, an unruffled buck would oblige him by coming down the trail.

The important thing about selecting a runway to watch is to make sure it is being used during the hunting season. There are many kinds of deer trails, and some of them appear mighty appealing to the hunter, even though they have long been abandoned by the animals. Some well-defined runways can be found in the vicinity of winter deer yards, but the whitetails that made them dispersed last spring. Other trails lead to farm fields and have been actively used through September, October, and possibly up to the deer season. Such trails are used mostly during the evenings, nights, and early mornings, and daytime watching here would be useless even if the animals still enter the fields, as they sometimes do during the open season on them.

There are short, summer runways from thickets to watering places, where a doe with her young walk daily during the hot summer months, either to drink or feed on the succulent water plants. Many of the trails deep in the country simply lead to the more open lands where summer's tender grasses are appealing to the whitetail. Such runways are little used as the grasses become sere in fall. I once sat on such a deer path that looked more promising than anything I had ever seen. It snowed a couple of inches the night before the opening of the deer season, and I was somewhat dismayed because there were no tracks in the trail the next morning. I left the stand at noon in disgust. About three days later I chanced upon the stand again, and still there were no deer tracks in the seemingly good runway.

There are trails, however, in the less hunted country, which are often used by whitetails in the fall, especially during the initial days of the hunting season. Bucks are more prone to use them only at night, or during damp weather or times of precipitation even in broad daylight. These cross-country runways, like old tote roads of the early cut-over country days, ramble on for great distances, and are joined here and there by other trails. They seem not nearly as common or well-defined today as they were during the decades after the logging era, the brush fires, and the subsequent birth of the ideal whitetail habitat. Such runways were, and to some extent still are, the highways used by the whitetails when traveling from one area to another. Bucks may follow these for a considerable distance during the rut, but the does and lesser deer use them only for convenience in getting about their established grounds.

These long deer paths traverse the better going along ridges, in broad valleys, the margins of large swamps and lakes, and through flat semi-open country — always where there is considerable view to one or both sides. When the whitetails are enjoying complacent living, they follow these established runways with considerable abandon, and even a deer flushed from a distance to the side might pick up one of these long-established trails and follow it in its escape to safer grounds.

The confirmed trail watcher has an envious position among hunters. He is little concerned over weather conditions except as they might affect his comfort. As long as there are deer in the area, his chances for seeing them are equally good with or without snow and on quiet or noisy days. The hunter, here, puts in full time under least exertion. His only care is to pick a comfortable, dry seat, with a full view of the runway or the intersection of two runways, and to be so stationed that any wind will carry his scent away from the trail.

The hunter can dress heavily for the occasion of a very cold day since his only walking will be to the stand. And a small fire can be both practical and cheerful, but fire tending should not become his major concern. Enough wood should be gathered at one time for the day so that the hunter need not leave his stand periodically in quest of fuel. Actually, the noise made in getting up a supply of firewood is not as alarming to deer as one might think. These seem natural noises and, once they are stopped, the animals are no longer concerned about their possible source. Nor does the whitetail show any fear of a fire. Strangely, too, it does not associate man with a fire. I have seen a deer look at a smoking fire with the same indifference whether a man was in attendance or not, if the man remained motionless.

On a particularly frosty morning, when even the slightest noises took on big proportions in the quiet, crisp air, I was huddled over a small fire on the terminating slope of a long, high ridge. I sat on the trail where I could best command a view of the cross runway in the wide valley below, and the fire was slightly to my right so its smoke would give me no trouble. The frost in the cold valley was snapping twigs on the tall aspens, and a lone hairy woodpecker could be heard in the frigid, thin air.

I sat statue-like, for the slightest movement on the crusted snow of the trail made a crunching noise that caused me to wince, so I made no attempt at watching the trail to my back. Then, across the fire and through the screen of lazy smoke that hovered over it, I could see the hazy forms of three large deer at the base of the ridge making their way to the valley at my front. They were only about fifty yards to my right, and I frantically tried to discern a buck among the trio.

No matter how I maneuvered my head, I could not free myself of the pall of smoke that surrounded it. Even as I leaned back and far to the side, the movements of my body seemed to suck the smoke directly at me. I finally got to my feet and, half blinded and coughing, I made a dash to escape the little inferno, but my whitetails faded into the thickets before I cleared my smoke-filled eyes.

Then, as I walked back and stood before the fire, I noticed the trail was heavily tracked just fifteen feet up the ridge from where I sat during my cold vigil. These were the tracks of the three deer. They were following the trail down the ridge and, as I sat smack in their path with my back toward them, they halted to study me by the fire. They were not alarmed but, for the sake of caution, they merely turned around as silently as three ghosts, backtracked themselves for about 200 feet up the trail, and went down the slope of the ridge to bypass me. Even as they went by so closely to my right, they walked slowly without showing a hint of suspicion or fear.

I recalled hearing a slight noise to my back a few minutes before, like the sound of a chickadee doing acrobatic performances at the tip of a dried twig. This, apparently, was all the noise the animals made when they gingerly retraced their steps. I concluded that whitetails are not afraid of a fire nor the trail watcher, especially if the two are so close as to appear as one. In this particular case, there was little distinction between the two, with the smoke curling about me as though I were a stump. And to climax my complete disguise, I smelled like a smoldering stump, too.

Trail watching in the sandy jackpine country and the cedar lowlands is a close-quarters situation, and the hunter cannot expect to command the view he gets in the more open deer areas of hardwood and aspen. Runways are more commonly used by the deer in the dense evergreen growths than they are in the less forested areas.

When I first tried trail watching in the heavy jackpines, there was some difficulty in conforming my hunting to a strange and new, cramped habitat. I followed a narrow tote road cut through the scrub pine growth that was as dense as the bristles on a hair brush. I paused at a good deer runway crossing the road. There was no snow on the ground but the disturbed pine needles indicated plenty of recent traffic here. This would be the spot where I would spend the forenoon.

Before settling down to a vigil in these gloomy depths, I wandered up the road a bit to get a lay of the terrain and sort of appraise the situation. Scarcely 200 feet farther was another good runway traversing the road and running parallel to the first trail. This was enough to warm the heart of any hunter. But the two equally good runways posed a problem. Which should I take? Or should I compromise and stand on the narrow road in an attempt to cover both? I reconnoitered the trails for a half hour in hopes that I could find where the two converged, but they never seemed to approach each other, any closer than they did at the road.

There is nothing like making a firm decision when selecting a stand. Any uncertainty about your choice gnaws at you so that in time you become uneasy and wander off seeking something better. And you might keep this up all day long. So back to the narrow tote road I went, with the thought of taking a stand on the road between the two runways. I leaned against a jackpine that was crowding the very edge of the lane and took up a relaxed and comfortable position. My head kept swinging from left to right with the precision of a pendulum, and I felt I had both runways pretty well covered.

A thick floor of pine needles cushions sound pretty much the same as freshly fallen snow, and I could expect no warning of an approaching deer. Even a red squirrel scampered about with no more noise than a shadow.

I must have had my head in the middle of a swing when something caused me to jerk it back to the runway on my left. My gun was at my shoulder when a long-geared buck had already made the crossing. All I recalled of the flick of image was a form zooming across the road from one wall of dense, dark green to another. There was no sound and all that remained was the swaying branch of a scrub pine where the buck had crossed. I began to recollect that his heavy, bleached rack stood out prominently against the dark background.

Maybe I turned my head to the side in disgust. At any rate, it was just in time to see another buck arc across the lane in the same direction on the other trail. He vanished like a phantom even before I had the gun halfway up — a long-geared specimen with even more massive, bleached antlers than the first.

One does not easily shake off the results of a nightmare such as this. Two hundred yards of view is a fair command from a stand back in the more open country I had always hunted. When I tried to straddle these two runways, I found I could not do justice to either of them, even at a hundred feet. Then I suddenly realized that jackpine hunting is something more than just hunting in jackpines. I left the congested, dismal scene and struck out over a ridge where going was good along an old trail. Here the pine growth was less heavy than on the slopes to either side. Soon the ridge tapered downward toward a valley, and I found myself on a gentle slope over-

looking a considerable expanse of open area broken here and there by a few bushy, scraggly trees.

The open area, like a half circle ahead of me, was surrounded on all sides by a luxuriant growth of pines. Instinctively, I sat down on the slope. This was it — a good command of considerable ground, and a few distant shots to my front indicating there were hunters stirring about. It felt good to be able to extend my vision farther than I could throw a stone. I was comfortably seated on a hummock well padded with soft pine needles, with my back propped against the trunk of a tree. An occasional shot in the dark green jungle to my front kept me alert and hopeful.

Even the faintest noises in the hushed woodland take on exaggerated dimensions to the straining ear. But there came a dull, soft sound like something stepping on a rotted log that was distinctly different from all else. A slight swaying of low-hanging bows caught my attention, and I was all set. I waited, but there was nothing more. My eyes kept scanning the edge of the clearing to the sides. There was just a suggestion of movement in the thick growth to my left. Then I made out a series of rapid leg movements of running deer skirting the opening and about fifteen feet in the jack-pines. The deer never broke into the open, nor ever revealed a flash of white as they filtered silently through the growth. Soon all movement was absorbed into the darkness of miniature tree trunks. Right then I concluded the white-tails of this difficult habitat stick to cover, and the only way to get at them is to take to the woods likewise, and accept the close quarters of jungle hunting.

The most engrossing experiences of the deer-minded hunter come most favorably to him when he sits quietly on his stand. If the whitetails edge by the stand, wary as usual but not spooked, they present a picture the ordinary outdoorsman does not often witness. Everything the white-tail normally does in his routine of living is steeped in caution. The animals seem to have a complex of being followed or watched at all times. The fact that they sometimes will pause at a stand indicates they tarry often along the route. Even after they have loitered in one spot for several minutes, they will not let down their guard for even a moment.

Deer will pause at a stand in an uneasy mood at times, as though they have some reason for suspicion but are uncertain as to the cause of their restlessness. They might look in the direction of my stand, maybe give me a hasty glance, and turn away. Then, as an afterthought, they jerk their heads back to look me over again as though the strange object warranted further scrutiniz-ing. It appears, too, that they might suspect the strange object and hope to verify any suspicion by surpris-ing me while I am in motion. As long as I remain frozen in position, and they do not scent me, they will remain for awhile, but their suspi-cions bring on nervousness, which builds up to fear. Then the deer shift about aimlessly, start to move out in unison along the trail, and finally break into full flight — seemingly afraid of fear itself.

A spike buck, apparently flushed by drivers from an area about a mile away, stopped near my stand during a deer season when only forked bucks were legal. He stood for at least fifteen minutes, quite composed, and his only concern for danger was from the direction of the country he had just evacuated, for he glanced regularly at the trail that brought him to me. Finally, he nipped at a few shoots within his reach, then slowly left the trail to browse his way up a hillside. While he was still less than a hundred yards from me, I could see him enter a hazel brush thicket where he stood for a moment. Suddenly he dropped to the ground as though his legs gave out, and he rested in his bed without making any adjustments for his comfort. I had previously believed there was more care taken in selecting the site of a resting place, and that the animals went through more of a ritual in bedding down.

The last deer I saw bed down was during the hunting season of 1963. I was watching a runway crossing when a small-antlered buck came toward me on a trail that skirted a beaver pond. The animal moved rather briskly along the high ridge, slowed down a bit, and finally stopped. He edged off the trail a few yards and dropped to the ground on a projection overlooking the pond. There he was over 250 yards away, basking in the late afternoon sun, much out of practical shooting range of my .30/30 with its peep sights. I was hoping for someone to come down the trail and start the buck toward me, but nobody came along. Finally, I decided on a stalk, but the buck left his couch just as I rose to my feet. A deer watching from his bed has things pretty much his way.

If a doe and buck come quietly down the runway, the buck usually follows the female rather closely. When a similar pair comes running by the stand, obviously flushed by other hunters, the doe is likely to be far ahead in the lead. Sometimes she will stop and look back expectingly. When the two are spooked, together with any lesser deer that might be with them, the wary buck seems to know he is the prime target, for in his hasty escape he is likely to strike out on his own, although later he might rejoin the group.

Does show much concern over their fawns and their interest in them is best observed by the trail watcher. Often, I have seen a walking or trotting doe stop short in the runway before my stand, turn around completely and, with head held aloft and big ears stiffened forward, search the trail with great anxiety. When the doe lowers her head, turns around, and slowly proceeds on her way, I can be sure her young are trailing along, though it might be a few minutes before they arrive.

There are some odd moments of the day when the less-harassed whitetail is plainly loafing — a time when it has no inclination for feeding, bedding down, or stirring about. A group of deer might stand in a thicket, relaxed and listless, much like resting cattle, with apparently a lack of anything else to do for the time. Even when they idle in one spot for a half hour or more, they leave behind them scarcely any more tracks in the snow than if they had passed through the area without stopping.

The low sun was already screened by the white birches around my stand as I scanned the grounds about me. I discerned the fuzzy outline of a deer standing in the distance behind a scant growth of hazel brush. I detected no movement whatever, but the more I studied the form, the more it looked like a big deer standing broadside to me with its head lowered to the ground. I had seen a buck in such a posture some years before, and he reminded me of an old, worn-out plow horse too weary to hold up his head. I thought then that maybe the buck was resting his neck from the burden of a heavy rack.

The outline of the object did not change during the several times I scrutinized it, and I began to wonder if it was a deer after all. Finally, as I was ready to leave my post for the day, I put a cartridge shell to my lips and gave a shrill blast. A head jerked upward above the hazel brush and there was a nice buck standing at full attention looking at me. He pranced off with tail erect, let out a couple of husky snorts, and then he was gone. I went over to study his tracks and found a spot where his nose made a slight depression in the snow, but there was no gouge in the snow deep enough to indicate the deer was eating snow to quench his thirst. Obviously, he had been half dozing, and when I roused him from his drowse, he was as fresh and wide-awake as any buck. The completely idle whitetail during deer season is not a common sight; such a study is reserved for the man on watch or the patient still-hunter who probes the backwoods country.

One of the rarest sights to come across my stand was two big, plump spike bucks that had enough mass in their antlers to make them at least eight-pointers. The twins were bigger than average mature deer, and their heavy, slightly curved spikes appeared to be about fourteen inches long. The pair looked a bit ridiculous, like overgrown billy goats, with bleached, flat spikes that were as heavy as the beams on big forked antlers. Big as the animals were, the strange pair went by unscathed, for there was not a single necessary fork on any of the beams.

One can hastily conclude that something went wrong with normal antler development here. However, it is more probable that the animals were early fawns of the year before despite their great size. Their large, ivory-colored, flat spikes were characteristic of the beams of bucks that roamed this region at this time. It is certainly not likely that two mature bucks would still travel as twins even had they been fortunate enough to have escaped hunters in all that time. There is much that can influence the size of deer and their antler formation, and parentage plays an important role here. The ten-point buck I got here a few days later was also bigger than average, and the flattened beams of his ivory antlers were as heavy as those of the twins. This prime animal could have been the sire of the overgrown pair.

Trail watching calls for more perseverance than it does skill in comparison to still-hunting. It also requires less expenditure of energy and less knowledge of the hunting grounds than is expected of the participants of an organized hunting group. By virtue of the few requirements imposed on the trail watcher, this type of hunting should have a much wider appeal than it does. It is an easy way out for the newcomer into the ranks who seems not sure of himself, or else is not all fired up for joining the gang in the all-out chase. It is befitting the older men and the physically handicapped who have the zest but lack the stamina necessary for the more rugged participation. And it is also appropriate for the man who likes to withdraw from the hub of the chase and enjoy the luxury of easy hunting.

The Hunter as Nature Observer

Too often the man becomes so involved with the hunt and the hunters that he misses much of the actual joys of being out in the autumn woods. Filling the legal bag should not be the foremost and sole purpose of any hunt, for if it is, then the outdoors will attract men only as long as there is some material gain to be wrested from the outdoors. Some of the thrills and surprises the hunter experiences in the woods come not from shooting his game, but from unusual observations made in the interludes of his hunt. And the trail watcher, sitting alone on his stand, finds mental occupation in the natural activity of any wildlife about him. If deer alone attract his attention, he will soon become bored of the lonely vigil. Trail watching is not for him.

Not many men today are accustomed to the utter silence of the woods; in fact, few there are who can endure the absence of sound for a prolonged period such as one experiences on a lonely stand, especially during the early or late hours of the day. In our modern civilization we have not only come to tolerate the sounds of our whirling machines of progress, but we have actually accepted them as being inseparable from our good living. The mass of our population finds itself in a sort of vacuum when subjected to the hush of even semi-wilderness country. It feels uneasy, depressed, and, in some instances, frightened by this strange environment.

All of this reflects our loss in appreciation of the outdoors. We are pseudo-outdoorsmen rigged in the latest accouterment from the sporting goods stores, making free use of a few cliches of the trade, and passing ourselves off as good as the next outdoorsman. Material success becomes the measuring stick of the value of a hunting trip, and the man who bags his game the first day is termed "lucky." He can leave the woods in triumph after a minimum contact with the wilderness, though he extracts from it nothing more than bare poundage in venison which, in all probability, he will not greatly relish eating.

If Thoreau was an extremist for his curiosity in even the smallest facets of nature's wonders, then the ordinary outdoorsman of today is also an extremist in his willingness to remain aloof from the world in which he hunts. There is a precious silence in the woods, but this silence has become a vacuum to our jaded ears. In this eerie silence the trail watcher, once his senses become attuned to the muted activity about him, hears sounds, detects life, and smells odors of an untrammeled and mysterious world.

The easy-going trail watcher has ample time on his hands for the close observations not afforded the man on the move. The hunter in motion must exercise his eyes and ears to their utmost if he expects to intercept his game by surprise; and in his concentration he must allot a precious portion of his attention to selecting a noiseless and advantageous passage in his pursuit. This leaves him little opportunity for a ground-level study of wildlife; and much that goes on with the woodland creatures at this time of the year is very near the ground and sometimes below it.

When a man walks up to his stand in the morning he might be impressed with the lack of any visible wildlife about him. He is, perhaps, not aware that he comes as an intruder, and his encroachment at least temporarily alters the habitat about him. Like a squirrel hunter entering a grove of oak trees, he must sit down for a spell and wait for the woods creatures to resume their interrupted industry. After a half hour or so of quiet, the lone hunter becomes accepted as part of the surroundings. Now he can catch glimpses of unrestrained animal behavior, and many of these observations will be the more interesting experiences of his hunt.

You do not sit very long before a blue jay suddenly starts screaming in the distance. There used to be a belief, and still is among some hunters, that the bird is rudely roused from his tranquility, most probably by approaching deer. The same is often said of the raucous cries of the raven. About all that can be truthfully said about these birds and any aid they unwittingly give the hunter, is that they do keep the man on the stand alert.

It is surprising the amount of unseen activity going on in the deep grasses of snowless ground as one strains his ears to catch the sound of a snapping twig in the distance. Many times I have heard warning sounds like that of an approaching deer, and I was kept on edge for minutes as the sounds persisted, but the deer never came into view. Then I caught the movement of some-thing in the grass at my very feet. Sometimes the industrious mouse was so active that I was tempted to leave the annoying fellow to himself and seek another stand.

But I concluded that if I could deceive a timid mouse and put him at such ease, then a deer at much greater distance would hardly take offense at my presence. Mice are like other inhabitants of the outdoors, and to a large degree like whitetails themselves. If I make a slight motion with my foot, the little rodents become frightened and I will neither see nor hear their stirring for some time. Then after a few minutes, there comes a subdued rustle followed by a long silence, a seeming mouse venture to test if all is clear again in the little mouse kingdom. After a bit, the rustling begins and continues as before, and maybe it is joined by the activity of other members of the family. But I can always put down the din by merely moving my foot in the grass. After a series of these threats, the mice will disperse to the remote extremities of their kingdom, for like whitetails, they too have runways — small tunnels in the grass that take them to various grounds of their bailiwick.

There are times when the crunching of dried leaves by mice puts me on guard for a buck crashing down the runway, but this diminutive noise only a few feet away comes louder to my ears than the noisiest buck carelessly crashing through a thicket a few hundred feet away. After one strains his ears till he hears a constant tinkling as of cow bells in the distance, his ears play him false, and the loudest sounds come from the smaller animals of the forest. In such a case, I find it best to get above the level of the ground and seek a perch on a stump or log, or else stand with my back propped against a tree.

Red squirrels, too, can be very distracting, for once they are on the move they scamper back and forth in your area, and they might remain in your hearing range for hours. Yet, you must listen to them, as annoying as it is at times, for a similar noise could be made by a deer. Sometimes a sudden outburst of a medley of noises breaks the calm of your watch as a pair of gray squirrels starts a family rumpus in a nearby tree. You wonder what domestic troubles gray squirrels could possibly have in this lonely outpost. Here you have a privileged seat in this family quarrel, and you watch it with prying interest. But the quarrel ends as abruptly as it started and, with some measure of relief at the apparent reconciliation,

you turn your attention to the hunt. All in all, these busy rodents, both mice and squirrels, keep the hunter alert and amused. A deer stand could be mighty dull without these stirring creatures.

Weasels are fascinating animals to watch. They are the Lilliputian gangsters of the forest, prowling during the day as well as during the night. Like mink, they are always in a hurry to make their circuits. These tireless hunters abound in energy, searching out every clump of grass, hollow log, or rock crevice on their route, and always running as though they were behind schedule in their hunt. They do not linger long in passing my stand, and if the ground is bare of snow I see the white bundles of energy pass from my view about the same time that the sound of the patter of their feet leaves my ears. Sometimes, even before the weasel has quite left the area, he comes back to reinvestigate a half-rotted stump, as though in his haste he forgot to ferret out a particular cranny. After he has completed this more thorough examination, he scampers off quickly to take up his hunt where he left off. I have never seen a weasel that was not in a hurry.

Once I came upon a white-pine stump whose roots were considerably exposed above the ground. The snow about the stump was dotted with weasel tracks, and as I studied this veritable weasel haven I found the reason for this concentration of tracks. Someone had dressed out a deer here, and the weasels were feasting on the viscera of the animal. There was an abundance of snowshoe hares and field mice in the country at this time, but even the warm blood-loving weasels will sometimes accept an easy handout and camp at the site of the stale and insipid remnants of a kill.

Weasels darted in and out of the maze of stump roots, and I set my gun down to watch them. I usually carried a trap or two with me when I hunted in those days, as I often tended my trapline during the hunting season. Fortunately, I had a trap with me, and here was a chance to make a set and watch the weasel step into the trap.

This was a family of short-tailed weasels, much smaller than the common or long-tailed species. On several occasions I have seen these smaller carnivores in family groups. The long-tailed weasels are bold solo hunters, and they are less content to tarry long at a stale carcass.

Even in the days when ermine pelts commanded a high price, trappers and fur houses made no distinction between the two species in this area. The large long-tailed and the smaller short-tailed were simply small or large weasels. Despite the limited knowledge I gained from my school-day traplines, I recognized some differences in the two species. The long-tailed weasels were the more common where I trapped; though they varied somewhat in size among them, they were always the largest. The short-tailed fellows were easily recognized by their shorter tails. They seemed to live in family groups and often tarried for days where food was available to them.

There must have been at least a half-dozen black-tipped tails and as many pairs of beady eyes darting nervously about the stump roots as I watched. Plainly, they were unwilling to leave their stronghold, though they were considerably aroused by my presence. One weasel kept thrusting his head through an opening in the stump roots, and I decided to set the long-springed size No. 1 trap at his door. Then I sat back a few steps to await his curiosity or defiance, whatever it was that caused him to poke his head through this entrance at regular intervals.

Before I had quite settled down, the little beast poked his head out and skimmed over the trap so rapidly I could not see the movements of his feet. As I moved my arm toward him, he skimmed backward over the trap without springing it. His feet moved so quickly that he did not exert pressure long enough to put sufficient weight to bear on the pan of the trap. So I raised the pan higher and adjusted the trigger on its very edge. I was now determined to outwit the saucy little fellow and add his pelt, and possibly those of the rest of his family, to my fur collection.

Now I merely crouched on my knees a few feet from his threshold, and the pert fellow was out again guarding his entrance. Each time I moved my hand toward him he retreated backward as before, but he would come out almost as I withdrew my threatening hand. His legs skipped about the trap with lightning speed, and when he did pause before his retreat, he managed to stand on the jaws of the trap or else on the portion of the pan that gave him the least leverage to trip it. It took about a dozen arm motions before I could inveigle the weasel into springing the trap.

This interval in my deer hunting was not very remunerative, financially, for the rest of the weasels decamped one by one. Perhaps the female I had taken was the dam of the others, and she boldly held my attention while her grown litter escaped unnoticed.

The weasel is a determined hunter and once he has his mind on his quarry, the bloodthirsty fellow is not easily deterred from the chase. I watched a snowshoe hare as he bounded over a ridge to enter the tangle of speckled alders in a frozen bog. A few seconds later a long-tailed weasel came hopping along the hare's trail and, as he entered the thicket, paused, nervously standing on his haunches, as if he had to decide quickly which of the beaten runways to follow.

Then he made short sojourns on the various runways, always returning to the starting point for a fresh reconnaissance. The black tip of his tail, floating along the network of the hares' highways, marked the irregular progress of the noiseless killer. In time he expanded his search to a wider radius, and he would be gone for several minutes. Even when I threw dead tree branches at him, he remained undaunted and continued his frenzied search for the hare, which now remained frozen with terror somewhere in the depths of the bog. Yet the terror-stricken hare was protected by its own helplessness, for the impatient pursuer in his haste could not easily detect the white coat of his sitting quarry against the snowy background.

More than an hour had elapsed, yet the tenacious hunter occasionally came back to where his hare had entered the lowland thicket. It was as though he came back to revel in the spot where he had last seen the snowshoe hare disappear into the alder growth. This was a lean afternoon for this persistent prowler. Subsistence does not come easily even to these diligent hunters, for with weasels, as with most Northern carnivores, it is feast or famine during the winter months when wildlife activity is at a low ebb.

Roaming bears are not commonly seen by hunters during the normal temperatures of a deer season even in our most northern areas. Occasionally, if the weather turns mild and snow is scant or absent, a bear will leave his den, but because of the relatively few roaming bruins, few hunters even get to see the animals' tracks in the snow. Bears are not easily run down by tracking, for they cling to the rougher terrain in a direct route out of the country when on the move. Unlike deer, bears necessarily roam a much wider area in their quest for a limited food supply for their enormous appetites. Through the course of these long rovings they become acquainted with a far-flung domain, and they have in mind a definite hideout at some extremity of their grounds when danger threatens them.

Not all bears leave their comfortable dens even when warm weather brings them from their stupor. One day I paused on a sharp ridge to take a temporary stand overlooking a series of lesser ridges crisscrossed with wind-blown timber. The fallen timber extended beyond the hills and into a large wooded marsh — a country more suitable for bruins than whitetails. After one spends some time searching the more distant grounds about him, his eyes quite naturally seek relief by resting on some nearby objects. This object was an old white-pine stump planted on the very apex of the steep ridge, and there was a sharp decline toward a valley on one side of the stump. Here was a hole about eighteen inches wide and somewhat less in height. I never quite outgrew my childhood penchant for prying into the darkness of hollow logs, burrows, or anything that has the appearances of a sanctum for some retiring forest dweller.

I promptly thrust my head into the black hole and almost collided with the swaying head of a drowsy bruin. He did not seem fully aware of any danger brought on by my intrusion, for he lay in his snug bed, his eyes less than wide open, and his head moving very slowly from side to side as though he were attempting to lull himself into sleep and thus dispel the hazy image before him.

The bruin showed not the slightest signs of alarm or concern, for he lay seemingly contented like a fat sow in the comforts of her wallow. I knelt before the entrance to the den, and from less than two feet I uttered a few soft-spoken words in a low, monotone voice, but I got no reaction from the sleepy occupant. After a half hour I left my indifferent bruin to himself, feeling that if I loitered around much longer he might wake from his lethargy and decide to leave his winter quarters. I had nothing against this bruin or any other, and killing him would give me no satisfaction or pride.

When I arrived at the car, my partner was already there waiting. My story of the bear in its den interested him to the point where he persuaded me to lead him to the scene. As much as both of us had hunted, it was the first occupied den either of us had found. There was no guarantee the animal would still be there, but we decided to expend the hour of available daylight in this nature study.

The snow was melting rapidly, and we had some difficulty in following my tracks back to the hills. Here, much of the snow was already gone from the southern slopes, so we disregarded my tracks, and I led the way up to the apparent ridge, but it was not the right one. The grounds were familiar enough, but one rise looked like the next, and in the anxious search our conversation must have reached a high and rousing pitch. We heard a deep underground rumbling coming from a stump on a hill crest, and I recognized the spot immediately.

The bear, in his tight quarters, had to maneuver himself into position for a quick evacuation of his den. His front paws and head had to be thrust through the opening, and his hind legs placed directly under his body for the spring that brought him out in one long leap. A bear is not graceful when in full flight, but he does cover ground in a hurry over the roughest terrain. In making the obstacle run of the downed popples, he simply ran in a straight line, breaking the smaller obstructions and glancing his muscular shoulders off the heavier tree trunks on his route. We heard him crashing along the edge of the swamp long after he was lost to our view. By now he was as wide awake as ever.

There was only the den to investigate now, and we found it to be not more than eighteen inches high and about three and a half feet in circumference. It was well lined with leaves and snugly accommodated this particular bruin, which weighed around 250 pounds. We guessed that the bear had some difficulty, after squeezing into the entrance headfirst, in turning around in the small compartment to face the opening again.

All the bear dens I have ever found were located in spots where a hunter is not likely to pass, such as on steep slopes overlooking a small valley or in the deep grasses of a dry marsh filled with woody debris. Hunters normally follow ridges where they can see to either side, and they find little occasion to go into a deep, small valley when they can scan it from above. The deep marsh grasses with their rough grounds and fallen timber are bypassed by most men.

Sometimes the dens are not more than a hollow stump with little or no protection from above; they could be mere excavations under wind-blown trees; especially if the upturned roots offer some protec-

tion from the wind, or if several tree trunks topple over a slight depression in the ground, the bear has a ready-made den. This particular lair we studied was well selected. Though it was on a ridge, the den opening faced the small ravine and could not be seen by anyone following the crest except by sheer chance or by one moved by more than ordinary curiosity.

Sometimes a fox comes down my trail, alternately trotting and pausing in his search for food. He investigates clumps of weeds, likely spots for mice, then proceeds on with nose held high as he continually sniffs the air. Of the two species we have, the gray fox, at one time more common in northern Wisconsin, now seems to cling to the swampy backcountry, and the aggressive red fox has spread from the farmlands into much of the wild habitat that saw only the grays. If a fox pauses very long before my stand to sample the air, he probably has detected my scent. Without further investigation, he leaves the hot spot for the country beyond. As numerous as foxes are in some areas, they are far more difficult to study closely in an undisturbed state than are deer.

Brush wolves, too, are rarely seen by the trail watcher, and in all my sitting I have witnessed only three of these shy species. One was trotting down a distant hillside on a path leading to my stand. Somehow he became suspicious, for he stopped short with ears erect and nose up. After sniffing the air in all directions it appeared he could not account for his uneasiness. Like some suspicious bucks I have encountered, rather than seek to justify his reason for uneasiness, he turned around and scampered back up the trail. Neither foxes nor wolves remain long enough in view for close observation, for they filter through your area like mere visions, and the slightly swaying brake ferns that mark their exits seem the only proof the animal has been there.

The daily routine of the snowshoe hare can be studied from a stand overlooking a speckled alder swamp. No animal seems more concerned with its safety than this great provider for the prowling meat eaters. As he silently nibbles on tender shoots in his swamp world, he pauses at regular intervals to strain his ears for the faintest noises. Sometimes he freezes into a motionless, white ball for an hour or more as he basks in the warmth of the winter sun. His days are filled with idle time, and whether he feeds, hops about, makes an energetic spurt across his kingdom, or merely sits, his actions seem not too purposeful.

In late fall and winter, Lepus is most at home in a silent world muffled by a deep blanket of light snow gently draped over a bog's resilient floor of sphagnum moss and such heath growths as Labrador tea, swamp laurel, and bog rosemary. His runways, like a labyrinth of trenches, are deeply pressed below the snow line, and the snow-laden hedges arch over his highways to form enchanting tunnels. He travels these avenues noiselessly even when he sprints along them, as he often does for no apparent reason, and if he can be seen at all as he hops about, it is the black tips of his ears that betray him. At times I have watched a hare dash down his snow-packed runway, and when he stopped short in his sprint, my eyes sought to see him continuing far down the trail.

Camouflage is his greatest asset, and that, together with his fleet legs and splayed feet, is the only protection nature has afforded the wilderness species. He is not as cunning or courageous as the common cottontail rabbit, and his one recourse when danger confronts him is to flee his enemy. Nature has endowed him with little capacity for trickery in escape or evasion.

Prolific Lepus, like the lemming of the northern tundras, has extremely fluctuating populations, perhaps more so in the past than today. The last heavy population peak I observed was in the late 1930s, and the hares were then numerous beyond belief in northern Wisconsin's Sawyer County. I recall one early spring, possibly in March, when I witnessed a hillside swell in motion with a horde of shaggy hares. Like the hillside with only remnant patches of snow, the swarming animals were mottled white and brown with a wide degree of variation in individuals from nearly all white to the brown summer pelage.

The same year, in August, a great plague ended their upward spiral. I was picking blackberries in one of the many burns when I smelled a great stench coming from the direction of a nearby swamp. There on a slight rise alongside the wet meadow were the bodies of hundreds of hares, some reduced by time to mere legs and hide, others apparently dead only a few days, and some few dying before my very eyes. The hare population was reduced to almost extinction in the country I had hunted, and since then it has remained relatively low and confined mostly to the lowlands.

The era of the extremely ups and downs in the snowshoe population here has not occurred since.

The stolid porcupine leads a life devoid of all but what is necessary for his bare existence. His packed trail leads from a log shell or the hollow at the base of a standing tree trunk. His subsistence comes to him more easily than it does to most of the wood folk, and he has virtually no natural enemies except for a hard-put bobcat, and this silent stalker is confined mostly to the evergreen swamps where he finds the snowshoe hare a more acceptable prey.

On sunny, frosty mornings the porcupine likes to scale the topmost branches of a tree to receive the benefits of the low November sun while he gnaws away at his frosted dinner of bark. On a still day I can hear him as he shifts about on his precarious perch. He eats only the inner bark, and the discarded thin outer bark falls silently down to mar the snow below. I do not begrudge him the many aspens available to him, but I feel a bit less tolerant of him when he is atop a prime pine or maple tree.

The hunter anxious to try his gun on a living target accounts for the most casualties in the prickly species. This has undoubtedly kept the bark eaters in check on my hunting grounds, for the porcupine population has been quite consistent over the years here, with neither a marked scarcity of the animals nor an overabundance of them to cause an appreciable amount of tree damage.

Mink do not tarry long in view during the colder months. I have seen only one from a deer-hunting stand, and he followed the ice ledge along a stream and never paused or slowed his pace all the while in passing. The hurried weasel travels an irregular and uncertain path, guided in his course by favorable game prospects he encounters, but the equally restless and energetic winter mink merely glosses over his grounds as he makes his regular rounds. He seldom stops to investigate anything along his route; perhaps this is because he has made the same circuit many times in the past. And so he patrols his beat as from a sense of habit, or as though he were out for exercise. Only when he comes upon promise of game in this routine run does he change to the determined hunter and relentless killer for which he is known.

I once saw a mink wrestle a large walleyed pike in a mad fury of spray, fur, and fins, in the shallows of a lake. So engrossed was he with his attack on the walleye, which weighed about six pounds, that I could not distract his attention with my shouting. He finally succeeded in dragging the struggling fish from the shore waters to the bank, and with his victim beside him, he held his ground with a defiant display of teeth while I stood only a dozen feet away. After awhile his rage cooled off some, but he remained stubborn and would not leave the fish until I deliberately walked toward him. Then he disappeared in the grass, and I traced his slow progress by the movements of the luxuriant lakeside growth. When I thought he had finally abandoned his spoils, I saw him farther down the trail alongside the lake, and he was still interested in his unfinished business. The mink was unwilling to part with this booty, and I walked off to let him return to wallow in his kill.

Otter, built much like mink, though larger, also make their regular routes of the waterways. Because they move in a much larger area than do mink, they find it necessary to travel cross-country considerable distances to other waterways in making their long circuitous trips. But unlike mink, otters usually travel in pairs, and they tarry less along their route during the cold months than they do in summer.

The only pair of otters I saw during a hunting season was on snowless ground, and the animals were bounding, one closely behind the other, across a valley filled with sere brake ferns. Mink bound with very little upward spring, but the otters leaped high into the air so they could see above the dense growth as they traveled. Their leaps were short, but buoyant and graceful, and their dark coats glistened in the sunlight as they bobbed over the dead ferns.

A partridge sometimes breaks the late afternoon silence with its rapidly beating wings as it makes for an aspen tree near my stand. The bird uses its wings to balance itself while it strains for buds within its reach. It feeds busily and noisily with no fear of an enemy from below. Frequently, it loses its balance while swaying on a supple twig, and it must struggle with wing beats to regain its posture. Wing-feather tips grating against slender branches come as commotion and din to the ears of the hunter accustomed to the lesser noises of the forest. The partridge flutters off across the hill and settles in the next valley, and all is quiet as before.

My eyes were trained on the valley below me one morning after a three-inch snowfall had whitened the drab landscape. Suddenly, I was startled by a bullet-shaped object coming toward me at great speed, emitting a hissing sound as it cut the air. It landed with a thud on the hillside just twenty feet below me, and I thought this was it for sure — a missile from outer space threatening me and my deer stand.

Cautiously, I approached the dark object half buried in the snow; then I recognized the feathers on the strange mass and I carefully picked it up in wonderment. The limp partridge was unconscious, and carrying it up to my stand, I set it down on the soft snow. In about two minutes the bird opened its eyes and showed signs of life, and a few minutes later it took off on its wobbly flight over the valley. The birds commonly seek the protection and warmth of deep snow, and they plunge into it with wings tightly folded and head pulled in close to the body. Apparently, this partridge overestimated the depth of the snowfall. Accidents among forest creatures during their normal existence are not common, certainly not to be compared with the traffic kills on the highways.

The man on the stand becomes at least a casual bird watcher in spite of himself unless he is completely devoid of any sympathetic feeling toward wildlife. A playful and friendly chickadee pops out from nowhere to console and amuse the lonely hunter. Sometimes he flutters at the end of my gun barrel as if to show his complete confidence in me. There is no other bird I know whose body and activity can be studied in detail at such close range. These are the least distracting creatures that come to me.

Both the hairy and downy woodpeckers are active on frosty, sunny days. The smaller downy is a dead ringer for the hairy woodpecker in all respects except size. Their high-pitched peeek, peeek, as they dip from tree to tree, and their noisy tattooing on tree trunks as they search for grubs, fills the void of a snow-blanketed valley. Occasionally, in the more heavily wooded country, a big pileated woodpecker laboriously wings in undulating flight across the lowlands. His flight is almost silent except when he brushes past dead twigs as he bobs through a narrow passage in tall timber.

Early in the morning I sometimes find a great homed owl still on his perch at the edge of a swamp. He looks like a big gnarl on a dead tree, saving his energy for the one big swoop necessary for surprising the fleet-footed snowshoe hare. After the last traces of dawn finally yield to daylight, the big owl quietly shoves off from his perch and returns to the seclusion of tall evergreens far in the swamp. He has had lean picking during this vigil, but tomorrow night or the next, he will gorge himself to a state of stupor.

Some of the smaller birds can be easily passed off for sparrows, but if you are a trail watcher of long standing, you learn to take more than just passive interest in even the least life about you. Among these ever-bustling little fellows, I identify the white-breasted nuthatches conducting thorough searches in bark crevices of tree trunks for nourishing, minute grubs. The golden-crowned kinglet, even at a dozen paces, is a drab nondescript bird, and a flock of white-winged crossbills fluttering about the spruce trees can be ordinary sparrows unless studied at close range.

My area is sometimes invaded by pine grosbeaks, robin-sized birds of an uninteresting dull plumage when seen from afar. In open light, when observed at short range, the males are predominantly rosy red, and they appear handsome when seen in the surroundings of barren trees and snowy background. Undoubtedly, the male pine grosbeak is often carelessly mistaken for a tarrying robin when seen in November, or else the first robin of spring if seen in February.

In rarer instances, and only in certain areas of scattered jackpine and spruce growth, I find the bold Canada jay fluttering about me. He looks like an overgrown chickadee and, like this little clown, he has little fear of man. Once he locates me in his pine habitat, I am not without company for the day.

One might think that nature overlooked color protection for some of her forest creatures. The cardinal stands out sharply on a sunny day against a background of snow, but I seldom see him so favorably exposed. On a dark day in the somber woods he is not a flashy bird at all, and he is difficult to discern when he sits without movement in the low evergreens, his favorite winter haunts.

One does not often take time off to watch a soaring bald eagle for minutes at a time, but at one of my stands near a big lake these majestic birds are quite common. Studying these eagles does not interfere with my trail watching, for the birds make no noise in their gliding flight, and I need not keep my eyes on them continually, for they cruise the lake shore during much of the day, and I can watch them at odd moments.

The white heads and tails of these great winged carnivores burst into bright flashes when the sun strikes their feathers at a certain precise angle. In their easy flight, the words "stately" and "freedom loving" come as natural attributes of this emblematic bird. Yet, these graceful and symbolic birds do not perform their effortless flights just for my mere enjoyment. They come here annually, just as winter sets in, to search for and prey upon the cripple ducks left in the wake of the duck hunting season. As soon as the ice starts forming on the lake, the wounded ducks clinging to the shore water, being unable to fly, are forced to take to the protection of the shoreline growth.

Here, they are easy prey for owls, foxes, mink, and the other predators, and the eagles coming from great distances join the raiders for a fresh, tasty repast. There are many fewer ducks on this lake than in the past years and, consequently, fewer predators find an easy handout here now. Still, the northern bald eagles come to this lake as from sheer habit, for I seldom see the birds do anything more than scour the lake margin, rarely indicating by their flights that their mission is more than patrolling the lake. Eagles have a relatively long life span, and it is possible the older birds make this yearly pilgrimage because of past experiences of more bountiful days and easier living.

When deep snow and bitter cold come early, the deer hunter finds wildlife activity reduced to bare essentials. Many creatures, in deep stupor, wait out the winter in snow-covered dens, and the wildwood becomes deserted save for those forest denizens elected to carry on. Now one sees the less trivial side of wood life, for every movement of creature is of significance. Activity is motivated by pangs of hunger and the will to survive, and energy for all else is niggardly expended. Here is wildlife in bold, stark relief, slowed down in pulse, and stripped of the exuberances of summer's lush living.

There are other observances the idle trail watcher makes in his unconstrained mood. Unlike a man occupied in active participation of group hunting or serious still-hunting, the idler finds time to extract what color and beauty he can find in the drab November woods. Color at this season is subtle, indeed, yet any variation from the sere brown of fall, with or without a snowy background, can be detected at once if one affords the time for this consideration. The bud-tipped twigs of the forest trees are already tinged with a mere suggestion of next spring's bursting leaf buds. Nature is never devoid of color, though in bleak November the various subdued hues must be studiously separated from the overall drabness of the landscape.

I paused one hunting season on a high rise that overlooked a bog densely shaded with tall, dark black spruce. It seemed a dismal scene in late November, and I recalled the life and color of this orchid sanctum that I visited with my camera so often during the past June and July. Here, in this moss-carpeted darkness, I found the white splashes of water arum spathes, the maroon pitcher plant blooms with their silky, delicate petals, and those members of the orchid family, the pink stemless lady's slippers and the showy orchis. Deep in the depths of the bog, on the sunlit floating margin of a small, deep pond, whose infirm bottom consisted of suspended decaying vegetation, there were two other members of the orchid family, grass pinks and snake mouths.

On the firmer ground in the glades of this isolated plant preserve were the blooms of the swamp heathers — the white of the Labrador tea, the crimson-pink splash of the bog laurel, and the tiny, white spherical blooms of the bog rosemary tinted with a mere suggestion of crimson-pink. All these moisture-loving plants parade their blooms in turn through the months of midsummer when the warmth of the outer world finally permeates the depths of this cool wilderness stronghold. It is my guess that such isolated bog habitats will be the last of our untrammeled wilderness to yield to our aggressive society; for, at present, there is little monetary gain to be wrested from these soggy plant kingdoms.

Now, in comparison, the familiar bog seemed bleak, indeed. The dark spruce trees approached a darker, lifeless green, and there appeared little in the somber scene to attract the eye. As I stood there looking at the overall gloom, the sun broke through the leaden sky. Now, I could pick up bits of color here and there. The younger shoots of clumps of red-osier dogwoods, growing at the edge of the bog, revealed a brilliant haze of red as the sun struck their branches. In subdued contrast were the waxy, olive-green branchlets of the straggling round-leaved dogwoods and the warm yellow of willows.

Even the mottled, speckled alders that fringed the margin of the soggy jungle gave off a warming glisten of dark bronze. And from the border of a small adjacent flat, filled with marsh grasses, came the bolder color of scarlet-orange. This was the persistent fruit of the winterberry or black alder of the holly family. At times I have seen an entire flat, neither swamp nor highland but somewhere in between, glisten in extravagant scarlet-orange. From a distance, a single black alder shrub laden with berries closely hugging the branchlets stands out like a red-garbed hunter planted in the midst of a thicket.

When the snow is fresh and sparkling with frost, and the sun floods the woodland slopes, one can see tinges of color in tree trunks and branches of common trees. There is some color variation in the several species of poplar tree that is so common to most of our Northern states. The American aspen is grayish green, and sometimes the whitish bloom is so pronounced as to give the tree the appearance of a dull-colored white birch. The large-toothed aspen shows a slight glow of buff in its bark, and this is more discernible when the two trees are seen side by side. There is a very definite gradation of more buff or light bronze in the dark of the balsam poplar.

White birches can be chalky white, especially when the species take over a favorable sunny hillside, and they can be dull white with a slight sheen on the thin outer bark when found alone in other dense growth or when they are not sufficiently exposed to sunlight. The striped maple or moosewood, quite common on Michigan's upper peninsula, has dark, smooth, olive-green bark marked with light lines. Subdued hues are difficult to describe, and even the greens of the forest have many gradations, which can be readily differentiated but not described. The singular green of the striped maple bark is of such a green.

To me the black ash is the least appealing tree of all. Perhaps this is due to its environment of wet, unfriendly woods where, through centuries of bog evolution, firmer land was formed. The first hardwood to take root there was the black ash. There is little to attract one to these gloomy, watery lowlands, where neither flower nor animal life find a suitable habitat.

The slender, clean boles of the Norway pines, usually preferring the tall sunlit ridges, radiate a warm, ruddy glow to cheer the hunter on a cold day. Often I sit with my back propped against the friendly trunk of a Norway pine to watch the valley below. Maybe I am influenced more by the trees than by deer prospects in making my choice here. There are certain stands that appeal to me more than others, and I always prefer those that give me a variegated landscape, for merely sitting quietly with an inactive mind and little to observe can become boring and even depressing. Though one might be assured his deer will come by sometime that day or the next, he will not enjoy those many hours of idle waiting unless he finds some channel for diversion.

The trail watcher not only becomes a keen observer of wildlife about him; he also has a grandstand seat from which to study the good hunting techniques as well as the foibles of the hunters who go by in parade, and he silently passes judgment on the manner of each. All receive a degree of sympathy, the good hunter and the bad — the good hunter for wasting his diligence on grounds so well covered by the trail watcher, and the careless man for his artless approach.

It may seem strange that so many hunters can pass a stand without seeing the man at his post, but this is a common occurrence, especially if the latter is dressed in less than brilliant red, or the daylight is poor. This sometimes gives the watcher a feeling of superiority over his fellow man.

Actually, man has only his sense of sight with which to detect the hunter high on his stand, who in all probability is partly concealed or blended in with a stump or tree trunk. A deer has keener sight at a greater distance than man, it can detect slight movement much more readily, and it has, in addition, the use of its nose plus the ability to pick up sounds not easily revealed to the human ear. In spite of all this, the whitetail will still blunder past the trail watcher.

It is not surprising, then, that the man sitting on a vantage point is not always seen by the hunter passing below. And this poses a problem in backwoods etiquette. Should the trail attendant acknowledge his own presence to all comers? He could start a friendly conversation that might ruin precious time. If he ignores the situation, the intruder might linger on the grounds for quite some time — a rather unhappy state that could develop into embarrassment for both men. For a man can feel mighty uncomfortable when he finally discovers that both he and his grounds have

been under surveillance by another. And the first comer feels some guilt by allowing the situation to take place. My own practice is to simply stay put and watch the hunter go by. If he looks in my direction, I get up or wave my hand at him to let him know I am not legal game.

Most of the eager redcoats stick to the beaten path of a runway. Some move with utmost caution and others walk at a brisk pace and are soon out of my range. In the course of the day's hunt, these energetic men must cover many miles. Since they hike right along, they do little more than scan the trail ahead. Thus, instead of watching the runway at one point, they follow its entire length and have the chore over with. It is part of our present tendency to do things in a hurry.

A deer hunt is hardly complete without a day or two reserved for serious trail watching. It is a change in pace that can round out the experience and pleasure for every hunter. And he will be putting in his best time, for the hunter is more mentally alert when he is most physically relaxed.

Running Down Your Deer 5

THERE was a time when hunters took considerable pride in their ability to pursue and bag a specific deer. This was more practical several decades ago than it is at present. The increased number of men in the field today and the many backwoods roads now penetrating the deer country are not generally conducive to this type of hunting. Though there are some untrammeled areas where the determined hunter can attempt to run down the deer of his choice, somehow this phase of solo hunting is becoming a lost art.

Most huntsmen, when they come upon large, fresh tracks, will follow them hopefully for a while. Usually they give up the chase after they come upon the tracks of the bounding animal. However, I am here referring to the man who carefully studies the slots in the snow and decides from them that here is the big deer he will attempt to take. This is

his quarry and he will not deviate from his persistent chase. Usually, if the tracking is started reasonably early in the morning, the hunter can hope to bag his deer the same day.

Of all types of hunting, this is the most specialized. Only a rare combination of characteristics and background produces the kind of man who will dog his quarry from dawn to dusk, if necessary. Many a determined tracker might wear off his keen zest for the chase of the big buck by evening, but after a night's rest and composure, his determination is restored and he picks up the trail next morning with a happy outlook.

The many hunters I have known who considered running down a particular deer as a thoroughly practical method of hunting had common qualifications. They were exuberant, stout-legged young men, and if not so young, they still retained a love and capacity for endless walking. They were ardent hunters with an unusual knowledge and appreciation of the outdoors. Chances are they had taken their share of deer in the past, and now they decided to pit their physical endurance, determination, and woods lore against a marked animal, usually a prized buck. These men who set their minds on taking specific deer were neither supermen nor attention-seeking nonconformists. They were merely pursuing an ancient but effective method for taking most wild animals. The scattered few Nimrods today who prefer to run down their bucks in country favorable for this type of hunting still find the method as practical as ever.

A wolf, bear, deer, or even a snowshoe hare senses a crisp image of danger when first put into flight by the intruding hunter. After the dash to apparent safety, these animals soon regain their composure and are in top mettle again. This is the normal experience of most animals, and it has become very much a part of their everyday living. In fact, an animal might be spooked several times during the day, as a deer might be during the hunting season, and yet maintain the alertness and bearing necessary for self-preservation.

But the one thing an animal cannot mentally cope with is being persistently dogged by its enemy. The steady pressure put on by a tracker eventually disarms the quarry. The animal's normal senses necessary for its very existence become fogged. Curiosity, lack of courage, and bewilderment take over, and the hounded animal wallows in helpless confusion.

My first experience in taking advantage of this weakness in animals came many years ago. I had a new size 1 ½ trap set for foxes near the carcass of a dead calf in our pasture. Ordinarily, a No. 2 trap is used for foxes, but I had successfully taken both red and gray foxes in size 1 ½, if I selected only those traps with stout springs.

Several inches of snow had fallen during the night and the next morning, from a shed top in the farmyard, I scanned the set with binoculars. There were fox tracks around the calf carcass, but no fox in sight. After putting on a pair of skis, I approached the set to within a few hundred feet. Foxes had tramped about the dead calf, and I wondered why the trap was not sprung in the soft snow. So I promptly investigated. There was no trap or drag to be found, and the freshly fallen snow revealed no traces of a fox escaping with trap and drag.

So back to the house I went. Whenever a trapping situation

confronted me, I could always depend on my brother John for help. Together we went back to the pasture. He looked at the numerous fox tracks and then circled widely around the area. He paused a bit and, pointing to the ground, called to me. There were signs, half obscured by the newly fallen snow, of something being dragged toward the fence line. We followed the faint trail to the thick poplar growth on the other side of the fence. There, in a dense clump of hazel brush, was the drag. Judging by the signs in the snow and the chewed and trampled brush, the animal was held for some time but escaped with the trap after the wire holding the trap chain to the drag was twisted free.

This was a pretty good-sized brush wolf, my brother concluded. It, and perhaps its mate, had come to feed on the calf during the storm. The fox is credited with being trap shy, but he is bold enough to take bait most any time he is hungry. A brush wolf seldom takes bait unless he is driven by sheer hunger. And even then he usually succumbs to this ignominious act only at night under cover of a snowstorm.

It was still early in the morning. My brother suggested that I take the single-barreled shotgun with a few rounds of heavy shot, pack along a sandwich, and take after the wolf. He promised me that I would run him down if I kept after him all day.

This was a new experience to me, and with young legs and stout heart, and goaded by a $20 wolf bounty, I took off with buoyant stride on my skis. The tracks led northward through swamps and valley thickets, and the behavior of the animal seemed no different than that of any brush wolf. After about three miles of tracking, I came to a dense spruce swamp where the trail was lost in the labyrinth of snowshoe-hare trails.

After circling the northern end of the swamp, I came upon the first running tracks. I had flushed my wolf from the spruce jungle, and from now on I was to keep him worried. Since the powdery snow was only about ten inches deep, the skis were of little help, so I abandoned them at the edge of the swamp.

The wolf had chosen to follow the scant timber growth on the ridges now, and after following his trail for less than a quarter of a mile, I saw where he paused on a high point to watch his tracker. He veered to the left or right now, unmindful of direction, for he sought the easier going on barren hills or trails. As I pressed on, I noticed he paused more often in his uncertain flight. He no longer behaved like a true brush wolf.

The chase led me to a road, and the dangling trap chain occasionally left a mark alongside the ruts. Pressing on rapidly where the going was easier, I was surprised to catch a glimpse of the big wolf just as he bounded off into the brush at a road bend. Had I been ready with the gun I might have gotten in a quick shot at less than seventy-five yards. But it was early in the afternoon, and I had high hopes of taking the muddled wolf by nightfall.

Even as I left the road on the track of the harassed animal, I saw him slink over a knoll. He paused on a small rise and turned around to watch me. Then, as I continued on, he proceeded halfheartedly. He entered the bay of a large lake just below the rise. The going was good on the wind-packed snow here, and I thought the brush wolf had finally won the chase.

From about a hundred yards out on the lake, the wolf turned around to watch me. I sat down for a moment to appraise the situation. Then I removed my jacket and heavy overshoes. My thought was to make a fast dash down the slope and onto the lake, gun ready, and maybe get in a shot at reasonable range. The dazed brush wolf was nervously absorbed in every motion I made, and even as I ran toward him he made only a few steps and then paused to watch me again. He was completely licked. The fifty-pound male died easily when shot from about sixty yards.

I digress in detail on the behavior of a brush wolf harrowed by a persistent tracker because this is somewhat the reaction of any animal in such a situation. True, the wolf was hampered by the trap on his forepaw, but his behavior for the first three miles of escape was quite normal. If left alone, he undoubtedly would have freed himself of the small trap one way or another, even at the cost of his toes. However, once he knew he was being continually dogged, he lost all sense of balance and behaved very much unlike a member of his rugged species.

Any depth of snow up to a point that does not hamper the movements of a hunter is suitable for tracking down a deer. If the snow is of such depth that the tracker is pretty well exhausted by the time he first spooks his quarry, then the hunter is at a considerable disadvantage.

It is worthwhile, when picking up your deer track in the morning, to attempt a careful stalk until the animal is jumped. If conditions for a quiet approach are ideal, this should not be overlooked. Under situations not conducive for a quiet approach, the tracker might best follow the slots rapidly until he jumps the deer. From there on it is merely a case of putting on unrelenting pressure. After being flushed a few times, the deer becomes nervous and starts losing his poise. Individuals of the species differ greatly, and the pursuer never knows just what to expect. Old-time trackers tell you there are about as many quirks in a tracked buck's behavior as there are bucks.

Usually, after the animal is put into flight a half-dozen times, more or less, he begins to sense a pattern in this series of disturbances. The animal becomes ever conscious of his pursuer and anticipates his approach with careless curiosity. Soon the hunter is able to flush his game at close range, and he flushes it more often. The perplexed deer makes no attempt at a complete getaway, but merely lumbers on ahead of the hunter, pausing frequently to watch the approach of his tormentor.

Some hunters prefer to sit down for a few minutes at this point, knowing that the waiting buck will exhaust himself from sheer nervous tension. From here on the hunter can expect to get in a favorable shot some time or other as he continues to jump the deer at short intervals. If the shot misses its target, the deer usually

breaks into full flight for a considerable distance, but after he is followed he eventually slows down again to resume his former sluggish behavior.

Men who pursue a buck in this manner have various theories for the animal's strange conduct. Some believe the deer becomes accustomed to being followed and merely attempts to keep a safe distance ahead of the tracker. After awhile the animal becomes careless at the game and meets its doom. Others prefer to believe the deer is merely curious, trying to understand the strange behavior of a man who dogs him at every step. Deer, like cattle, can become very inquisitive at times. I have had a circle of bug-eyed cows crowd me while I was busily engaged setting a fox trap. And I recall three deer eyeing me in wonder as I chiseled a fishing hole in a small lake in the backcountry. So deep was their curiosity that it took them some time to snap from their trance even as I ran toward them shouting and brandishing my ice chisel.

Curiosity causes the downfall of many a whitetail, and it no doubt enters considerably into a buck's behavior when being dogged by a lone hunter. However, it is more likely that the faltering buck succumbs to a strange mixture of fear, curiosity, and frustration and not to any appreciable degree of physical fatigue.

I recall the first buck I tried to run down when I was a mere lad. While still-hunting some ridges on a crisp morning, a buck in top spirits jumped from his bed on the next ridge and crashed through the popples in the valley beyond with an apparent attempt to leave the area in all possible haste. I followed his bounding tracks for nearly two miles through thicket and open country, and in all that distance he paused briefly only two times. When I finally jumped him from his bed, I reasoned he had nearly an hour of rest and undoubtedly was in shape to duplicate this long sprint. I promptly gave up, fully convinced that I was no match for the fleet-footed whitetail. Later I learned it was not my speed or even my endurance I was to match against this prince of the forest.

6

Snow Tracking

EER tracking, like other types of solo hunting, is becoming less common as more hunters enter the woods each year. The tracker likes elbow room and, in fact, must have it. And his spirits sag mightily if, after following a set of slots until he is entirely engrossed in the pursuit, he finds someone else has muscled in on the trail ahead of him. Very definitely, tracking in an area congested with hunters is discouraging. But the tracker, by virtue of hunting alone, has flexible plans, and he can pick his spots. Hunters have a habit of shifting about from one area to another. These random movements can bring a heavy concentration of men in a locality, while another equally good territory might by chance be nearly or entirely abandoned. Since the army of hunters indicates its presence by the automobiles parked along the roads, a man knows before he sets foot on his grounds just what the hunting pressure in the environs is like. And even when he sees a sprinkling of parked cars along the road, he is likely to find little company if he walks a half-mile back in the country.

Tracking snow comes all too infrequently, and the inveterate tracker will not pass up this opportunity for a pleasant and often profitable hunt. It is possible to have snow-covered ground throughout the entire season and yet not have good tracking, for more than mere winter precipitation is here involved. So seldom does one find even one or two days during the deer season that lend themselves to this very specialized hunting, that when such a day comes, my partners will find me politely bowing out of their company.

The very best time to pick up a track is early in the morning after a snowfall of about four inches has ceased sometime during the night or very early in the morning, though a lesser snowfall will suffice if there is already a layer of not too crunchy snow beneath. Such a track will be fresh, the deer will likely be not far off, and he will not have been molested. The weather should be warm so the snow will be heavy and noiseless, and if the branches and trunks of the forest growth are mantled with white, so much the better for a close approach to your game. All this does not pamper the comfort-loving hunter, for he can expect to be ready for a happy change into dry clothes after the chase. But, dressed properly in wool, the man can be at least reasonably dry for the few hours he will be out.

A track picked up at such a time will not take you very far, for the whitetail, like the hunter, does not like to push his way through snow-laden thickets. All conditions are tops for tracking down your game, and it is most probable you will have the country to yourself at this time.

My first experience in tracking under such conditions happened quite by accident. Three days of a snowless deer season had already passed, and I was to meet my hunting companions early next morning at the intersection of two backwoods roads. Meanwhile, about six inches of wet snow had fallen during the night, clinging loosely to all cover from brake ferns to heavy aspens. It was a world of white, and I wondered why I ventured forth on such a day. At daybreak, I turned off the blacktop to follow a side road, where I was first to break trail with the car.

Before I had driven very far, I saw my first deer slots in snow for that season, and I had the usual urge to look them over. So I pulled to the side — in fact, much too far to the side — to allow passage for the vehicle of some other such overzealous hunter as I, who would be sure to enter the road after I had pioneered the trail. It was a lone animal with big tracks, and it crossed the road to enter a thicket whose branches bent down with the heavy weight of clinging snow. After looking at the forbidding white jungle, I was quite satisfied to continue on and join my companions. But the old car was mired in mud and snow, and even as broad daylight came, no one else entered the side road.

What an unhappy situation to confront. Then, it dawned on me there was nothing else to do but follow the deer track. Perhaps, after I returned, the fair-weather hunters would be surging in and I might get the car back on the road with some help. The idea appealed to me more and more, and I even became elated over the prospects of following a deer that was completely relaxed and possibly bedded down not too far off.

So I entered the woods with utmost caution, evading all possible snow drenching as I followed the tracks that I strongly suspected were those of a buck. The meandering trail indicated the animal was not making a long cross-country trek. And he wasn't, for I jumped the buck from his bed less than 200 yards from the road. He was facing his tracks as he got to his feet, making no more sound than a snowshoe hare. We must have seen each other at about the same time, at a distance of no more than fifty feet, although it appeared considerably further in the snowy jungle. The quick shot, as he whirled around for the takeoff, took him at a forward angle high back of the shoulder blades, and the bullet lodged in his neck. It is strange how some unhappy situation often diverts one into the path of success. Once I had the buck alongside the mired car, my troubles were over. Nobody passes up a hunter who needs help with his buck, and in this case, his car, too.

Although a fresh track picked up in the morning gives a man the advantage of following an unharried and composed animal, tracking can be good any time during the day if the snow is soft from above-freezing temperatures and if it is of sufficient depth to muffle the ordinary sounds made by the hunter's feet. A falling snow, however slight, coupled with this setup is definitely an asset for a close approach to game. During a bright day, any track not going into the sun is best for the hunter; he can see best with the sun at his back, whereas the whitetail, like man, is handicapped when looking into the low November sun.

The tracker is interested in following freshly made slots, for if he picks up a track around noon that was made early in the morning, the deer could be a considerable distance away and, perhaps, already flushed by some other redcoat. What the hunter seeks is to intercept the trail at a point near his quarry so that he can put every effort into the short stalk. It is more likely that a man can give more attention to a short hunt than he can to a considerably prolonged jaunt, for as time wears on he becomes careless even without realizing it.

The age of tracks can be appraised in most kinds of snow conditions. During a thaw, the slots rapidly lose their sharpness, and the hoofprints melt and expand more quickly on the compressed leaves underneath. Sometimes they may appear relatively fresh in deep snow, but the same trail leading under shade of evergreen growth is old and the imprints still frozen, indicating they were made before the thaw. And those tracks on a melting southern slope look ancient, while the ones in the valley made by the same animal appear still fresh.

As the warm day progresses, the hunter observes a deteriorating change in all tracks, including his own. It is only during such times as when the temperature hovers around the point where there is little thawing, and the imprints remain fresh longer, that the man must be more discerning. Even so, he need not be fooled by any old tracks for long, for he will soon pick up some clues that will aid him. The fresh trail will cross signs made by wildlife such as hares, rabbits, squirrels, and also other deer.

The age of a man's footprints is more easily ascertained than that of a deer, and if the two cross each other, the hunter, with a little study, should gain the needed information here. The hunter is aware of any tracks made by other redcoats in his area, and he can make a fair judgment of their age by comparing them with the fresh tracks he himself is constantly making. Therefore, he will gain some knowledge of the age of deer slots by observing whether they are made over a hunter's tracks or whether the hunter's tracks are made over them.

Tracking is less productive in dry, powdery snow, for now the air is crisp and the whitetail's senses are much keener. The sign in dense growth remains fresh in appearance even for a few days, and only by delicately feeling with bare fingers can one discern the crust of age on the disturbed snow. And the fresh sign in the open country can appear ancient if there is even a slight breeze stirring. Nothing looks as old as deer slots filled with snow. The tracker who is necessarily ever conscious of the weather soon learns its effects on aging deer slots under varying conditions. Deer pellets found along the trail, can also be of help. They are moist, black, and glossy when fresh, and become dry and dull brown with time.

Identifying the Sex

Very often a man will select a particular deer track to follow because he is sure its imprints are those of a large buck. Most probably his belief is largely influenced by the large size of the animal's hoof marks. Yet, two of the biggest whitetails I have ever seen, with proportionately big feet, were does. Actually, there is no reliable or practical method of discerning the difference between a buck and a doe track if the slots alone are observed.

Some hunters think the buck's front hoofs make a rounder impression than those of a doe, but the shape of hoof marks can vary greatly in the individual animal according to its stride and the nature of the footing. The toes appear pointed when the deer walks slowly in firm, but damp, earth or on a thin layer of snow or dust. And they look much rounder in deep snow. The sprawling toe marks emphasized by the imprint of dewclaws of any running large deer are readily accepted as being made by a big buck.

It is my belief from long experience that a heavy-necked, large buck with extremely weighty antlers makes a deeper impression with the tips of the toes of his front feet. This can be observed only in the walking tracks on soft ground or in shallow, soft snow. Since the toe tips sink deeper into the footing, the tracks have the appearance of being somewhat rounded.

But one's chances of finding such heavy animals these days are rather slim, and this exception might well be ignored.

Some few woodsmen are quite accurate in picking out the mature buck's footprints from the tracks of a band of deer. They select the most straddling stride in the group, then they look for a light drag of hoofs between each step. These two peculiarities in the same set of tracks are pretty certain to be those of a big buck. This slight deviation from the prints made by does and fawns becomes discernible only as the buck attains full maturity. The younger forked bucks do not have these characteristics so pronounced as to be of any value.

A close inspection of the feet of dead does and bucks of various ages will satisfy most men that the tracks these feet made did not in themselves give any clue to the identity of their owner's sex. Any recognizable difference between the tracks of a big doe and a big buck comes not from the individual animal's hoofprint, but from the way it is planted.

A sure way to recognize the trail of a buck is to actually see the animal make it, and a second best bet, if one is fortunate enough, is to find where the animal urinated. A doe haunches back and urinates in her tracks, often with a wide and irregular spray, while a buck's urine comes straight down to perforate the unbroken snow. Even as the animal moves on, the snow stains remain to determine the animal's sex. Both of these clinchers are far too remote to be of great use, for one finds a buck's urine stains in the snow about as often as he sees the animal itself.

There is, however, a general behavior pattern in the mature animal that helps distinguish its sex. A lone, walking track made at night, following the more established runways and traveling in a definite direction, is usually made by a buck in search of does. I have followed such tracks early in the morning, with a man on a stand where we surmised the animal would pass if it had not already done so. When we met with success, the cross-country traveler was a buck.

The lone buck afoot during the day seldom uses old runways, but prefers the easy going on barren hills, semi-open pasture lands, or tall growth where there is little underbrush to hamper his movement. Occasionally, he enters a very dense thicket in quest of a receptive doe, but if he meets with disappointment he continues on.

Sometimes a very wary buck will abandon the easy going of the open country and confine his courtship wanderings exclusively to rugged country. Like a bear, he will crawl under windfalls and pick his way through almost impenetrable growth, but in his long ramblings he will still hold to a rather definite course of travel until he accepts the company of a group of deer because of a prospective doe in the bunch. Now that he is out of circulation, his movements are limited, and singling out his tracks from the group becomes the problem.

It is natural to conclude that one of the two sets of large tracks traveling together are those of a buck. This is a happy thought, but only a guess. As a youngster, I accepted this common belief and followed two large sets of slots in the hush of freshly fallen snow. The pair was bedded down in short cover, and I quickly spotted a big, uneasy doe rise to her feet, her ears searching in my direction. I concentrated on the "buck" still in his bed, and he was likewise bald. Both ran off silently as ghosts, their big white flags held high and quivering. I felt there was something strangely wrong here; perhaps they were widowed and sought each other's consolation.

Does naturally live in family groups, and the family can consist of the old matron doe with her latest fawns and, sometimes, those of the spring before that are now quite mature at about one and a half years of age. In such a group there could be a spike buck still tagging along with its mother. During the hunting season some of the members could be killed, and the remnants of the small family might appear not at all related to each other. There could be a spike buck and an old doe, or two fawns with a spike buck traveling together. And when a larger pack is dispersed by hunters, one might find a combination of several related mature does gathered in the regrouping, or a lone odd doe or fawn still separated from the band.

The trail left by these small bands confronts the tracker. Is there a big buck among them? There could be, if one of the females is in heat; otherwise, the buck shows little interest in the band. He is not the family-loving sire so often depicted in calendar pictures, but rather an independent and self-concerned Romeo.

The Tracker as Hunter

Tracking is still-hunting, and all the care used in the latter is employed plus the additional task of yielding some time and attention to the course of the trail. It is as though one were hunting as usual, but in a direction and over terrain not of his choosing. The hunter can frequently get so involved in following the slots that lead him to the left and right at random that he can become more of a sleuth and less of a still-hunter.

The tracker must assume his quarry is close at hand, probably within the distance of fifteen minutes' stalking time. Many whitetails have been jumped prematurely by the overanxious man because he hurried at the very start in an attempt to pick up time lost since the deer made the tracks. But the whitetail, being always in his element, does not lay unnecessary tracks when at ease. So the tracker starts his hunt from the moment he intercepts the slots and decides to follow them.

He will search the broad area in the general direction of the progress of his game, and when he is convinced it is not within sight, he will follow the tracks with his eyes on their furthest point within his range of vision. This point is his goal, and he then picks the better going to reach it, even if it means swinging in a wide detour, though at times it could also be reached by a short cut. Now the tracker's eyes are free to search about as he slowly moves on to his goal. Here, again, he pauses to scan the grounds in the direction of the deer's progress, looking also far to the left and to the right, and concluding with another goal to attain. This studying of the terrain to the sides, especially the higher grounds, is necessary all the more when following a single set of tracks that might well be those of an old buck. The experienced fellow has a habit of circling back and bedding down on an elevation overlooking his trail. Whether the whitetails be bedded down, browsing, or just idling, the unhurried, loitering tracker, carefully probing in the direction of the animal's movements, can expect a favorable approach if tracking conditions are good.

Once the animal is jumped, even when not seen by the tracker, chances for a further successful stalk are greatly reduced. The hunter now would have to take on the additional odds of tracking a roused animal. If damp weather and noiseless conditions prevail, the animal might settle down so that another tracking attempt would be worthwhile. After a few unsuccessful tries to approach the animal, the hunter might well make up his mind to leave the track or else plan an all-out attempt to run down the deer.

Sometimes a track, especially if it is suspected or known to be that of a buck, is followed by a man with another flanking to one side, or two additional men, one flanking each side of the tracker. This extra manpower does not double or triple the success possibilities of the stalk. The tracking now becomes more involved, for it is not probable that the several men can move with the stealth of the lone tracker. Each man diverts some attention to the progress of the others, and unless the flankers are far to the sides, much of the same ground is studied by all the men. The group, if spaced too far apart, soon loses sight of each other, especially when the deer tracks veer sharply to one side. In this subsequent confusion, the buck has the odds for an easy escape. He could get the scent or hear a sound from any of the scattered men, yet only one man might be in position to see him.

If two or three men are available when a lone track is intercepted, presumably that of a buck, and all the men are thoroughly familiar with the country, some strategy can be employed. There are general crossings where bucks commonly pass, either through their own accord or if gently prodded by a lone tracker. Such crossings are generally nondescript, but by long experience a hunter knows these animals frequently pass through such areas. These spots are sort of gateways to another territory the animals often frequent, like the country across a highway or a railroad, areas of swamps, wooded ridges, or even semi-wooded pasturelands. The bucks leave their grounds to enter a different habitat and, because of the country's geographic makeup or from sheer habit, they enter such territory nearly always through the same entry point. This is not an established deer runway, for a buck seldom uses such trails during the day except, possibly, for a very short distance when crossing them.

When such points of probable passage are known, it is a simple matter of having them manned before the tracker proceeds with his task. Even when the going is a bit noisy, this is one of the most effective ways of getting a specific old patriarch when ordinary tracking methods fail.

Unusual Hunting Methods

7

THE types of solo hunting described in this chapter have largely become lost somewhere in the big change to the more popular group hunting. Nevertheless, they were effective in their time and probably would serve as well today. The hunters I know who have used these methods have long given up this more strenuous game. Now, with aging joints and heavier stride, they hunt as eagerly, but they have slowed down and joined the quiet ranks of the still-hunters.

If the whitetail deer followed a definite pattern of behavior when being pursued by the hunter, the tales of the chase would be somewhat drab even to an outdoorsman. Only the precise hunter would be successful, and the nonconformist would, indeed, be an odd duck. But, fortunately, in no other hunting does the individualist come into his own as in deer hunting.

These unconventional hunters simply went after their game in a most direct manner, disregarding all the niceties of accepted still-hunting rules. They moved rapidly with little attempt to pick the easier and quieter going. Instead, all attention was directed toward one objective: seeing a deer.

A deer is not always fearful of a man as such, but he is fearful of the man whom he recognizes as an enemy. And his picture of an enemy does not often come from the sight of a running man, a trout angler engrossed deeply in his trout stream, or even noisy, harsh-voiced pulpwood cutters. To the deer these may look and smell the same as an ordinary hunter, but they do behave differently from the enemy man, the hunter. Undoubtedly, this was the subterfuge used by these singular hunters, whether or not they were aware of it.

I know a man who, in his younger days, was the most unorthodox hunter ever to push an old octagonal-barreled .30/30 through an aspen growth. He had the knack of surprising so many bucks in their beds that I enviously accused him of poor sportsmanship. Now, as I reflect on the success of his unusual hunting technique, I am pretty well convinced that even he, at the time, was not aware of what made his method click so well.

He was an energetic lad, blessed with muscular, tireless legs, and he had only two natural gaits: a brisk stride and a fast, short-stepped trot. The trot seemed the least tiring way of covering ground for him, and he covered a lot of country in his hunting. He dressed lightly in soft woolen trousers and a heavy woolen shirt, but he wore no coat or jacket that might hamper his movements. His footgear usually consisted of lumberjack rubber pacs, preferably without the leather uppers if the snow was absent or scant. Thus attired, he could slink over the tall ridges at a smooth lope that was both rhythmic and surprisingly noiseless.

After analyzing his unusual mode of hunting, I can see that he had inadvertently stumbled upon some pretty good tricks for surprising a bedded or browsing buck. In the first place, he covered a lot of territory, and he followed the ridge tops where bucks were most often bedded, and from the high vantage point, he could also scan adjacent ridges and hillsides for his game.

A whitetail might readily recognize danger in the familiar swish, swish sounds made by the usual stride of a hunter, but the rapid patter made by the feet of a trotting man might produce more curiosity than alarm in the animal. I had some experience that seems to bear out this point when I was tracking a badly wounded buck late one afternoon. The crippled deer managed to keep a distance of several hundred yards ahead of me for a full half hour. On several occasions, I caught a glimpse of him as he went over a ridge, but I could not approach him close enough for a finishing shot. Daylight time was short, and I decided to attempt running the buck down. With my head bent over the bloody trail, I buffed my way through thickets and over windfall tangles for about a half mile before I came upon my exhausted and bewildered buck and was able to dispatch him.

Despite the noise I made, I recalled flushing out no less than four deer at very close range during this half-mile sprint. Being seriously bent on overtaking my quarry, I paid no attention to the animals scurrying to my left and right. Had I attempted to glance ahead as I charged through the brush, there might have been some easy shots at ridiculously close ranges. I doubt very much if I could have come so close to these deer had I covered the same distance in my usual still-hunting.

The fast-moving hunter also reduces considerably the effect of an adverse wind on his quarry, and on a relatively quiet day it is conceivable that the man might keep ahead of his own scent. A buck, bedded down in a hillside, depends much on his sense of smell for warning him of danger. If a hunter suddenly appears on the scene, the surprised animal is likely to remain in his bed hoping to get by undetected. All these factors taken together could prove very effective for the dog-trotting hunter endowed with keen vision and quick reflexes.

Once, while pausing on a hillside to watch a creek bottom below me, I heard a continuous crashing in the brushy flat to my left. It sounded like a deer drive in progress, and I felt like a gold prospector who had just staked a fertile claim on this vantage point. I waited smugly, perhaps with a faint feeling of guilt, expecting a big buck to pop out any minute. The noise of the crashing, as it became nearer and louder, converged on a single point. Now the brush shook like a moose was pushing his bulk through it, and out came a hunter as though happy to break out in the open. I recognized the man at once, and did not question his mode of hunting. It was the middle of the season and he already had three bucks hung on the meat pole for his hunting party.

He is another type of renegade solo hunter, and some few still follow his technique today. They brush aside any attempts at fooling the whitetail by stealth, and instead put all their efforts into seeing their game. In their hurried hunt, they cover more territory than several hunters combined, see many deer, most of them within shooting range, but all of them running. These tireless young men must be endowed with better than ordinary vision, be quick on the draw, and be good shots on a running target.

There was an artifice used in my early years that might have been old as whitetail hunting itself. Over the years, I learned of only several other instances where this technique was employed. Whether from sheer ignorance of accepted deer hunting procedure, or from youthful exuberance and hunting zeal, when starting a deer, my brothers and I would run after it or attempt to intercept its course if it veered sharply to either side.

We had taken several deer by this artless, direct approach before we conformed to conventional hunting. It was especially effective if the animal followed the contour of a hill or followed a valley that turned sharply to either side. We would lunge through the brush to cover the escape route, and in many instances found our deer standing as though it were quite willing to let us run by. A spooked deer very often pauses briefly after an initial short run to appraise the situation before taking off in determined flight. The animal seems to become absorbed in a man crashing through the thicket; after all, this is not the cautious, slow gait the hunted animal has learned to recognize in his enemy.

One deer season, as I walked briskly down a dirt road, bent on watching a deer trail for the duration of the opening day of hunting, a buck walked slowly across the road about 200 yards ahead of me. His thick neck was arched back like the neck of a caribou, and his large antlers extended protectively over his sleek back. It was a picture that still haunts my memory, but undoubtedly, the vision was somewhat magnified through young and imaginative eyes.

The huge animal followed a natural runway in a shallow valley, and I ran parallel to his direction of travel with the hope of intercepting him. Going was good over the half-open country, and when I estimated I was well ahead of my prize, I cut in toward the runway. He was not yet in view, so I laid flat on my stomach in the deep grass and awaited the arrival of my dream buck. Something went amiss for he never came, and I began to suspect he had already passed this point.

Slowly, I raised my head to get a better view of the runway. There, on the trail to my left, about seventy-five yards off, stood my magnificent buck like an iron deer on the lawn of an old estate. He must have seen me, or at least part of me, moving in the grass. I dared not move my head, much less attempt to get on a knee for a shot, for now the big fellow became nervous. Yet, he did not stir from his tracks but moved his raised head from side to side completely mystified by my strange conduct. It was just a matter of who would wait out the other. The buck won out, for I could not hold up my head indefinitely while lying flat on my stomach.

As I exposed myself in attempting to get on a knee, my fair prize pivoted slowly on his hind legs and trotted off from whence he had come. Perhaps he was still not completely convinced I was something to be feared, but he decided nothing could be gained by further exposing himself to a mysterious something that emitted the odor of man. This generally seems to be the response of many a whitetail when he confronts a man who does not behave at all like man the hunter.

It is obvious that the types of solo hunting here mentioned are not for everybody. They fit only the hardy, keen-eyed local youngster who knows the haunts and habits of deer on his familiar hunting grounds. In fact, most uncommon hunting methods are stratagems evolved by some native hunter. He stumbles upon an easy kill in an unusual situation. Maybe it happens to him again in a parallel circumstance, and he figures he has got this deer hunting business reduced to a simple formula.

Alas, this is not the case. He pursues this strange stratagem so long as it proves productive, and its productivity usually declines as the young hunter becomes an older hunter. He is now less willing to expend the strength required for such energetic attempts. So, with most of his hunting years still ahead of him, he pursues his game with careful stalk and stealth.

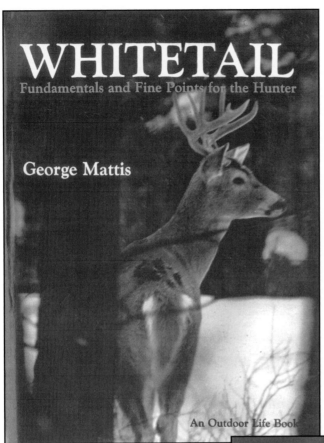

Dust jackets from the original 1969 printing of WHITETAIL and the revised 1980 edition. Mattis dedicated his book "To the hunter whose heart hungers for the sight of a bounding buck, the first snowfall to cover the sere woodland floor, or the somberness of a November woods." WHITETAIL has sold more than 500,000 copies.

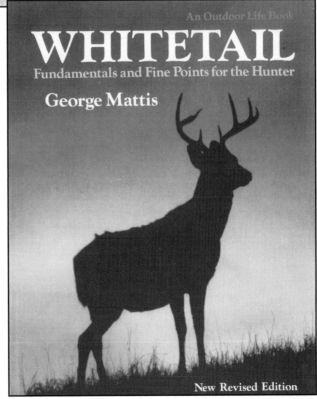

Mattis' home in Birchwood, Wis.

Photo Courtesy Francis Mattis

Rob Wegner Photo Collection

As a 16-year-old in October 1921, Mattis shows off a northwoods coyote, often referred to then as a "brush wolf."

Photo Courtesy Francis Mattis

Mattis served as a light-tank driver with the Third Armored Division in Europe during World War II and received the Purple Heart. Except for his years studying journalism at the University of Wisconsin and his military service term, Mattis never missed a deer season.

Photo Courtesy Francis Mattis

Mattis in 1962 at his comfortable Birchwood bachelor home. "I just married the great outdoors," he often said.

Photo Courtesy Francis Mattis

Photo Courtesy Francis Mattis

Although Mattis enjoyed the camaraderie of deer camp, he was clearly a still-hunting proponent. In one of his many passages explaining the advantages of still-hunting, Mattis wrote, "The individual who goes it alone is unfettered by time limits, appointments, or any of a dozen things that can come up when he is part of a group. Being strictly on his own, he is free to change his tactics or direction of travel to suit the occasion anytime he desires, and he suffers no loss of hunting time in making these changes ... The still-hunter learns to become self-reliant, observing, and somewhat of a lay naturalist, and, as a consequence, he develops a keen appreciation of the outdoors."

Photo Courtesy Francis Mattis

Mattis studied whitetail behavior year-round. Here, armed with his 35 mm camera, he snowshoes along a trail leading into a northern Wisconsin deer yard.

"A man does best with a gun he has complete confidence in ... " Mattis wrote. For him, that meant the venerable .30-30, although he acknowledged that many calibers provided more power. "The gun is the right weight for me, especially for still-hunting, and I am aware of, and willing to accept, its limitations." Mattis was all in favor of good telescopic sights, and eventually added a 2x scope to his Winchester.

Photo Courtesy Francis Mattis

Mattis learned much of his hunting skill from his brothers. Here, brothers Francis and Tom pose with a Wisconsin buck from the late 1920s or early 1930s.

Brother Tom with a pair of Northwoods bucks.

Photo Courtesy Francis Mattis

Photo Courtesy Francis Mattis

Photo Courtesy Francis Mattis

An unidentified hunter helps Tom Mattis drag out a heavy-beamed trophy.

George Mattis didn't dwell on trophy hunting in his writings. These photos are silent testament to just a few of his successes in a hunting career that spanned the better part of seven decades. One clue to Mattis' success is this comment: "If the solo hunter scores better, it is because he hunts better."

"There are more tensions released, anguishes soothed, and racking decisions realized on our fishing waters and in our deer forests than in the offices of psychiatrists or family consultants, or in the offices of all the other trouble shooters for our ailing humanity."

— GEORGE MATTIS (1905-1982)

Lucky Breaks

8

*O*NE of the happy aspects of deer hunting is the indiscriminate manner in which Lady Luck metes out favors to the men in the field. All too often, the sallow-complexioned city cousin stumbles onto and bags a handsome buck his first time out, while his host, a veteran of the woods, is humbled with a blank season. This is often termed "beginner's luck," but if one thoroughly examines every situation in which a fluke kill was made he might discover that the deer was caught off guard by something the hunter did, even though it was done inadvertently.

These pleasant interludes brighten the prospects for every man in the woods, but somehow these breaks seem more often to drop into the laps of novices. And it could be because the inexperienced hunter has not yet learned the accepted rules of hunting. The crafty buck might well cope with the standard strategy of the true-to-form hunter, but he often becomes confused and meets his doom at the hands of a blundering beginner. This element of luck seems far more prevalent in whitetail hunting than in other outdoor pursuits. Certainly a fox hunter, wolf trapper, duck hunter, or trout angler becomes more proficient with experience, and there is little here to compare the beginner with the veteran.

But who can say with any degree of certainty which man will fill his bag during the coming deer season? True, the veteran hunter has the edge in the long run, but his margin of success seems rarely in proportion to his experience and accumulated woods lore. This is a fortunate situation for the ever-increasing ranks of newcomers in the field each season. For, if only the hardy, more woods-wise members of the hunting clan were successful season after season, there would be little to encourage fresh membership in the army of hunters. And the eager, but untried, lad might never learn to thrill to the season's first snowfall, the sight of fresh deer tracks, or the glimpse of a whitetail bounding over a ridge.

The first easy kill that comes to my mind happened many years ago, and it could have had its counterpart in many farmsteads in whitetail country. My two older brothers, still in their teens, were already eager and able hunters in 1920, and my father, who loved the woods more than the hunt, felt somewhat relieved that his sons could well take his place. He had been threatening to hang up his old gun after every season now, but somehow he always got caught in the spirit of the hunt and invariably ended up with at least a few days in the woods. At that time a resident deer hunting license in Wisconsin cost only a buck, and it could be obtained anytime during the hunting season.

There was always that final hunt, I recall, but finally in 1926 he definitely made up his mind he would not hunt that fall. The season had only two days to go, and he weathered those booming reports coming from all sides while he did the farm chores. Even those inevitable long hunting discussions that filled our evenings did not sway him from his decision.

Three of us boys were hunting that year, each in a different direction, for bucks were especially scarce, and we thought our chances were best if we went our separate ways. We always had a large tripod set up in the yard during deer season, and a buck displayed here told of the success of some member of the family. The tripod was the first thing we checked when returning from the hunt. So far, nothing suspended from it. But as I returned home late in the afternoon before the final day of the season, there was a brute of a ten-point buck filling that long-vacant spot.

I wondered which of my brothers had this good fortune, and I studied the big hulk from all sides. Just then, my two brothers entered the yard toting their guns as though they were also just returning from the day's hunt. They quickened their steps when they saw me standing alongside the trophy. Before a word was exchanged, it was awkwardly obvious that the successful hunter was not one of us. It had to be dad.

And it was. While he was busy about the barnyard that morning, he saw the buck browsing just across the road in the brushy forty fenced for fall pasturing. This had happened many times before — a buck walking across the open pasture or else loitering in some thicket in plain view from the yard while we were combing the big country far beyond. This was too much temptation for dad. The buck, unmolested by hunters in this wilderness pasture, might stay put for the day. After the chores, dad drove off for his license. Two days of hunting would suffice for him and this would be the final tapering off.

So the old Swiss army rifle was again brought down from the attic. The buck was no longer in view, but dad went out to look for him. I don't think he ever considered shooting at even a walking deer with the heavy gun, so he naturally sought the standing target. He hunted slower than anyone I ever knew, and all his kills were at close range. The forty acres of brush land would take care of his day's hunting, and if the buck still remained somewhere in the enclosure, dad and his bulky musket had a good chance of bringing the old stag to his end.

The buck was still there feeding only a few rods from where he was earlier in the morning. The brace shot on the fence post brought him down with a clean neck hit, and the hunt was over before dad even entered the enclosure. He hitched up a horse to drag in the animal the short distance, and his gun was back in the attic before noon. With that stroke of luck, he very appropriately yielded the hunt henceforth to his sons.

I must admit I had my share of windfalls, and most of them came in my early years of hunting. In looking back, I wonder how I was able to score at all with so much excess of youthful energy and impatience, and so little in knowledge of both guns and hunting. Hunting skill played practically no part in the taking of my initial buck, but the experience made me a confirmed deer hunter.

It was my first season of hunting. My older brother, John, was already an accomplished marksman with a fund of woods lore and a trapper's knowledge of wildlife. John, even as a lad, was one of the confirmed still-hunters of the area, and he took part in few deer drives.

This particular fall, I hunted with him on the first weekend of the deer season. We hunted within walking distance of the farm, making short drives to each other over familiar grounds. By mid-afternoon each day, he would pause at some runway and set me all agog with its glowing possibilities. I ended up at the stand for the balance of the day, and John was happily free to go on his own.

At that time, deer hunting did not have quite the grip on me it now does, and I went back to school the following Monday. Meanwhile, my brother had gotten a fine ten-point buck, so he felt he could spare some time making drives to me. A promise that I could use his new .30/30 rifle was all the inducement I needed to skip school the next day.

John was to drive a thicket adjacent to the west pasture fence line, and he directed me to the tote road that led through the thicket and crossed the main road running east and west. I was to stand near the road intersection but south of the main road. This would give me ideal shooting since any buck he might flush would certainly pause before making the crossing. John started me off in ample time for me to pick a suitable stand, one that offered proper concealment and good vision of the tote road to the north. Above all, I was to remain motionless until he came through in about half an hour.

He no doubt loaded me with more advice before I went bounding off down the frozen dirt road to the stand, but none of it seemed important. It was a chilly morning and the

thin covering of snow was crusty and noisy. Within ten minutes, I must have paused momentarily at five or six different stands, never quite able to decide which I should take. Then I decided the hard snow was much too noisy, so I plunked myself on the dirt road smack in front of the runway. A few minutes became tediously long, and I became uneasy. Soon I began to shuffle about, pausing only at intervals. I paced back and forth, and as time went on I stood less and paced more. Then I began briskly patrolling a good length of the road with not too much thought on the hunt.

When I remembered to glance up the tote road as I was passing by, it was just in time to see a buck trotting toward me. He came to a sudden halt about 150 yards off, raised his head like a startled gazelle, stamped a nervous forefoot a couple of times, and with tail twitching he took off parallel to the road and toward the pasture fence. Then, for the first time, I realized I had completely ignored my brother's detailed instructions, and a cloud of guilt hung over me.

I didn't waste much time in remorse, however. The buck skirted the road in a straight line, keeping to the thickets, but he never made any attempt to go back toward the driver. He made great arching leaps and seemed suspended in midair momentarily before he came down crashing into the dense brush, but he was actually covering little distance in his serial capers. I took after him down the road and kept pretty well abreast of him for the 250-yard sprint to the pasture fence. Here he decided to cross the road rather than jump the fence and enter the pasture clearing.

All I remember is a muddled buck leaping across the road about twenty feet in front of me. I cannot recall whether or not I had time to come to a complete stop before I shot. In fact, I am not sure if I fired the rifle from my shoulder or from my hip. But at the resounding boom of the .30/30, the buck hit the frozen ditch on the fat side of the road head-on with the impact of his long leap, and there he lay in a heap. Examining his hulk from a distance, I found he was hit high on the neck, just above the vertebra, and close to the shoulder. It was not a fatal hit, by any means, but the bullet at such close range delivered a temporary knockout punch. His nose mushroomed against the solid bank of the road ditch and he was completely out with hardly a muscle quivering in his sleek form.

When my brother arrived, I had my plump six-pointer in the middle of the road and was proudly standing guard over him. Suddenly, the animal woke from his daze and struggled to his feet. John quickly dispatched him through the neck and he was down to stay. Instead of the expected congratulations on my good fortune, my brother asked what I was doing so far from my stand. Glowing with pride, I innocently related the whole story, convinced nothing mattered as long as I got the buck.

Brother John listed in detail the errors of my conduct at the stand, including my failure to finish off the deer after it was temporarily stunned. It appeared that even my fleet-footedness came in for no praise. For some years after, in looking back to this first kill of mine, I felt some hesitancy in listing it among my deer hunting successes. But later, I learned that not all deer are taken by well-executed plans or diligence in the field. Some of the personal experiences I here relate concluded in successful hunts. The kills were as legal and worthy as any, but somehow they always left me with a feeling that I might be hard put if I had to play the game on more even terms with my quarry.

There was the time, some years ago, when a happy turn of events the last few minutes of the hunting season climaxed one of my best years. Wisconsin had a forked-antler buck season that year, and I was down to the last hour of the ninth and final day. I was seated on a ridge with my back against a stump watching a spruce swamp. Two does had been browsing there during the afternoon, and I could think of no better place to spend the dying hours of the season.

Late in the afternoon the does had browsed their way out of the area, and the swamp became cold and dismal as the pale sun filtered its powerless rays through the aspens. A snowshoe hare, with lingering patches of brown, silently made his way through the bog on a well-beaten trail. He paused at the speckled alder growth that fringed the swamp, and his motionless form soon became a part of the lifeless bog.

Here was a chance to settle for a hare dinner, and I jarred the silent bog with the sharp report of my .30/30 carbine. Lepus made a few convulsive kicks with his long legs, and both he and his swampy kingdom were enveloped in silence again. I could have picked up my token kill and called it the end of another season, but there were yet some twenty minutes of shooting time left and I would see the season

out. So I sat down again with a feeling of obligation, counting the minutes off and scanning the opening in the spruce growth below.

There were but a few minutes left and I felt definitely relieved when I got up with determination and half slid down the slope to pick up my snowshoe hare. His body was still warm, and I decided to dress him out on the spot. Laying my gun against a low-sprawling speckled alder, I proceeded with my task, working in a kneeling position on the bog's matted floor.

The job finished, I straightened out from the tiring crouched position. Directly in front of me, near my stand on the ridge, stood a large buck with massive antlers, watching me in bug-eyed wonderment. Even as I reached for my gun, he cocked his head slightly from side to side, completely engrossed in my odd behavior in this remote swamp jungle. He was an easy target at about fifty yards, standing slightly quartered to my left with inquisitive head held high. With blood-sticky fingers, I squeezed off the neck shot that brought his hulk down to his tracks.

There were about two minutes of shooting time left, according to my wristwatch, when I wrestled the buck into position on his back with his hindquarters downgrade in preparation for field dressing. I thought of the inexplicable quirks of fate that so often decide, even in the last few minutes of the season, whether the hunt shall be discouragingly fruitless or a glowing success.

I was about to sink the knife into the taut skin of the deer's belly just below the tough gristle of the brisket, when a hunter suddenly loomed over the crest of the hill. With heavy breath, he proceeded down the slope toward me. For an instant, I felt the guilt of a man caught red-handed dressing out another man's deer. But the gentleman promptly extended his hand to congratulate me. He studied the twelve-point rack with more interest than one would expect from a total stranger. Then he told me his story.

He had been following this same buck back and forth over a limited area since early morning, and had caught several glimpses of his slinking form during the long, persistent stalk. The big fellow knew he was being tracked, but he refused to leave his bailiwick, nor did he run or become panicky at any time. His steady stride kept him at a safe distance ahead of the hunter, and with this deliberate pace he calmly selected his route. In his careful meandering he came upon me there in the swamp thicket. But for the brief moment when his caution yielded to curiosity, he might have survived for another season with the advantage of this additional experience gained in the ways of eluding the hunter.

If the term sportsman broadly includes all those adept in hunting, shooting, or fishing, then its application is most inadequate to this hunter who cheerfully helped me dress the deer and drag it to the road. There is always the winner and the loser in every game of chance, and it is so with whitetail deer hunters. But the man who loses and genuinely shares the joy with the winner is, indeed, a rare gem among hunters. It is my hope that this deserving man, and other hunters of his generous caliber, are blessed with a windfall, no less than mine, thrust across their paths to brighten some unexpected moment of theirs in the field.

One fall a younger brother, Tom, and I spent considerable time still-hunting together. We usually hunt abreast over country with which we are thoroughly familiar. Before proceeding with our hunt, we took time off to drive a small triangular thicket. This area of about fifteen acres lies in the midst of good whitetail country, and with hunters stirring about, a harassed buck often seeks refuge in this neglected nook. We had been driving deer from the pocket every morning, and once we recognized a single-antlered buck among them. Somehow, the driver was never successful in putting the animals by the man on the stand, although we varied our tactics every morning. Since the ground was barren of snow, somewhat of a rarity for a deer season in upper Wisconsin, we were unable to locate the exact spot from which the deer were flushed. It began to appear that we had something more to contend with than mere chance in making this short drive click for us, but what that something was we could not guess.

This particular morning we parked the car at a sharp point of the area formed by a fork in a backwoods road. The two roads bounded the triangle on two sides and the far side of the area was shut off by a lake. We made our plans while still in the car, and it was my turn to make the drive. Tom was to take the road to the left and stand on a ridge near the corner of the thicket against the lake. I was to wait at the car for ten minutes and then walk through the area keeping somewhat to the road on the right. Near the lake, I was to swing left and complete the drive to the stand.

Tom was already on his way before I had my gun from its case. The gun loaded, I studied the steep incline ahead of me. Well blended in a clump of scrubby red oaks, still heavily clothed in sere, ruddy leaves, were two deer watching me intently from the hill. I was able to make out the silhouette of small antlers and the forepart of one of the animals against the sky. The rest of the buck's body and all but the doe's head were lost in the rusty oak foliage. Quickly I dropped to my knee for the long shot. The coarse front bead pretty well covered the entire shoulder of the buck at the distance, and I let the shot off, holding high on the shoulder.

The oak leaves quivered a bit, a few flashes of white melted into the scattered aspen growth in the background, and there remained nothing for a second shot. Tom, who was only a hundred yards up the road, came running back thinking I had an accident. But he was happily relieved when he saw me scanning the hillside. We walked up the long slope, and I stepped off 167 yards to the red oaks on the crest.

On his second or third jump the buck had spurted blood widely on both sides of his trail. Surprisingly, the bloody trail led us nearly 300 yards, much of it downhill, and we came upon the dead animal at the other extremity of the area near the lake. But I was completely confounded when we saw no antlers. My brother looked at me in wonder. I seized the deer's ear and raised its head from the deep bed of leaves in disgust. There on the underside was a single, small three-point antler. We probed the hair on the buck's head and found the other antler was broken off flush with the skull, perhaps the result of a dueling match with some heavier-armored combatant. So started a successful day, even before the hunt got under way.

Deer are taken in all sorts of situations, some of which can be disconcerting to the serious, conscientious hunter. After a fruitless week of hunting one season, and his keen zest for the chase somewhat tempered, brother Tom took an afternoon off to do some neglected shopping. About three miles from home and only a mile from town, he noticed a buck feeding deep in a corn patch just off the road. The farmer, also an avid hunter, was probably far in the hinterlands combing some remote, untrammeled area in search of the wily whitetail, while, ironically enough, a corn-fed buck was to be had practically in the shadows of his farm buildings.

Here was an irksome situation since Tom had no gun with him.

There was considerable traffic shuttling back and forth on the road, most of it made up of restless redcoats seeking new hunting grounds. Tom decided it would be useless to drive back for his gun, for surely some hunter would spy the handsome prize in the meantime. So with heavy heart he drove into town, did his shopping and returned home, taking a short cut on a dirt road that bypassed the small cornfield.

Even after he was home for some time, the thought of the buck still thrashing in the dry cornstalks kept gnawing at him. He decided that if he would allay his troubled mind and guarantee himself a peaceful night's rest he had to return to the cornfield and see if, by any slim chance, the buck might still be there. Despite the lapse of about three hours since Tom had seen the buck early in the afternoon, the deer was still in the roadside corn patch busily stuffing his plump body and apparently undisturbed by the open season on his kind in the country about him.

Tom parked his pickup, left the motor running, and walked off the road without further ado, loading the gun as he went. The preoccupied buck finally raised his head in mild concern, and Tom took him through the neck at less than a hundred yards.

Hitting Them on the Run

9

THE standing shot at reasonable range is always to be desired. No one need apologize for knocking off his game with a well placed hit even if his resting target is less than fifty yards off. That is the aim of the hunter — to be able to set himself up for a clean, humane kill. One can well say that most deer, by far, are killed standing or walking at about fifty yards in any brushy or wooded country, and the large portion of the animals wounded and lost to hunters is the result of shots made at running deer at any range.

The time has come, I believe, when the hunter must reconsider the common practice of taking the running shot simply because it offers him some chance, however slight, to get his deer. With an ever-increasing army of hunters in the field, this snap shooting at fleeing game is becoming less acceptable from the standpoint of hunter safety, for one thing. And the hunter, for his own well-being,

cannot afford the impact brought on the public by hunting casualties resulting from inconsiderate gun handling. Aside from this, we have a simple matter of conservation and economy here.

Our wildlife is not unlimited, and today's hunters must be aware of the fact that any deer saved from a crippling loss is theirs to get later.

The practice of shooting at any running deer has too long been accepted by many as a standard hunting procedure. Actually, a very small fraction of the men afield is qualified for this type of shooting even at relatively close range. Hitting a running target with any degree of consistency does not come easily to the man whose gunning experience is limited only to his annual deer hunting outing.

Yet, there remains the temptation to shoot at a running deer if the hunter is reasonably sure he can down it, and he is satisfied no other hunter is in his line of fire. The presence or lack of good tracking snow should also be a factor in making the decision. Because such shooting possibilities do arise, I am including this discussion and presentation of facts on hitting a deer on the run.

There has been much written and said about the science of shooting at running game, and some of the theories expounded can be conflicting when applied to different men. One hunter I know says he always shot back of the running deer until he learned to lead his game. Another equally good shot on the moving target tells me he used to shoot ahead of his deer when he took the recommended lead, so now he simply aims at the forepart of the animal's front quarters. He has been scoring good hits since.

This sounds confusing, but the confusion arises from the manner in that the same theory is applied. There are some solid, cold facts about the distance a running deer can move while the bullet is en route to its target, but the use of these facts should be tempered with good judgment and adapted to one's personal gun handling.

There is no point in going into detailed technicalities, for the hunter has to decide on the spur of the moment how he will hold his gun on that particular target, and he will learn to do it quickly only through the habit of practice. But the hunter should know a few simple facts concerning the velocity of his gun, and the possible speed of his running game, and then he can translate them for his personal use.

Here are velocity figures for the .30/30, 170-grain bullet:

Muzzle	100 yards	200 yards
2220 ft. per sec.	1890 ft. per sec.	1630 ft. per sec.

If the whitetail travels thirty miles an hour at a right angle to your fire, here are some approximate distances it will move while the bullet is en route:

Bullet travels	200 yards	100 yards	50 yards
Deer travels	14 feet	6 feet	3 feet

These figures, though sufficiently accurate for the situations described, are certainly not applicable to the normal situation confronted by the hunter. Most often the speed of a running deer is far less than thirty miles per hour, and in most cases the animal's flight is not at a right angle to the line of fire. Judging the required lead is a mathematical problem that can be solved for one's practical purpose. But then there are other factors, variable with the individual, which also add to delayed time for the bullet to reach its goal. And it is in these where the rub comes in. If the gun discharged itself the moment it was held on target, the problem of leading running game would be relatively simple.

Nerve reaction to the sight picture, reflex action to set off the trigger, and the movement of the gun's mechanism until the cap is ignited add up to an appreciable lapse of time. The human element of nerve reaction and reflex action, or the time it takes the hunter to get off his shot after he has decided to shoot, is the big factor in hitting running deer, especially at close range. This loss of time is largely eliminated, however, when the hunter follows the running target with his sights. If he does not follow his target, then he will definitely shoot behind, unless he allows extra lead for the delayed time in getting off his shot.

There are times when the hunter cannot follow the game with his gun because of the obstruction of heavy tree trunks. He might then train his gun on an opening through which his game must pass and hope to let off his shot just as soon as his target comes into view. This nearly always results in poor hits or complete misses, and this can happen at very close range where the time a bullet

travels to reach its destination is a negligible factor in scoring a hit.

The few times I tried such shots on running deer convinced me that my reflexes are too slow for even a fair hit at close range. I had an exceptional opportunity to try this out once when three deer came running by me. The two does were in the lead, and I could see them plainly only when they dashed through a small opening thirty yards away. The buck was trailing the females by about fifty yards, so I had ample time to cover the gap and await him as he emerged from the tree trunks.

I sighted for the middle of the four-foot opening and fired just as the buck loped into sight. Down he came like a collapsed tent, but before he was quite stretched out, he started to raise himself on his forefeet. The second shot broke his neck and put him down to stay. My running shot scraped his backbone just over the kidneys, fully two feet back of the mid-shoulders I was hoping to hit.

Since I led the deer by two feet and still my shot trailed his shoulder by two feet, the buck had moved four feet between the time I decided to shoot and the time the bullet had reached its destination. Perhaps three and a half feet of this distance could be attributed to my reflex response, and not more than six inches to the time it took for the bullet to reach the deer.

Had I been able to follow the running deer with my sights, I would have scored a fair hit without leading, for when the gun follows the running deer, it is moving with the target even as the shot is released. Any brief pause at the trigger squeeze results in shots behind the target. This happens when one snap-shoots at a running deer as it breaks through a small opening, and it also happens when one inadvertently pauses in his swing for the brief time it takes to pull the trigger. This is the fault of the gunner who hits his deer far back or else misses it entirely even when he takes the necessary lead.

Assuming that the hunter can ease off the trigger when his gun is in swing and on target, then he has only to take the necessary lead to compensate for the movement of his game while the bullet is in progress. This distance for proper lead is invariably exaggerated by most hunters; And the man who follows the target with his gun but allows too much lead is the one who shoots ahead of his deer.

The difficulty lies in approximating the speed at which the deer is traveling. Somehow, every hunter is unduly impressed by the interesting fact that the whitetail can travel at a speed of thirty miles per hour. Using this bit of information, we find that the speedy deer covers forty-four feet per second, or a bit over six feet in the time it takes the .30/30 bullet to reach him at a hundred yards. All this, though mathematically true, is a far cry from anything normally applicable to the deer hunter in wooded country.

Of all the running deer I have seen in my time, only about a dozen of them were going at what I estimated was their top speed. In each case, they were running through a clearing, carrying their heads low, and scampering over the ground in a straight line like a scared brush wolf surprised in the open. If any whitetails could be timed for the thirty-mile-an-hour sprint, these few should have well qualified. Seldom does a whitetail run at his top speed even when he is thoroughly frightened, and it is very questionable even then if he can come anywhere near thirty miles per hour when he has to pick his uncertain way in the thickets.

The running deer, with his white rump and flag bouncing with every jump, might make a forward progress of only fifteen miles per hour, and the hunter assumes the animal is traveling full speed. Then, too, even when the deer runs at a right angle to the hunter, it veers to the left and right in picking its route, and the speed of forward progress is thus considerably reduced. The common flight of the whitetail is definitely to the general front, with varying degrees of quartering to the left or right. In such cases, even when the animal is laying fast tracks, its speed across the line of fire is not very great and little or no lead need be taken.

At fifty yards the deer seems an ideal target, maybe something to be hoped for by the man who likes to believe he gets his venison with shots at a far greater range. It is self-satisfying to pace off the long shot, but not all hunters bother to measure the distance to the close kill. I have taken deer at less than ten yards, and the farthest I ever shot one was 167 yards off, taken with an open sight. Even with this unusually long shot for brush country, I find the deer I have bagged over the years have been taken at an average distance of forty-five yards.

This, I grant, is close-range shooting, but I believe, when comparing it with other hunters, it comes pretty near the average for all deer kills in dense cover. Forty-five yards on an open field seems ridiculously close, but when the target is even partly concealed by an obstruction, the distance invariably seems far greater. A deer in an open field, even at 200 yards, presents a sharp picture, and the sharp picture gives one the impression of nearness.

The same animal, if it can be seen at all in a scattered growth 200 yards away, will appear hopelessly remote for even a chance shot. Actual pacing of such distance is the sure way to learn the exact yardage. After some experience in measuring, one can become adept to the point where he is not too easily misled by the makeup of terrain.

Getting down to field probabilities, it becomes obvious that the hunter scores most of his hits on running deer when the target is less than fifty yards away, and if it is moving across his line of fire, the speed of the animal is ten to fifteen miles per hour. If the gun is following the target and is held on the front of the deer's shoulders, little or no lead is required for a good hit. The hundred-yard running shot very definitely requires a lead, but the theoretical six feet is usually a gross exaggeration and hardly applicable to one's normal hunting experience. Those countless shots at the more distant fleeing whitetails can be largely written off as mere hunting exuberances and they should be discouraged. True, they take a large toll of deer by virtue of the number of such shots fired, but few of the wounded animals are ever recovered by the hunters.

There is a matter of sizing up a shooting possibility and getting into position the instant a deer is sighted. This has to be developed so that it comes instinctively. A standing deer allows one time to make the necessary preparation before the shot is released, and sometimes these steps can be made methodically and with deliberation.

The shot at a running deer requires independent coordination of legs, hands, and eyes. The legs must place the gunner in an unstrained position for shooting; that is, the game should be brought to the left of the right-handed shooter. If the game is too far to the right, a quick pivot with the left foot thrust ahead will bring the hunter into good position. If there is an obstruction ahead, the same result can be achieved by stepping backward with the right foot to make the pivot to the right. This must be accomplished without conscious effort, for the hunter has to bring his gun up into position at the same instant.

While position is taken and gun brought up, the hunter's eyes must not be removed from the target, for even in the split second the eyes are away from the running deer, it will require time to locate the game again. Very often, as I have experienced, the deer could stop short in the brief time one takes to watch his footing. Most men have missed opportunities for standing shots because they lost track of the target and assumed it had escaped.

As long as the hunter does not lose sight of the progress of his game once it is identified as legal, there is little chance of him making the grave mistake of shooting at something other than the object he first identified as a deer. With numerous men afield, it is entirely possible for two men to come to close quarters without being seen by each other. A whitetail is flushed and disappears to the side before a shot can be taken. The anxious hunter, avid for success, draws up hastily to shoot at a moving object stirring in the direction where his deer disappeared — but now it happens to be a man and not a deer. After game is lost to one's vision for even the slightest moment, it must again be identified beyond any doubt. The hunter can save himself time and care by keeping his whitetail in view once he ascertains it is legal game.

Somewhere in the distant past there evolved the custom of shooting with one eye closed as though one might thus concentrate his vision through the one shooting eye. Even to this day, youngsters pick up this habit to carry on a practice that has more tradition than merit.

It is especially advantageous to have both eyes open while shooting at a running deer. It takes two eyes to give one the perspective needed for gauging depth, and without this third dimension the senses for judging speed, distance, and direction are largely lost to one's vision. Aside from this, one can obviously follow his running game better with the use of both eyes, especially since he will be handicapped somewhat by following it over the barrel of his rifle.

The less obstruction one has on top of his barrel, the easier it will be to keep the running target in view. From my own experience, I find nothing better than the aperture sight with the big opening for use in thick cover shooting. The larger aperture will likely be more operative even during snow or rain, weather conditions common during deer season. One has only to concentrate on lining up two objects, the bead and the deer. The aperture can be completely ignored after one has accustomed himself to bringing up the gun in practice aiming.

When one's hunting includes farm fields and forest clearings as well as the brushy habitat fringing them, then he might well use a low-powered scope if he expects to attempt running shots. My two-powered scope is good for running shots in the open or in sparse cover, and here I have some advantage over the aperture sights in which my scope is of help in identifying legal game. If I had just one choice of sights for my hunting, this would have to be it.

Most anyone can become adept in the science of shooting deer on the run at reasonable range. It is not a case of just blazing away at a whitetail, hoping that by dint of a long string of shots one can occasionally score a hit. There is a matter of discipline in using the trigger finger. This I first observed even before I was big enough to hunt.

I accompanied my oldest brother to a deer stand one Saturday with the solemn promise that I would sit quietly by the fire and cause him no concern. This was a bigger promise than I could easily keep, for I soon tired of my confinement. After a long, dull period of nothing to do but stir up sparks from the burning pine knots, I was roused from my play when my brother slowly brought up his gun to his shoulder.

His serious look meant that a deer was coming, and I rose to my feet to see my first antlered buck. He loped slowly along the trail with his head lowered, not at all like I expected to see the noble creature. I anticipated the roar of the .35, but nothing happened. The deer was well past the stand and bounding away from us, and still there was no shot. Finally, as I decided there was something wrong with the gun or my brother, the long-delayed blast came. The buck had apparently escaped, I thought, but my brother ran down to the trail, and I was happily free to join him. There the buck lay on the runway only a few yards from where I had last seen him.

When I asked why he didn't shoot when the deer was much nearer the stand, my brother said there was no use shooting until he had his sights lined up on the buck.

This finger discipline marks the distinction between the man who shoots with resoluteness, and the man who simply shoots. The trigger squeeze comes naturally when the bead is superimposed on the front end of the deer. Hair-splitting accuracy is not required on a target this size at close range, and the careful, slow trigger squeeze used on a standing shot cannot be used on moving game.

The limited number of hunters I know who are good shots on running game did not come by their talent accidentally. You will find them training their guns on bobbing chickarees, scampering red squirrels, or running rabbits. The man who will not occasionally be tempted to flex his shoulder muscles on an imaginary running deer is perhaps not sufficiently interested in acquiring the knack of hitting his game on the run. Perhaps he should not attempt it.

Hunting in Milder Climates

10

EXAS, Michigan, Wisconsin, Minnesota, and Pennsylvania have long been recognized as big whitetail states, with New York, Missouri, Maine, Virginia, North Carolina, and Arkansas not too far behind. Other states with good whitetail populations are Vermont, Mississippi, Georgia, Florida, South Dakota, West Virginia, Alabama, Louisiana, and South Carolina.

It is difficult, if not impossible, to list the states according to their deer populations since there is no accurate count of the animals made, and any figure given is an estimate at best. And there are, of course, some regional changes in the animal's population over its broad range even during a period of a few years.

The whitetail is pursued in his milder southern habitat as well as in the snowy northern states. Weather fluctuations being what they are, sometimes the northern hunter, whose

season usually includes some portion of the last half of November, spends at least a few days afield without even tracking snow. And again, those in the milder climates below the snowy area might have at least an occasional experience of treading quietly over the white stuff. I have hunted at times in over two feet of snow at below-zero temperatures, and a few years later have been uncomfortably warm on the same hunting grounds wearing a shirt and light shoes to walk the snowless ground.

Generally, though, it is only in the extreme northerly areas of the United States that the whitetail hunter can expect snow and freezing temperatures to be the rule during his hunt. That leaves a vast area of whitetail country where the hunter experiences little or no snow on his grounds. To northern hunters, snow, at least sufficient for tracking, is most welcome. Many feel a keen disappointment if the deer season opens with bare ground, not realizing that this is the usual condition in most of the whitetail's range.

Frankly, I prefer the bare ground because it makes for comfort in the field, and it does not pose the problem of a crunchy, noisy crust that seems to be the inevitable result of an early snowfall except if the temperature remains at an even, cold level. And if the temperature is such that the snow is powdery dry at all times, then it could be pretty nippy, especially for the slow-moving hunter.

The whitetail adapts himself well to the thickly populated areas and the farmlands of the East, the South, and the central states. For one thing, the milder climates here favor growth of almost impenetrable vegetation for the protection of deer. Then, too, many of the trees in this vast area are nut-bearing and the whitetails winter on crops of acorns and beechnuts when the crop is abundant.

The deer has infiltrated our strictly agricultural states where even his relatively small numbers there pose a problem to the farmer. Some states such as Indiana, Illinois, and Iowa, long without this large game animal, find the whitetail is back again in sufficient numbers to not

only warrant, but require, an open season on the expanding species.

It was once thought that the whitetail properly belonged to the wilderness and his movement into the agricultural areas was adventitious. Now it is obvious that deer follow in the direction of their food supply, wherever that might be, and with protection they become established there as elsewhere, though obviously in not as great numbers. The hunting seasons are very short in such areas, and hunting by limited permits is often the rule.

Hunting the heavy agricultural areas is pretty much the same in any of our states. Take Iowa, for instance, with its preponderance of farmlands and its relatively scarce deer habitat. The whitetails are necessarily concentrated in what cover there is, such as the timbered or brushy river valleys, especially in the northeast along the Mississippi River and in the southwest along the Missouri River. Even the scattered valleys of the lesser inland rivers afford limited deer habitat.

The gun-hunting season, by permit, is necessarily short, and the shotgun with slugs must be used. Because hunting is on a permit basis, deer hunters here are likely to be found with the same shotguns they used for rabbits, pheasants, and ducks during the earlier seasons for this game. Consequently, shotgun scopes are not as common here as in those states with heavier deer populations where the individual can expect to hunt every season.

Due to the limited expanse of any deer area in Iowa, especially in the state's interior, driving is the common method used by hunters, and the walkie-talkie is popular in this group hunting. Drivers are thus able to alert the standers when a deer is started and advise them in what direction the animal is going.

Unlike some of our strictly agricultural states, most of our other densely populated areas have an appreciable amount of marginal lands so that a heavier deer population can be maintained for the hunter. There are, for instance, many national forest lands in the Appalachian Mountains and in our southern states. Other state-owned lands furnish hunting grounds for the gunner in a day when posted lands are becoming common. Permission can usually be arranged for hunting the many vast private timber holdings that compose much of our deer habitat.

Whitetail country even within a state can be extremely diverse, and the hunter will simply have to adjust himself to the section he hunts. Take the small state of New Jersey, for instance, with its three quite distinct whitetail habitats. The northwestern section is mountainous, with the Kittatinny Mountains and the Appalachian Trail running in a northeasterly direction. It is a country of pleasant valleys, low mountains, small rural communities, and farms. The hardwood ridges are covered with oaks, pines, and maples. Even the populated counties around Newark and nearby New York City yield a few bucks for the New Jersey gunners.

South of the Appalachian ridges we drop down to the scrub pine country of south Jersey. This dwarf conifer covers the highlands, and the swamps have thick stands of red cedar, wild magnolias, and catbriars so thick only a deer can crawl through them. Cranberry bogs, sphagnum moss, hollies, and blueberries are part of the deer's habitat here.

To the east of this are the plains — an area of extremely sterile soil on which scrub pine and oak grow in profusion but seldom attain a height of over five feet. This is the country of deer clubs, and driving is the order of the deer season here in this jungle of stunted trees.

A Jersey drive is something to remember. The drivers use horns, bells, whistles, and other frightening noisemakers to get the whitetails out of their cover. Ten or 12-gauge shotguns with No. 4 to No. 00 size buckshot are used in the state of New Jersey, and no one will argue that this is the preferred combination, especially by the brush beaters for their quick, close shots.

The mountains or hills, the swamplands, the river valleys, and the farmlands bordered with woodlots or wild-grown marginal lands are whitetail country in much of the East, and the states here, including New Jersey, are favored with diversified deer habitat. And here the apple orchard is as much a part of the deer's environment as the oak ridges or the farm fields.

Hunting the farmlands or the eastern mountains is pretty much the same regardless of their precise locations. Certainly, the whitetail recognizes no artificial border such as a state line. It is the terrain and cover of his quarry that determines the method of pursuit used by the hunter.

The Appalachian Mountains, extending southward from southern Quebec, Canada, and including such famous whitetail hunting spots as the Adirondack and Catskill Mountains in New York, offer some of the best wilderness deer habitat in the East. The Allegheny Mountains of northeastern Pennsylvania, which are also part of the Appalachian chain, are a good example of what the redcoat can expect to encounter in eastern mountain hunting. Though not as rugged as some of the Alleghenies farther west in Pennsylvania, one must be in good physical condition to climb these ridges if he is to hunt this excellent deer country.

This section is made up of hills and valleys with many dairy farms sprinkled throughout. Much of it has heavy, thick stands of poplar, grey birch, scrub oak, red maple, and buckbrush growing in patches between the hardwood forests and the farmed plots. The edges of these patches, that can comprise from four to twenty acres, are good places to look for buck rubs and deer trails. About the only way to hunt these farm side thickets is to drive them or else take a stand right in the brush. Your visibility is very limited, but if you get a shot it's likely to be at a buck and at close range.

The top of the ridges is usually sprinkled with conifers, mostly white and red pines, and shooting is difficult in this heavy stand. Below the pines are the hardwoods such as red and black oak, sugar and red maples, wild cherry and black birch, while the various viburnums make up the undergrowth. During a good year for acorns the forest floor is torn up by deer that feed on the generous bounty.

Binoculars and scoped rifles are the order here where one can expect to see deer at a great distance across a valley. The hunter who has practiced on woodchucks at 300 yards during the summer can use this experience here to good advantage. If there is snow on the ground, the deer are quite easy to see on the hardwood hillsides up to 500 yards away. Often a hunter will plank himself down on one ridge and spend the day scanning another ridge several hundred yards across a valley.

A friend of mine who usually hunts this area and takes his share of deer says he is a stickler for staying in one spot. He picks a place that looks good, the area of a few fresh buck rubs and other deer sign including used trails. He builds a low blind almost as carefully as one builds a duck blind, and here he rests in a comfortable reclining position almost completely under cover. He has taken most of his bucks with this method, and all of them have been killed between 11:00 in the morning and 3:30 in the afternoon — not considered the best hours for taking the whitetail. His explanation for his strange success

is that during these hours most hunters go back to their cars for lunch, a coffee break, or a confab with the boys at the roadside. This constant procession of men back and forth between the road and the hinterlands keeps the whitetails on the move, creating a golden opportunity for the man under cover on a good stand. The woods are filled with restless hunters who find it most difficult to remain stationary for any length of time. The resourceful, patient, and determined hunter will take advantage of this weakness in his fellow hunters by clinging to one spot so as to intercept the deer moved by them.

The whitetail population in any state is naturally confined to such areas as provide food and cover for them. These could be the rugged river bottoms with their timbered and brushy growth or any hilly nonarable lands.

Missouri and Arkansas, two good deer states, have fine habitat for the animals in the rugged Ozarks as well as elsewhere in the states. And both Missouri and Arkansas are favored with considerable spreads of national forests. The many species of oaks here produce an abundant crop of acorns for the deer. As soon as the nuts are ripe and start dropping to the ground, the whitetails leave the bottomlands and make for the oak ridges. Arkansas produces a good many trophy whitetails.

Acorns and beechnuts are important foods for the wintering whitetail throughout his range, especially where there is no snow cover. In the northern states deer sometimes paw into two feet of snow to uncover and feed on this nourishing mast. And if the nut crop is poor or lacking altogether, the deer must feed entirely on winter browse. In the milder climates, especially around farmlands, when the natural nut crop is scarce, the animals will often raid the farmer's cornfields.

Wherever the whitetail lives, the hunter must learn where it feeds and where it beds down. Still-hunting, trail watching, and some form of driving are used throughout the animal's temperate range. Where the northern hunter might bemoan the lack of snow, as is sometimes the situation, because he cannot readily track a wounded animal, the hunter in the milder climate accepts and adjusts to this situation. Too often reckless shooting results because the hunter has good tracking snow. He unthinkingly gambles on chances for scoring a good hit simply because snow is there to help him track down and recover a poorly hit animal.

In any of our bare-ground deer-hunting states, the use of slugs in shotguns requires that the quarry be at close range. The impact of a slug on an animal at about fifty yards readily brings him down. It is not too difficult to track down a wounded animal on bare ground if one makes the determined effort. The snow tracker simply looks for bloodstains in the deer's trail, but the bare-ground tracker must stoop over and carefully search the ground for any specks of blood, and look for any fresh disturbance in leaves or twigs that might indicate the route of the fleeing animal.

Generally, the hunter who sticks doggedly to his stand will have the edge over the man who shifts about. The early morning sees many standers, but after an hour or two most of them become restless and start moving about. Then they take deep probes into the deer country both to escape the mob and to find where the deer are holding out. The man resigned to watch a good spot has all these drivers working for him.

In much of the South, except possibly in the Appalachian Mountains, which extend from Canada as far south as northern Alabama, the whitetail is found in such dense cover and wet terrain that tactics unusual to other areas are commonly employed. Dogs are used by many hunters here for driving the deer to standers. Often this is the only recourse to take if one is to have any success in such areas as the low coastal regions of the Carolinas, Georgia, and Florida, or the wetlands of the lower Mississippi River.

As in regular driving with men, driving with dogs can be very simple with just a few local men and dogs involved, especially if the area and habits of the deer are well known. The drive can include many men and dogs in a well-organized hunt, and the chase can take on the air of an annual social affair with much ado. There is some prejudice against hunting deer with dogs in the South, and much of this could stem from the problem arising when the dogs, unmindful of area boundaries, enter grounds where they are not welcome.

The Appalachians of the southern states offer opportunities for the still-hunter who walks the deer trails or follows the ridges to watch the valleys to the sides. This hunt can be mixed with a good deal of pausing every time a big hollow needs to be thoroughly checked.

There is also wide use of tree blinds in areas of the southern states, and these afford the stander a better view of his grounds while he is under concealment. And in some sections of the South and Southwest the deer and turkey seasons run concurrently, and the hunter using a gun such as the .270 with a bullet of 150 grains is armed for both.

Whitetails in the Arid States

11

*T*HE whitetail is found in sizable numbers throughout much of the West and Southwest; and in parts of Texas he is abundant. Although the western and southwestern states have both the whitetail and the mule deer, the two animals have their own particular habitat, and they are, therefore, seldom found together. The mule deer lives in the high, open expanse of hills and mountains with their scant growth; the whitetail clings to the lower timbered country and the wooded or brushy river bottoms. And in his home here he is as wary and crafty as in any other part of his far-flung domain.

The whitetail's habit of skulking and of mistrusting any stealthy action in a man is best appreciated by the western hunter who has observed the behavior of the whitetail and the mule deer. From my own experience, I find an interesting comparison in the two game animals.

During recent years I have been taking annual western trips into the game country during the summer months. I arm myself with a 35-mm camera and 300-mm telephoto lens and stalk game as one would with a rifle. For the relatively few hunting hours I put in still-hunting or stalking mule deer, I have come up with some dandy shots of bucks lounging in their beds or does sizing me up before taking off in their stiff-legged, hairspring bounds.

I simply follow the edge of a deep gully, and like the Arizona whitetail hunter, I toss in a stone occasionally to start out a deer resting deep in the shade of a ledge. If I am lucky I can get a good snap of the startled animal as he attempts to negotiate an escape up a wash to the side of the steep canyon wall. In several instances I have caught a mule deer buck bedded down in the shade of the canyon not more than twenty-five yards away, and he merely eyed me passively while I adjusted the camera's lens for a sharp picture.

Once, while sitting with my binoculars on a long, gradual slope of sparse sage and other short growth in Wyoming, I studied a wending gulch about a mile off in a valley below me. It was midday and hot, and any wildlife activity should have been at a low ebb. Yet, I picked up the movement of what appeared to be a mule deer browsing in the growth of a wash. I decided to stalk the animal for a close-up picture, so I carefully studied the terrain, and I planned my roundabout approach. Once I reached the valley, I was able to keep some elevation between me and the deer. I slowly proceeded to the very edge of the wash where I had sighted the movement from the crest of the hill.

A spotted mule deer fawn edged its way up the side of the shallow gulch. Another fawn emerged from the scraggly growth to join its companion, and the twins moved in unison side by side like a team of well-trained miniature horses. I took a couple of snaps of them at about fifty yards as they slowly left their cover, thinking I had as good close-ups as I would ever get of a set of twin deer. The fawns watched me in complete innocence and wonder-

ment as they picked their way toward me with apparent curiosity. I never photographed wilderness deer at closer range, and I took some remarkable close-ups of the youngsters. Finally, the twins approached me so closely I had to back up in order to keep them in focus for additional snaps.

It took a little arm waving and yelling to send the pair scurrying back to the protection of the shallow gulch and its scrubby growth. Meanwhile, the doe never did show up on the scene. If she had, possibly the fawns would not have reveled so innocently in their strange experience.

I have never been able to approach the wilderness summer whitetail at such close quarters, and I have spent many hours in attempting it. I find the whitetails of northeastern Wyoming as wary of man as those of the North, East, or elsewhere. I think that anyone who has hunted both the whitetail and the mule deer will agree the whitetail is at least a bit more difficult of the two to take.

In these vast arid spaces the cover of the whitetail can vary from scant scrubby growth to dense brushy thickets, and it also includes the substantial timber of the mountainsides as well as the river bottoms. Wherever his range, this deer makes the most of the cover available to him, and sometimes this protection is scant, indeed. Though the whitetail is his cautious self wherever he may be, the quarry must be hunted according to the animal's local habits, the terrain he occupies, and the general climatic conditions existing during the hunt.

Generally speaking, a whitetail hunter is a whitetail hunter throughout the deer's national range. He is no different from a trout angler, such as I, who has long fished the upper Great Lakes trout streams, yet finds himself at home on any western mountain stream. A good hunter adjusts to any situation for taking his deer. It is just a case of presenting himself to best advantage in any whitetail country.

Still-hunting and trail watching are the more common methods of pursuit in much of the West and Southwest, although small group driving is done of necessity in getting the deer out of any dense cover.

Unlike the deer of heavy thickets in the East, the whitetails here usually leave no well-defined trails between their bedding hideouts and their browsing grounds. On dry, bare ground, it is difficult to locate the daily route of this game animal since it usually travels over a broad area rather than on a narrow well-marked trail. Such routes commute between the bedding spots on high grounds and the brush valleys where the animals feed. Runways could also lead between two valleys or feeding grounds. Any of these broad runways could cross a wide saddle on a ridge or low passes in rugged or hilly country. It is only through careful study before the deer season that one can locate a good stand to take for his hunt.

Much of the whitetail's habitat in the arid states consists of patches of thickets surrounded by almost barren area. When deer leave these thickets, either of their own free will or else by being driven out, they will make their exit through a projecting brush point to enter the open country, and they will enter the next cover at its nearest projecting point. If there is even some slight growth scattered between these two juts, this will be the normal travel route of your quarry. After the hunter, in his preseason reconnaissance, locates the travel route between the deer's daytime bedding area and his nightly feeding grounds, he must select a stand windward of the runway. His best hours for trail watching are naturally the mornings and evenings, especially if no other hunters are moving about the area. Deer, after a night of browsing, move up to their resting refuge early in the morning, and they leave their shelter late in the afternoon to fill up on browse. If even a few other hunters are stirring about in the area, the lone trail watcher can profit by sticking to his stand during the entire day.

It is well to select a comfortable stand where one can sit for hours with little strain. A slightly reclining tree trunk makes a good backrest, and any terrain that allows your feet to come down a bit below your seat is ideal. Even raising your sitting position with a cushion, extra hunting apparel, or chunk of wood, gives you elevation so that your legs can rest outstretched and in a relaxed position. If the hunter is sitting in a cramped position, he will shift about almost continually, and he will not be fulfilling the true role of a trail watcher.

In some deer country, as in Texas, the watcher is legally permitted to sit in a tree blind to await the passing of his game. This is not nearly as comfortable as sitting on the ground where the hunter can occasionally flex his muscles or shift his position to relieve a confined and cramped body. Also, one's view is likely to be limited and his best shooting will be confined to a narrow arc from a perch in a tree. Some frown on this type of hunting, yet in many instances it is the only recourse for taking deer in very dense cover.

Watching the area of buck scrapes or pawings is a method of hunting, especially in the Southwest. A buck will return to a freshly made scrape several times a day during the rut, unless he is already preoccupied with a doe in heat. Here, the watcher selects a favorable stand on the ground or else he locates a suitable tree for a blind. If he is on the ground, he will have the wind to consider. The tree blind reduces any adverse effects of an unfavorable wind, and if the blind or perch is high enough, it is not likely to attract a deer's attention as animals do not readily recognize danger in a motionless figure in a tree.

The still-hunter in the arid country could have a difficult time of it unless he is well skilled in making use of all available cover, and he mixes in a good deal of watching with his walking. Often the ground is gravelly or is covered with sere aspen leaves or other dry vegetation, and quiet movement is almost impossible for a good approach to your game. The hunter must be resourceful and pick the situations most favorable to him.

Where there is a series of low hills, the still-hunter can skirt them, keeping just below their crests to avoid exposure to the other sides. As he rounds a rise, carefully and slowly, he brings in a new area to his view with the very minimum of his intrusion. Each time his scope of vision is changed, he pauses for many minutes to study any movement his eyes detect. A long-standing shot can be made from a comfortable prone or sitting position, in many cases, and the use of a gun sling is valuable here as in any long shots made at a standing whitetail.

Where the country is flat, and there is much open area between thickets, the whitetail can spot movement from a great distance. The hunter must follow the edge of the patches of growth so the sharp outline of his body is less pronounced, and he must settle for a very slow, smooth stride. He will pause often, especially as he rounds a thicket to gain a new view. It is at times like this that he finds his quarry completely off guard.

The whitetail, if he is not heavily pressed, is very reluctant to leave his home grounds when spooked by the hunter. This is especially true where cover is limited to scattered patches in great open spaces. Even if he is forced to leave his favorite bailiwick of mesquite or chaparral, the deer will eventually return to his established grounds before the day is over. This desire to return to his home area seems most pronounced where hunting pressure is least. The hunter seeking a specific animal or a trophy buck can usually wait him out if he has the patience.

Fortunately, in a dry and mild climate, whether the hunt is in December or January, the still-hunter can don light, soft footgear such as tennis shoes for an almost noiseless step. There is usually a wide variation in temperature from early morning to midday, but the still-hunter is better off when he dresses for the cooler part of the day and then slowing his hunt as the heat of the day increases; or he could carry any excess clothing in a light shoulder pack. He should never dress so lightly as to encourage a quick step during the chill of the morning or evening when careful hunting should be most fruitful.

Any river bottoms, creeks, and dry runs usually have deer trails along their banks, and these are good hunting spots for the still-hunter. Two men, moving abreast on opposite banks, can combine their efforts for a good hunt. Each is a still-hunter who gains the additional advantage of being in position to intercept a skulking deer spooked by the other member.

The big, noisy drive used in taking whitetails from dense cover belongs to the upper Great Lakes area and the East, though some form of the drive is used throughout the animals' range. When deer are hidden in patches of cover, wherever it may be, it is necessary to flush them out into the open for favorable shooting. A man might walk through a growth of chaparral, a mesquite grove, or through a deep canyon to start any game into the open for another man posted on a strategic point. Two or more men might hunt abreast, or one or two men might still-hunt an area while a third takes a stand on a runway to surprise any skulking deer stirred by the others.

The attracting of deer by antler rattling for a close shot is productive in the Southwest, but it is largely experimental elsewhere. The rattling or banging together of two antlers to simulate the sound effects of two bucks in combat belongs properly to the deer's rutting season. In at least some of the whitetail's northern and eastern range the rut is pretty much past its peak when the gun season on the animals is open. Also, the rattling of antlers to be effective would have to be used under ideal conditions in areas with relatively few hunters. These conditions most conducive for the successful use of antler rattling are found in the whitetail's southwestern range, especially the thorny brush country of south Texas. Deer calls, if practical at all, might also best be used where there are few hunters.

The effective use of deer lures, whether sex or food, is largely a matter of personal opinion. I have never used them myself, though I have heard pros and cons about them. If a hunter feels he profits from their use, this confidence he gains in them should be of value to him. And, again, I repeat, I prefer never to belittle another man's mode of hunting. Deer are taken in unusual situations by methods that might appear unconventional to many.

There are many subspecies of whitetails throughout the United States, some overlapping and mixing with others so that there is no sharp distinction in the subspecies in adjacent areas, at least as far as the ordinary hunter can observe. One of the easily distinguishable subspecies is the Arizona or Coues deer that seems to belong more properly to Mexico but whose range extends northward into parts of the Southwest. Even among the members of this diminutive subspecies, sizes vary from one locality to another.

A local friend of mine has head and feet mountings of a buck and doe of the mysterious little fantail found a few decades ago in the Blackfoot country of Montana. The heads and feet of these small, bug-eyed whitetails seem no larger than those of a two-month-old northern fawn. The buck has a well-balanced, dainty rack of three points on each side, and the ears of the midget deer appear very large for the small heads. I measured the heads out of curiosity and found them to be roughly eight and a half inches from nose tip to crown. This compares to eleven and a half inches for ordinary northern whitetail buck mountings I measured in the same manner.

According to the owner, the deer were taken in Montana by a brother in about 1943. If this information is correct, the fantails must have been very nearly extinct at the time they were taken. Elmer Keith in his book on big-game hunting says these deer were well-known in their particular habitat in Montana during the years 1917 to 1919. In his book, published in 1948, he comments they still may be there, or the hard winter of 1919-20 may have killed them off.

These fantails could have been related to the small Coues whitetail of the Southwest, or they could have been a separate subspecies entirely. Some authorities in Montana pass them off as mere whitetail runts, and not a subspecies.

12
Wounded Deer

THE ideal shot always to be hoped for is at a standing or walking deer at about 200 feet or less, preferably when the animal is in its natural, unruffled mood. The impact of the bullet at this range delivers such shock to the unsuspecting animal that even a fair placed hit brings the game down at the crack of the rifle. Undoubtedly, most deer are bagged at this close range, though not all of them are taken under ideal conditions otherwise.

The temptation, however, is to shoot regardless of the odds, and some hunters will blast away at a flickering tail with no thought of ever checking on a possible hit. This is something less than hunting; it is merely using one's hunting privilege as an escape valve for reckless abandon.

Somewhere in between the ideal close-standing game and the distant flickering tail is the target that accounts for most shots fired and most deer wounded. The number of animals left in the woods to die of gunshot wounds is not realized by the ordinary man. In the big emphasis to fill the bag, too many hunters refuse to pass up any shot regardless of consequences if it offers the slightest chance for getting their deer. It is unfortunate that these hunters do not linger in the deer country after the hunting season to learn first hand of the misery caused by trigger-happy shooting. And this misery continues until time or the rigors of winter painfully eliminate these maimed animals.

This deer loss does not include the large number of does and fawns killed and abandoned where only the buck is legal game. Man can be calloused beyond belief. I came upon a dead doe some years ago when a buck only was legal. In the fresh, early-morning snow I found the tracks of the hunter on his stand. The doe, still warm when I chanced upon her, had walked down the open runway and was shot from about a hundred feet. The man, apparently aware he was killing an illegal animal, did not bother to check on the carcass for further verification. Such an individual is, indeed, a dangerous mental invalid, and certainly should not be entrusted with a weapon.

The quickly dispatched deer, legal or not, is brought to a merciful ending, but the crippled animal may be seriously wounded or it may be less fortunate and escape with a bullet injury that it succumbs to months later. I have found the close, trampled winter quarters of several such handicapped deer that had finally died or else were killed by brush wolves.

Only once have I had the unpleasant experience of actually seeing a totally emaciated animal cling tenaciously to life when death was inevitable. The fawn had a front leg broken just above the knee, and the black, shriveled member dangled hideously with every move of the poor animal. It was late February and the snow was about thirty inches in depth. The deer, now reduced to mere skin and bones, lived in a popple thicket roughly fifty feet in circumference. All growth up to the thickness of a finger was completely eaten to the ground, and the bark of bigger popple was gnawed off as high as the fawn could reach. Such is the stamina of the whitetail deer.

This is the cruelty imposed on wildlife by the shot that just drew blood or merely nicked the whitetail. After all hunters have cleared the woods, this is the story remaining back of the scene that is politely referred to as the "inevitable cripple losses." But most such losses are not inevitable. The hunter, bound by his moral obligation, will concentrate all efforts toward bagging the deer he has wounded. In most cases, one's chances of finishing off the crippled animal are far greater than the probability of coming upon another deer during the remainder of the hunt.

During the deer season of 1959, I was hunting in Wisconsin's Burnett County. There were a good number of deer in this sandy, brushy country that was interspersed with numerous abandoned farm fields. A heavy concentration of hunters was on hand, lured on by the party hunting permit in addition to the buck season. There was a continual barrage of shots beginning at sunrise in the road-bounded section square, and the din did not taper off until nearly noon. I passed some time on my stand, counting the shots when the reports seemed heaviest, and I counted as high as twenty-five rounds to a minute.

Next day, my party and I returned for another try to the same place. We drove completely around the section in the early morning and found where only two deer were dragged over the snow from this area. But we found much evidence of wounded animals as a result of the unrestrained shooting of the day before. These cripples were to linger until they were killed by other hunters or until the winter's deep snow brought them to a slow death. Seldom does one ever take a whitetail that shows the healing scars of anything but the superficial wound.

Every man back of a gun knows pretty well what his chances are for hitting his deer. When the odds are negligible, it is far more satisfying for the thoughtful hunter to withhold fire. I do not believe many hunters ever make a fortunate kill under circumstances that they deem quite impossible. Yet, these few exceptions often rule the policy of the man in the field, and, as a result, he assumes a sort of bellicose approach to his game — a trigger-conscious gunner instead of a hunter. It is this segment in the army of redcoats that accounts for the heavy toll of wasted wildlife each season.

The obvious rule to follow in any hunting is simply this: Do not shoot unless you are willing to check thoroughly the results of your fire. This will take considerable time on bare ground, even if the bullet has hit a vital spot on the animal. A running whitetail can continue its sprint for over a hundred yards, even with a deadly heart shot, and in this distance it may leave little or no blood to mark its trail.

One season when the snow was of ideal depth, I found a chunky eight-point buck dead on a runway. He was killed by a well-placed shoulder shot, and the heavy tallow on his broad shoulders must have sealed the bullet hole, for there was just a sprinkling of blood in the tracks leading to the carcass.

A few days later, my brother Francis and I were still-hunting about a mile from the same spot. I came upon a freshly killed big doe, and I was somewhat puzzled since it was still early in the morning and I tracked no other hunters in the newly fallen snow. The deer was shot smack through the shoulders, its trail was well marked by profuse bleeding, and to top if off, any deer was legal game this particular season.

I pondered the situation for some time, then decided to dress out the animal and be on my way. Before proceeding with the task, I looked around to see if there was a hunter somewhere on a stand, but all I could see was fresh, unbroken snow all around me. Even after I slit the doe's belly open, I made another survey around me. Sure enough, there on a brushy hillside, about 150 yards off, was a man sitting on a stump. He wore the dark, dull red that so easily becomes a nondescript black on a cloudy day. This was, undoubtedly, the man who shot the doe. But why did he show so little concern while I was dressing out the animal? I walked up to the man slouched on the stump, and he raised his head with scant interest when I inquired about his luck.

"Saw only one big doe come down this trail early this morning," he said. "I took a shot at her but I guess I missed."

"Come with me," I said. "Let's follow your deer's tracks. It must be the big doe I was just starting to dress out."

The old man suddenly came to life. He slid off the stump and before his stiff legs recovered circulation, he half stumbled down the hillside in his excitement and hurry. The tracks showed the deer was standing only about a hundred feet from where the old man sat. There was no blood in sight, but a few feet farther the first drops fell, and farther on the trail was sprayed with red. The doe ran about 150 yards in an arc around the hill and then dropped dead in a little hollow where I found her.

The happy hunter, I soon learned, had never dressed out a deer before, so I finished the chore for him. His age also belied his hunting experience; he said he had hunted only once before and that was in his younger days. Like a few other redcoats I have met over my hunting years, he expected the deer to keel over in its tracks if it were hit. And when he first saw me starting to dress out the deer, he guessed I was merely building a fire by the runway. A simple hunter, indeed, but he is part of the multitude that makes up our hunting force.

Recovering Wounded Deer

When deer, such as the two mentioned, are lost to hunters even with snow on the ground, the loss of animals on bare ground and with poorly placed shots is something to consider. These two deer were not just wounded; they were killed. Any man with even bare elementary knowledge of hunting would have found them. So we will consider the means and possibilities of recovering the wounded animal — the one that, although handicapped by a bullet injury, is able to escape the hunter.

An experienced hunter who knows his gun can tell pretty well whether or not he has hit his deer when it is standing or moving slowly. He has formed the habit of squeezing the trigger only when it is dead on the target, and when he does not recall the perfect sight picture, he knows he let off the shot in carelessness or in haste. He is aware of the hit or miss just as he pulls the trigger, but sometimes anxiety rules his better judgment, and he lets the shot go for a miss.

Years back, when I used to complain to my older brothers about missing a standing deer, they handled my tale of woe wisely and with dispatch. "Did you hold the sights on the deer's shoulder?" I was licked with this line of approach. To say "no" was self-condemnation. If I said "yes," then my brothers agreed the deer was dead and they would help me drag it in. The fact is, I was not sure if I held on the shoulder or not and, as I see it now, it meant I did not.

The manner in which a whitetail reacts to a shot gives some clue to the flight and effect of a bullet. The animal will flinch when he is hit, but this can be observed only at close range. If a deer is standing or walking, he will likely run forward when hit. If, in this same situation, he is missed, then he will usually turn around and run back. The deer generally will stand long enough for a second shot if the bullet sails over him. A bullet close under the animal will make him jump straight up on hairspring legs, and he probably will swing around and run back.

There are several reactions a standing or walking whitetail might show when he is hit — a slight slumping of the body, lowering of the head, or a slow, irregular gait when walking or trotting. The running animal can be expected to continue his flight whether he is hit or not, and the fact that his flag is down or up is no indication of a hit or a miss.

If there is reason to believe a deer has been hit, the hunter had best get in what shots he can and get them in as quickly as he can, for if he is lucky to score another hit it may save him considerable time and energy in recovering the wounded animal.

When there is snow on the ground, the hunter should have little trouble in ascertaining the damage inflicted by his bullet. Both hair and blood are the important clues. Large, dry tufts of dark hair on the snow just back of where the animal stood would indicate a grazing shot over the back. This could be a mere cropping of the hair, for even a flesh wound on the back would likely bring the animal down for a moment. In this case, the hunter can follow the trail for at least a hundred yards to check for blood. If he sees none, he can assure himself the animal is not injured. Short, dark hair might also come from the top of the shoulders or the neck, but here, also, anything more than a superficial wound would stun the whitetail briefly. The deer could not be considered seriously injured despite on occasional drop of blood trickling down to the tracks. Long gobs of sticky hair and a trail of bloodstained brownish-yellow is the sign of the unfortunate gut shot. It is unfortunate because the deer's ability to run is not greatly impaired, the animal suffers much, and the wound is mortal. Short white hair in this instance is the very low belly wound. Long white hair, usually with little or no blood, is the grazing rump or tail hit, and the hunter has little consolation here.

Blood spurting to the sides is a good sign, for the hunter knows the deer will not get very far. The animal has been hit somewhere in the front quarters and most probably below the lower half. It is a matter of time before the animal succumbs completely so long as the blood flows freely. Frothy blood coming from the deer's mouth and nostrils is the mark of a lung shot. The deer may travel some distance, depending on the injury to its lungs, but the animal is seriously wounded and can be hunted down.

Much of the blood sign found on the trail of a wounded deer drops to the sides of the tracks or directly into them. This is not a happy sign for the hunter. A little study can aid the man in determining the nature of the wound. Blood from a broken leg trickles downward except for occasional drops to the side from the dangling leg, and the swinging of the loose leg will show in the snow.

The height of a bullet wound on an animal is indicated on shrubs or trees when the deer passes through them. Blood showing on shrubbery and trickling down the body to the tracks gives the hunter some clue as to where he hit his target.

From the scattered hair and the nature of the blood sign, the hunter has some idea of the task before him. There are many pro and con arguments as to the feasibility of taking up the tracks immediately. From my experience and that of veteran hunters I have consulted, it is entirely practical to follow your quarry immediately, at least for a short distance. An animal is temporarily stunned by the impact of a bullet even though the injury is not severe. If the hunter is quick enough to take advantage of this condition in the wounded animal, he might save himself a long chase.

I was neither alert nor quick enough to finish off a dazed buck when I scored a poor hit high on his hindquarters just below the spine. The blood dripping to the tracks was not too encouraging, and I followed the trail for about a hundred yards in order to learn the nature of the wound. To my surprise, the buck rose slowly from his bed in a dense growth only fifty feet ahead of me. He staggered away from me in a straight line, and I hesitated shooting him in the rump for he appeared ready to collapse any moment.

The next time I jumped him he was a good 150 yards off, and from then on he bedded down less often. Finally, he did not bed down at all, but held a steady pace just fast enough to keep well ahead of me. After a two-hour chase, I caught him as he was crossing a broad valley. Now I was less selective in placing my shots, and I was happy to drop the buck with a mid-body hit.

The hunter, if he is unsuccessful in finding his mortally wounded quarry for a favorable finishing shot immediately, might spend some time in attempting to learn the nature of the wound; for once the animal has

passed the brief stage of initial stupor, it has regained sufficient poise for a deliberate escape. The shock resulting from the injury does not come until some time later, and it comes sooner and with more impact if the wounded deer is not pressed.

If there are no hunters in the area and there is sufficient daylight time, it is best to wait for an hour or two before pursuing the quarry. In the meantime, the deer will be weakened by loss of blood, and if it is bedded down, as will be most likely, it will become stiff and slow in its reflexes. In the event that it is too late in the day to follow the bleeding track, and the animal is not seriously injured, the trail should be picked up the next morning.

Many men become discouraged too easily when they see the white-tail run off, apparently unhampered, or if they see very little sign of blood along the trail. Yet, such an animal could have received a deadly hit. I took a big lead on a running buck as he went across a clearing. He went by me broadside only 150 feet away, and it looked like a complete miss to me. After following his running tracks for 200 yards, I found a fleck of blood. Further down the trail were a few more red stains, and in the brush just off the clearing was my dead buck — the bullet severed his windpipe at the white spot close to the jaws. Even the heart shot does not always draw blood immediately; nor does the gait of the wounded animal always indicate a fatal hit has been scored.

The gut-shot animal can nearly always be recovered when there is snow on the ground. The whitetail is in extreme pain, and it strives to alleviate its discomfort by alternately lying down and moving on to escape its enemy. The hunter has his deer marked and he should go all out to finish it off. With snow on the ground, the animal can be tracked and still-hunted. The gut-shot deer is dull in spirit and slow in movement. When one or two men are available to flank the tracker, there should be little difficulty in taking the deer as it rises somewhat sluggishly from its bed. The wounded deer is a handicapped animal. It is less alert, travels more slowly, and stops to rest more frequently than if it were uninjured. When the hunter deems it practical to follow the slots of the sound whitetail, he will certainly find it advantageous to pursue the ailing whitetail. The deer with the broken leg, the hip shot, or the brisket wound should not be abandoned to a slow but certain death. If it is pursued with the stealth of the still-hunter, chances for recovery of the animal are good.

During the hunting season of 1964, I was unfortunate in inflicting a leg wound on an eight-point buck when the ground was without snow. It was early in the forenoon, and brother Francis and I were determined to run the animal down before nightfall. The buck bled profusely for the first mile we followed his trail; then the bleeding tapered off, especially when the deer merely walked.

The animal bedded down several times, indicating that he was weakening from loss of blood. Tracking became most difficult on the snowless ground, and at times only a fleck of blood indicated the buck's course along old runways skirting the many swamps. But we pressed on with determination. Once Francis got a distant running shot at our quarry. After about three hours of steady pressure, we came upon the exhausted and panting buck, and we finished him off easily. The leg shot, just above the knee, severed the main artery without breaking the leg.

Without snow, it becomes extremely difficult and sometimes impossible to track down the wounded animal. Yet, if hunting is to be a sport it must be tempered with humanity, and the hunter cannot ease his responsibility simply because tracking does not come easy on snowless ground. If one puts his mind to it, he can recover the more seriously injured deer, and he certainly should follow the tracks of an animal at which he shot. About 200 yards of trailing will remove any doubt from the hunter's mind as to whether or not he made a hit.

There is nothing like getting down on one's hands and knees in searching for hoof marks, hair, or blotches of blood on the leaves. When any of these are found, the hunter can mark the spot with a broken tree branch. From this point he can pretty well tell from disturbed leaves, broken dried twigs from the lower branches of trees, and the lay of the land, which direction the animal went.

Continued long-strides in the running animal, when no blood is found, are a good indication that the deer is most probably unscathed. Short, jogged leaps warrant further investigation. The healthy deer picks its route through openings in the brush, and is not averse to running up a steep incline or leaping over obstacles in its path. The ailing whitetail, on the other hand, might stick to the brush but prefers to follow the downward sloping terrain. And when his vitality begins to ebb away, he enters heavy brush, often stumbling through the dense growth. It is in the lowland thickets, the creek bottoms, and the swamps where most crippled deer are found dead.

Under usual situations, the only hits that bring a whitetail down in his tracks are those in the brain and spinal column, and probably in the kidney. The hit within a six-inch circle of the center of the shoulder usually drops the deer at once, also, but if the deer is running or edgy, it could travel for over a hundred yards before it falls dead.

Most hunters will check the results of their shots at a standing deer even if the target is a considerable distance off and the deer has fled. Yet some of these same men will snap shoot at running deer, and if the animal continues in full flight, they make little or no attempt at investigating the effect of their fire. The whitetail traveling at full speed when hit can maintain his pace for some distance and show no apparent injury even when critically injured. This results in the biggest loss in our wounded deer.

Merely pulling a hasty trigger at every running whitetail is the overt sign of eagerness and inexperience in the redcoat. The hunter takes a deliberate shot, for he expects to check thoroughly the results of his fire.

13

After Your Deer is Down

FTER you see your deer go down, it is a good idea to remain on the spot to see that it is down to stay. Should the animal attempt to regain its feet again, the hunter is in position to finish it off. There have been many tales told of hunters rushing out to an apparently killed deer, momentarily losing sight of the animal behind a thicket or fallen timber, and arriving at the spot where their prize was last seen to find it gone.

A buck hit in the antlers close to the skull, or any deer creased over its back or neck can be stunned momentarily only to recover and escape completely. Even a badly wounded deer could muster up enough strength to struggle off some distance to become lost or at least cause you some concern. All this can be avoided if you cling to your post to watch your downed deer for several minutes. This, of course, might not be entirely practical if the area is congested with men and you stand watch over your deer from a considerable distance.

Even as you approach your deer you should keep your eyes on it and be ready for a quick shot should it suddenly come to its feet. Once you are alongside the animal you can locate the bullet hole and appraise its effect on the deer. A final neck or headshot might be in order, especially if the head is not to be considered for mounting.

A prod in the ribs with the muzzle of the rifle is usually sufficient to ascertain if the animal is dead, but if the hunter is favored with a big heavy-antlered buck, he might want to exercise more caution before applying the knife. Hunting with a medical doctor, as I often do, I have learned that tapping the eyeballs of the deer with a fingertip will cause the animal to blink if it is still alive and conscious.

Deer have been known to get up and escape after being tagged by a hunter. This will not happen to the man who checks the placement of his hits and makes sure the animal is no longer conscious. A deer will occasionally kick and show signs of life even with a well-placed shot, and here one needs to wait but a short while before it is dead and field dressing can be started.

Many outdoor writers dwell at length on the possible danger of approaching a downed deer. A man with normal hunting precautions need have no great concern here, for a deer, like any wounded animal, seeks to escape rather than attack, but in its struggle it sometimes might injure the inexperienced hunter. Also, if you apply your knife in field dressing the animal while it is still conscious, the prick of the knifepoint could cause the deer to kick its feet to send the knife flying. This could result in your sustaining a nasty cut.

If the animal has been hit in any part of the front body cavity, it will be pretty well bled. However, if it has been hit in the head, neck, or toward the rear, the big blood vessels on each side of the windpipe should be severed, unless, of course, you expect to have the head mounted. In this case you can stick

the chest in the area of the heart. The carcass should be raised above the level of the cut to help in good blood drainage. Since venison should be cooled as quickly as possible, the draining of the warm blood, either from any cut or from the body cavity, is a desirable first step.

The once-a-year deer hunter cannot expect to be a professional butcher, and he will likely have some processor take care of his kill once he gets it home. But he can properly field dress his animal so that the processor can get the utmost from the deer. No processor delights in working with venison that has been badly treated from the start.

The deer is best handled if it is placed on its back on an incline so that drainage will be from the chest cavity downward toward the hindquarters. The cut is started at the lower part of the belly, and after a small opening is made into the abdominal cavity, two fingers are inserted in the slit to steer the knife in its course upward toward the brisket. The fingers also raise the belly wall to help avoid cutting into intestines or the bladder.

To do a thorough job of field dressing a deer, I take time to split the pelvis bone and remove the large intestines by cutting it free from its extremity. Splitting the pelvis bone takes a stout knife and sometimes considerable force. If this is impossible with the available knife, one should tie the large intestine with a string near the pelvis bone and then cut around the anus to remove the gut. This can be done with a pocketknife. The pelvis bone can be split later with a heavy knife or hatchet.

The chest cavity is often carelessly handled simply because it is not sufficiently opened for cleaning. The best way to get at this area is to slit the brisket alongside the breastbone (sternum). This is the point where the cartilage attaches to the breastbone, about three inches to the side of the breastbone on either side. This cartilage, easily cut even with a pocketknife, should be slit with the hide up to the base of the animal's neck. The cavity can then be partly opened so that the windpipe can be cut, or if the windpipe is already cut on the neck, it can be pulled out with the lungs and heart.

The diaphragm, the muscular tissue that separates the abdominal cavity from the chest cavity, must be cut close to the ribs. Any tissue holding the organs to the chest walls, and this includes big blood vessels, must also be cut. All the insides, now entirely freed from one extremity to the other, can be rolled to the side and down the slope in one mass. The carcass, still sloping downward from the front quarters to the hindquarters, should be turned on its belly with legs sprawled for thorough blood drainage.

If a clean handkerchief or any clean cloth is available, it can be used to wipe the deer's body cavity of blood. Contrary to common belief, cleaning the deer's inside with a damp cloth is most helpful if the moisture is exposed to air so it can readily evaporate. Getting rid of all blood is most essential since blood is the most active culture media for bacteria to grow on and contaminate the meat.

The liver and heart, especially of young deer, are thoroughly palatable, and many hunters claim these with some elation as a token of a successful hunt. Liver, even from an older deer, if sliced about an inch thick and soaked in salt water overnight, will have its bile extracted and make a good breakfast fare for the hunter.

Now comes the chore of getting the kill out of the woods. Many hunters consider this a menial, unpleasant task to be disposed of in a hurry so that the hunt can continue. And here is where a soft, but otherwise normal, hunter might succumb to a heart attack because of a combination of anxiety and physical strain. It has always been my contention that if a man has had the good fortune to bag his deer, he should afford himself the luxury of ample time in getting it out to his car or camp. This is part of the hunt, and it deserves a bit of consideration and planning.

Any arrangements for taking the deer out depend on the number of men in the hunt, the area hunted, and the original plans of the hunting group. In western or southwestern country, a four wheel-drive motor vehicle or a packhorse saves the hunter from a great part of the task of bringing in his deer from the rugged backcountry.

In much of the wooded and brushy deer habitat of the North, East, and South, the successful gunner can expect to exert at least some physical effort in most cases in getting out his deer.

And sometimes, where the country is mountainous or hilly, the task of getting the deer to the car or camp can be a consideration. Naturally, the hunter must be prepared for the conditions that confront him on his hunting grounds.

If two or more men are available, a freshly killed buck can be dragged with a man at each antler. With an antler hold, the forepart of the deer is raised sufficiently so that it will drag nicely, especially over snow, pine needles, sere grass, or dead leaves. Any additional men in the group might scout ahead to seek an easy route. If the two men dragging the deer carry guns in their free hands, the guns should be unloaded or at least have no shells in their chambers.

Any men to the front of those dragging the deer might profit by keeping alert with guns ready should they come upon another deer. Many a whitetail is flushed by a group of plodding men caught off guard. With frequent changes at dragging the deer, and rest periods at brief intervals, and the whole combined with an easy hunt, the task of taking out a deer far back can be a pleasant experience.

If less men are involved or available for taking out a deer, the chore need cause no great concern. The successful hunters simply take more time at the job. The time to take a breather is at the slightest sign of fatigue, not when one is forced by exhaustion to come to a halt. And if the deer cannot be taken out easily the day it is killed, it should be left during the evening and picked up early next morning.

When a deer is left out overnight, it should be prepared for proper cooling. Some hunters might drag the animal into a small hollow and maybe cover it with brush or leaves for protection. This might keep the deer hidden until next morning, but it is a sure way to ruin venison. The body heat trapped in a deer's body cavity and insulated by the animal's heavy coat should be released as quickly as possible.

The best way to do this is to lay the animal on its side over a log or several heavy sticks of wood so that air can circulate under the carcass. Then several sticks of proper length are placed in both the abdominal and chest cavities to hold the walls of the cavities apart so that air enters freely. Never should the belly skin be permitted to collapse and seal off air circulation from the inside of a warm carcass. When leaving a deer in the woods overnight, it is well to pay special attention to any landmarks in the immediate vicinity to help you find your deer early in the morning.

Even the lone hunter need not get panicky about getting his deer to his car. If he hunts an area alone, chances are he is somewhat familiar with the country and any back-woods roads or trails in the vicinity. When I hunt alone, I am always aware of the distance the deer will have to be dragged, and I do not stray into an area where this might be a problem.

It's a good idea, especially for the lone hunter, to carry a small nylon cord on his person. A spike buck or an antlerless deer can be dragged by tying the cord around the animal's neck and then making a half hitch around the deer's muzzle. The short cord, tied to a cross stick, allows you to pull the animal with both hands while raising its head and neck for better going.

This could be slow work, especially if you have no sling on your gun. But you must consider that the big task was bagging your quarry. You should now relax and take the easiest way out with your kill. No need now for any undue strain or anxiety. Many a hunter suffers a heart attack because he wants his deer at his camp or quarters in the least possible time.

Once the animal is out of the woods it should be properly cooled and kept ventilated. Hung on a meat pole, it will be well aired and keep fresh in cool weather. If the weather is warm, the deer should be hung in the shade with a cheese-cloth wrapped around it to keep out any flies. When the carcass is transported any great distance on a car, it should be kept cool and exposed to air on its trip. The hunter might best choose the cool of the night for his trip home.

Whether you take care of the venison yourself, or give it to a commercial processor, the head, if it is to be considered for mounting, must be left with ample skin, usually including the top of the shoulders to the front of the brisket. This gives the taxidermist sufficient skin to work with.

You will find your venison a delicious fare if you have taken the proper steps in caring for it while afield. Venison is as palatable as beef if it is killed, cared for, and processed with the same concern given beef. If venison has a strong, gamy odor and taste, it is the result of poor field handling on part of the hunter.

14
Buck Fever

BUCK fever comes in about as many different guises as there are men who succumb to this strange derangement of hunting behavior. In all its various forms, from simple loss of good judgment, which is buck fever in its milder phase, to helpless confusion and utter loss of composure, the malady is still buck fever, differing only in its effect on the hunter and the intensity of the attack. Sometimes the attack is so slight that the hunter honestly passes it off as mere carelessness in gun handling or just poor judgment in appraising the situation before him. Even in the most severe cases of bewilderment, the hunter will often search for some plausible reason to explain his unusual behavior.

This embarrassing seizure is pretty much confined to the inexperienced deer hunter, or more pointedly, to the hunter inexperienced in shooting deer, and only rarely will a man suffer a repetition of the severe attack. The overanxious fellow is taken by complete surprise when a big buck brushes past his stand without warning. Somehow, the hunter did not expect it to happen that way, and he is caught completely off guard. His reaction to this stunning experience could be anything from simple awe to uncontrollable and uncoordinated gun handling. There are some first-timers who can knock down the first deer they have ever seen with a slick shot through the head or neck and register about as much apathy as does a trout angler in absentmindedly dispatching an annoying deer fly.

The man most subject to buck fever is usually an avid, though untried, hunter with a keen zest for bagging his game. He is at least normally impressionable, and the sight of a timid, beautiful wilderness creature suddenly thrust upon him at very close range is a breath-taking experience.

The proximity of the deer plays a considerable part in stirring the hunter's emotions. A buck standing off a hundred yards does not cause the shakes in the novice that the same animal would induce if the hunter were close enough to see its wide-eyed stare, the details of its body, and its large, moving rack. Under conditions such as this, it is entirely possible that the hunter becomes so impressed with the beautiful specimen before him that he struggles with hidden inhibitions to kill such an animal, and he inadvertently shoots carelessly if he shoots at all.

Most hunters experience buck fever, at least to a small degree, when they are confronted with the first deer they hope to bag. I had a slight touch of it when I attempted shooting my first buck, and this despite the fact that I had seen many whitetails before I was old enough to hunt them. Naturally, it never dawned on me that I had buck fever. The prized animal stood off at about only thirty yards, and my first hurried reaction was to shoot. The animal did not drop and I wondered what went wrong. I was calm, but puzzled, as my handsome buck ambled off unharmed.

When I related the incident to my oldest brother that evening, he gave me a long-remembered piece of advice: "It isn't the noise of the gun that kills a deer. You've got to hit him." Then it occurred to me that I could easily bore a tin can at that distance, but when the chips were down I completely missed the buck.

There is a strong psychological association between the booming of a high-powered rifle and a mortally wounded deer struggling hopelessly to regain its feet. The sound of the shot becomes important to the anxious hunter, sometimes so important that he will mechanically blast away with little thought of holding on the target. Still, the hunter might remain quite calm and feel his reactions are normal and his ability unimpaired.

This is the common buck fever experienced by most hunters, although few men recognize it in this moderate form. Because it is not recognized as buck fever, the hunter could go on for several seasons thinking he is merely a victim of circumstances every time he misses his game at reasonable range. If this man is honest with himself he must admit he recalls no clear-cut image of his gun sights lined up on his target after he hears the resounding report of his rifle. Actually, he is unconsciously putting emphasis on the sound of the shot rather than on the placing of the shot. When this man is able to squeeze off the trigger without anticipating the gun's report, he is cured of this common but most persistent type of buck fever.

The more pronounced cases of this hunter's ague are readily recognized even by the victims themselves, though they may be reluctant to admit it at the time. And some of these experiences are prime examples of behavior breakdown in otherwise usually composed individuals.

Once, while hunting alone, I came upon four hunters standing at the intersection of a deer runway and a tote road. The man in the middle of the group was taking a verbal beating from his three partners, who all seemed to be shouting at once. Before I could approach the group to learn what the heated rumpus was all about, the three men left their browbeaten companion, waving their hands at him in utter disdain. Plainly, this abandoned man had committed a serious breach in hunting procedure. What did he do to warrant such abuse?

I sidled up to the outcast, half in sympathy and half in curiosity. It took some coaxing to get the story from the helpless individual, but he finally related the tale with childish remorse. His three companions made a drive to him and put two does and a buck down the runway and across the tote road where he stood. The animals came trotting down the trail single file and then stopped short before making the tote road crossing. Here they stood, seemingly for hours, while our defeated hunter appeared to remember only one thing, — to remain motionless while on the stand. The deer bypassed the hunter on either side of him, scarcely twenty-five feet away. They rejoined the trail immediately behind him and slowly proceeded on their way. And when they were gone, our hero mulled over the incident as though it were a mere dream. He did not recall even making any attempt to shoot. But he was rudely brought back to reality when his irate hunting companions stormed him for an explanation after one of them followed the deer tracks to the very stand.

This man had what might be termed passive buck fever. It was obvious to me that he had been so impressed by the sight of these animals fairly breathing down his neck that he had been overwhelmed with awe.

There is the other extreme of buck fever in which the hunter finds himself so emotionally bound that he seeks to extricate himself from the situation with vigorous but irrational action. Here, the sufferer is well aware of his helpless plight, but there seems little he can do about it. He jumps into action, and with trembling hands points his gun in the general direction of his quarry and blasts away. After the smoke has cleared, the echoes of his rifle shots linger in his ears for minutes afterwards — possibly for hours. The entire episode becomes a nightmare to him, and when he attempts to relate the incident to his hunting partners he has a difficult time of it. He is not sure how many deer there were, where they stood, or how many times he shot. Maybe several days, or even months, afterwards, he is able to piece together some hazy facts of the episode.

I know of one instance when the hunter was so hopelessly struck with buck fever that his story bore little relation to the facts. He said he emptied his gun at a big buck standing broadside to him at a distance of about a hundred feet. The handsome brute simply refused to lay down after being hit several times; but the hunter was not sure where the animal was hit. The bewildered man did not remember to look for blood sign in the snow, but promptly marched straight back to camp in disgust. Naturally, he placed the blame on his gun.

One of the more experienced members of the party went right back to the scene with the hapless hunter, thinking that despite the heavy discount that must be given the story, there was still enough substance left to warrant some investigation. If you have ever had occasion to follow a man to the site of such an incident, you know how uncertain the fellow is of any simple facts connected with his experience. The spot was found in due time, but it was the excited youngster who had to be shown where he must have stood when he sighted the buck. There, in the light cover of snow were a couple of ejected bullets — ejected without being fired. A brief search brought up the seven intact bullets, the entire load of the .30/30 carbine.

The buck-happy young man had not fired a shot at the deer, but in his intense excitement he had lost all reason and simply went through the mechanics of gun manipulation. He could not remember whether or not he had heard the series of shots. His mind was a jumbled mass of confusion.

Many hunters seem to believe that uncontrollable trembling is the sole symptom of buck fever. Actually, trembling is an outward expression of the emotions gripping some individuals, but there are those who can appear outwardly stoical while their senses are numb. Often the tremors come minutes after the hunter has fumbled his good chance at a deer. He may wonder why he missed his target when he recalls he was quite unruffled. In reality, he had buck fever when he first sighted his game, and the trembling came in the aftermath.

There are simple precautions the untried hunter can heed that will help him subdue his anxiety and jitters when he sights his first legal game. First, he must convince himself that he is as subject to the fever as is the next neophyte. When he humbly accepts this fact, he will be prepared to fight it. Then he must strive to be ever conscious of the use of his gun, for it is the proper use of his weapon that kills the deer.

When the man fully realizes the importance of placing his shot, he will strive to push aside his emotions and concentrate on the one important thing — lining up his sights on his gun before squeezing the trigger. If this bit of precaution is kept foremost in the hunter's mind, he will have less difficulty in applying it when the big moment arrives. Too often, the beginner thinks only of bagging his game in some vague manner, but he has no clear concept of how he will handle his gun.

There are those few individuals, and they can be mere lads or oldsters long past their prime, who are wholly unmoved when sighting their first deer over a barrel. I recall such a rare character who shot the first buck he ever saw when hunting for the species. He was a middle-aged man with no special love for the outdoors. Above his fireplace in his summer home, on one of Wisconsin's northern lakes, was a rack of antlers supporting a deer rifle that had never seen use. This particular year, because of agreeable weather, he remained at his summer cottage much later than usual. Since the deer season would open shortly, he decided to put in a few days trying for a whitetail.

This lukewarm hunter knew nothing of whitetails despite the fact that he spent many summers in good deer country. A younger brother and I agreed to put him on a stand on the morning of the season opener. We would spend the day still-hunting and then pick up our charge at the close of the day. There were two good stands several hundred yards apart on a long ridge that we considered, and we were undecided in our selection. Then it occurred to me that here was a chance for a short drive without much loss in time. My brother would station the man on one stand while he himself would cover the other. Accordingly, I remained at the road for a half hour while the two slowly circuited the area to their stands. I covered the flat thicket with rapid strides and then paused a bit to pick my way up the steep incline of the ridge.

There was a deafening boom above and to my left, and a suggestion of burnt powder came to my nostrils. Then I spotted our not-too-zealous hunter calmly standing atop the rise, and he showed little indication that anything had happened. There, about twenty-five feet below him, lay an unusually big eight-point buck, shot through the center of the white patch on its neck. Our guest hunter, meanwhile, continued to survey the valley below him as though the bagging of only one buck was somewhat short of his expectations. He appeared strangely indifferent to his success, and he could not be stirred into anything more than mere complacency, at best. That morning's jaunt sufficed him for all time, as far as I know, for he utterly lacked any zest for the sport. Certainly such a man does not succumb to buck fever, nor does he receive his proper share of enjoyment in pursuing the whitetail.

To the eager hunter belongs the chase of the whitetail deer. And the man who boasts of never having even a trace of buck fever when trying for his first deer, probably does not enjoy the hunt as much as his more excitable hunting partners.

15
The Buck

*M*OST hunters know the buck only from deer-season observations. The animal is pictured as a handsome, stout-necked specimen with an impressive rack to mark him as a lord of the herd. Such characteristics as intelligence, wariness, stamina, grace, and bigness are attributed to him, as though he alone represented these qualities in the species.

I suppose if bucks were without antlers, or if both sexes carried them, our buck would be a mere male, and the does and fawns would then receive equal attention and, perhaps, more preference because of their more tender flesh. But, as it is, the buck is the prince of the forest, the sought-after prize; and the does and fawns are the lesser of the species. Yet, aside from the period of the rut, the buck fades into the background of the deer family, and much of this time he lacks the noble appearance with which the hunter is most familiar.

It is only during the fall, when bucks move about freely in response to the rutting urge, that one can expect to see them frequently; in fact, they now appear more abundant than the actual ratio of their number to the rest of the whitetails. During the summer, the mature males are a bit reclusive, and the deer population seems to consist mostly of antlerless deer. This is the less picturesque side of the whitetail buck. Rogue that he is, he has little concern for the family, and the artist's conception of a prime antlered sire alongside a doe with her nursing spotted fawn is about as incongruous a picture as could be imagined.

During spring and early summer, bucks often live quite alone and apart from other deer. Even the yearling male, which has been following its mother since his birth, finds himself alone, for the doe now ignores her older offspring and turns her interest to the newborn fawn.

Bucks, if seen in any company at all, might choose to team up with other bucks for companionship. This seems to be a common tendency with them except for the rutting period, and even then they are commonly tolerant of each other.

If one studies the late-summer and early-fall deer feeding in specific fields during the evenings or nights, he can observe the inclination of bucks to feed by themselves or in the company of each other. Sometimes, one might find twenty or more whitetails in a field at one time, and there will be no bucks among them. This same field, at a later hour, might contain a half-dozen sires with few or no antlerless animals among them. Sometimes the bucks come to feed early, even in broad daylight. In such a situation, the does and fawns do not enter the field in any large numbers until the bucks have left. And if there is a mature male or two on the same field with antlerless deer, chances are these males will be feeding by themselves in some far corner.

Antler Development

Early in April, the tufts of hair on the male's head become more pronounced, and within a few weeks two knobby projections indicate the start of antler growth. Before there are any signs of sprouting branches, the straight, bulbous-tipped beams give the lean-necked buck the appearance of a giraffe. And the animal becomes even more grotesque as the knobby forks appear on the growing beam.

The thick, velvety skin, containing numerous blood vessels, encases the antlers and adds great bulk to the growing rack. During this growing period, the antlers are sensitive and pliable, and it is at this time that any injury to them shows up later as a deformity in the prime antlers. In August, in our northern areas, antler growth is completed, and the velvet-covered skin that nourished it now becomes shriveled. The buck presents a ludicrous picture when the peeling velvet sometimes hangs in fluttering ribbons from the rack.

The velvet from antlers is not always shed bit by bit in a slow peeling and drying process. On this I have some first-hand information, for once I found the complete velvet case from a single antler of an eight-point buck. It was during the middle of August, and I happened across the strange object that looked like a piece of dark suede leather.

The soft velvet was shed in one entire piece, and it split along the outside length of the beam to free itself from the prongs. The fuzzy growth was about an eighth of an inch thick and was substantial enough in body so that the projections covering the points of the antler stood out firmly on the discarded casing.

The curio was found in an open spot where the pasture grass was closely cropped. There was nothing nearby that the buck might have rubbed against in an attempt to free himself from this skin growth. The soft, damp condition of the casing caused me to believe it was shed that very day.

I brought it home in some sort of triumph, but the next day it was already beginning to shrivel and dry, and in a few days it lost its shape and the mummy-like skin was reduced to something that looked like a withered and twisted leaf. In this aged condition, it might not have caught my attention had I passed over it, and only the eyes of a naturalist could have identified it when found. I would guess that at least some velvet shedding takes place in this manner. Most bucks seen at this time are either in or out of velvet, and only in a few is there an indication of a gradual peeling off of the velvet.

There has always been considerable controversy over the manner in which the buck rids himself of the peeling skin, yet there need be no argument. Buck rubs do not normally occur in the northern states until October, at a time when the antlers have been free of velvet for a month or more. In short, the bush fighting is a sex urge building up in the males at the approach of the rut, and if any velvet is worn off or antlers polished in this process, it is an incidental occurrence at best. Anyone in deer country during the months of September and October can make this simple observation.

Buck rubs normally begin to appear in the North in October. The adult male is now at his physical best, and in his exuberance he becomes overbearing and bellicose. He paws the ground with his feet, fights a bush or single stout sapling to try out his antlers and, in general, works himself into a rage like a mad bull. All of these are, undoubtedly, instinctive acts incited in the animal to prepare him for competition in the rut.

Freak growth and abnormally small racks are the result of malnutrition or lack of mineral in the browse. Normally, one can expect racks of good growth for any particular year if the deer have been feeding well from early spring till the full development of their antlers. Yet, there is a wide variety in shape and development in the whitetail's antlers that are purely physical characteristics passed down to the progeny by the parent.

One of the sleekest, medium-sized males I ever saw had a small, perfect sixteen-point rack that hardly cleared his ears. This dainty set of antlers was ridiculously small for the size of the animal. A few years later, another such specimen with miniature antlers was taken from the same area.

In opposition to this, the widest-spread, most well balanced antlers I ever saw graced the head of the scrawniest buck ever to hang from my neighbor's meat pole. The animal was so gaunt that his backbone and ribs showed plainly through his heavy coat. He would have been a miserable specimen by spring about the time his winter coat was shedding. But considering his emaciated condition in mid-November, it is doubtful if he could have survived even the normal winter. The animal showed no marks of any previous injury that might have handicapped him. I gathered he was normal in all respects, but was physically run down because of his active participation in the rut.

Possibly an animal with such wide-spreading beams found it difficult to travel through the brushy country in which he was taken. If this were his handicap, then nature was already working to eliminate this misfit from his unsuitable environment. The buck with a large, spreading rack is greatly inconvenienced in running through thick growth, for he is forced to arch his neck far back so that the brush slides off his beams as he plunges through the thickets. Even then, he makes considerable commotion and expends excess energy in his travels.

One likes to believe that through necessity such sires handicapped by massive racks keep to the more open country. Yet the very largest set of antlers I have came from a buck I took as he emerged from a very dense spruce swamp. My brother, Francis, drove the almost impenetrable jungle toward my stand on a slight projection into the swamp.

The going was so difficult in the dark tangle that Francis had to crawl through much of the area. I could hear his progress plainly as soon as he entered the growth. Almost immediately I heard a similar crashing alongside of him, and I began to wonder which of the two was the hunter. Both noises were the same in every respect —

the sounds of laborious progress through a dense tangle, the swishing of branches, and the constant snapping of dead wood. Slowly and painfully the crashing came toward me, and they came abreast not more than a hundred feet apart.

Finally, I could see the alders to my left at the edge of the marsh shake as though a bull moose was blindly forcing himself through them. When I first caught a glimpse of the hulk picking its way through the hard going, I was not sure if it was Francis or a bear. I had never before heard a deer move so noisily as this. Once free of the alders, the huge buck lunged to the solid ground on the bank and stood as though he were dazed by the sudden appearance of open sunlight about him.

At about the time I dropped the fine trophy, my brother bounced to the bank on my right. During his drive, he never heard the deer because of the noise he himself was making. The massive antlered buck was a recluse of this swamp, yet he had great difficulty in traveling across it, even at a slow pace. Perhaps his rack was a burden to him, and he chose this stronghold for his lair, for here he might get by with the least movement. This specimen was also very lean.

Most of my stained or dark-colored racks come from the vicinity of evergreen swamps. The darker antler, generally, indicates health in a deer, and it could be the browse here contributes to the animal's well being. It has been conjectured in the past that the dark rack is a result of stain received when a buck fights evergreen saplings.

White, bleached antlers come, generally, with old age in bucks, although I have seen some mighty handsome white racks, indicating the age of the animals in these particular cases caused no deterioration in antler growth. Bleached antlers could also result from poor health in the animal, or, as is often the case, from the chemical makeup of the soil in the deer's environment.

The shape of racks can vary some in deer living in the same area, for their general form is innate in each individual. Under the hunting pressure of today, when deer are shunted about freely, the strains inherent in each animal become absorbed in the mass of whitetails in any given locality, and the individuality or peculiarity in antlers is largely lost. Such was not the case even thirty years ago in deer country I had hunted and still do.

A certain area regularly produced bucks with antler characteristics quite distinct from those of bucks in another locality separated by only several miles. Such spots were somewhat isolated, and their particular terrain was different from the surrounding country. One of these was a series of semi-barren hills alongside a lake. Most of the bucks taken here had flat beams and tines, somewhat resembling the shape of caribou antlers. They were smooth and white as ivory, usually well balanced, and the tines were exceptionally long. Eight years ago I killed my last buck here, and there was still the visible flatness in the beams and tines of the rack.

A rolling country, covered with a mixture of popple, prairie willow, and white birch favored a strain of whitetails whose racks were much the same except that the beams and tines in this case were round, and the tines were not as long. In the vicinity of a series of swamps covered with short spruce, we used to take bucks with beams extending far to the sides and turning in very little at the tips. The tines were very short, and the dark rack somewhat resembled a garden rake.

Today, I do not find these same sharp distinctions in antlers taken from these areas. In time, it is likely, there will be little difference, except for size, in all antlers in any big area.

It still takes the mature buck of four-and-a-half years or older to produce the heavier racks, and in these years of intense hunting, fewer animals attain this age. Due to closer cropping, the spike and four-pointer, usually one-and-a half and two-and-a-half years old, now generally constitute the great portion of the buck kill in northern whitetail country.

After the rut the antlers on bucks become useless, for now the males have no occasion to use them. The rut tapers off sharply with the coming of winter. The shedding of antlers is greatly influenced by the weather, and there is also some discrepancy in time of shedding among individuals.

In early February of 1961, which was a very mild month in an unusually mild winter in northern Wisconsin, I saw two bucks still carrying their antlers. Even during this easy winter with little snow, the animals were thin-framed, and the antlers seemed strange and cumbersome on the slim necks of the late-winter bucks.

One of our hunting party got a fat, large buck late in the deer season one fall when the month of November was as cold and snowy as any winter. The animal had already shed one antler, and the other came off when we used it in dragging out the trophy. Normally, most antlers are shed by our northern whitetails during the month of December.

What happens to deer racks after they are dropped, and why they are not found more often, always makes an interesting topic of discussion among hunters. I used to accept the old theory that they were gnawed away by some calcium-loving rodents like mice, porcupines, or chipmunks. One could take this for granted and let it go at that, and perhaps no great loss would be suffered by this easily acceptable conclusion.

When northern Wisconsin was covered with short growth and grasses after the numerous brush fires during the 1920s and 1930s, mice were extremely abundant. Any flesh bait set out by the trapper was invariably chewed up by the hordes of field mice before the furbearer had a chance of finding it. And I well recall my discouragement at finding so many of my trapped weasels chewed up by the hungry rodents. Any piece of garment, leather goods, or personal object not made of metal, if left outdoors even overnight, was ruined by the countless field mice.

Naturally, deer antlers were not an exception, for every one found at this time was sure to show signs of gnawing by mice. It is doubtful if the little rodents ate the entire antler, but the evidence of teeth marks on the structure brought on an apparent conclusion as to what happens to deer racks.

During more recent years, as our brush growth has attained young timber size, mice have become very scarce in most of the North country. I have lost leather mittens during a winter while trapping beaver, and when I returned the following June to fish trout in the beaver pond, they were still there entirely intact. Likewise, any other items I leave in the woods these days cause me little concern. If there are no rodents to chew up my knife handles, old leather jacket, or salty stiff socks that I commonly leave along the trout stream, then there are no rodents to destroy the shed antlers. Yet, the bucks' antlers are difficult to find today as they ever were. Therefore, I prefer not to make rodents the scapegoats for the mysteriously missing antlers.

The well-preserved antlers I have found were always picked up in a dry, sunlit area. During the fall of 1960, while I was hunting woodcocks in a sparsely wooded, closely cropped pasture, I found a well-preserved, bleached eight-point antler basking in the open sunlight.

It was so well balanced I decided to keep it. Then I decided to search around a bit, and only about ten yards from my first find, there was the mate, likewise exposed on the bare pasture sod.

These antlers, which were shed the previous winter, were still in good condition, but the tips of the tines already showed sign of some deterioration. The portions of the beams that rested on the ground were heavily stained from the earth's dampness.

Any antlers I found that were even in fair condition came from dry, sunny situations. Those I found in deep grass or leaf mold were covered with mildew, were porous, and showed such signs of decay that it was not difficult to crush them by hand. Most deer racks are naturally shed in the lowland thicket, the winter grounds of the whitetail. Here, in the dampness of the forest floor they soon disintegrate. During the hunting season for birds and small game, when the hunter might expect to find antlers, the ground is covered with dried grasses and leaves. Few men are in the winter deer country in early spring when the fallen racks are more easily found. When I think of the number I have found in the odd pockets of the woods during my ramblings, I am convinced the shed antlers simply lie on the ground, become enveloped in the damp mold, and finally yield themselves to the soil.

The whitetail deer, like other creatures, sometimes deviates from the normal in its body characteristics. Some individuals are long-legged and slender, some are smaller than others of the same age, and some few are short-legged and chunky. The last type, if males, often are referred to as swamp bucks, but this could be a misnomer. Of the number of bucks I have killed in or about swamps, two were extremely long-legged. Only one was stout as a cob, had a short, heavy neck, and had shorter legs than most deer. On the other hand, I have seen chunky bucks taken from the high grounds far from swamps. The belief seems to be that the stout buck, perhaps handicapped by his short build, seeks the seclusion of a swamp for protection. Possibly in times back such strains might have persisted in isolated areas for a time, but at present the characteristic appears rare, and if found it might be on any type of terrain.

Because a mature buck spends much of his time apart from the females and young, he is considered something of a sneak, as though he mistrusts even his own kind. But is he really endowed with inherent perception that stamps him as a smarter animal than the doe? Perhaps not. By virtue of being isolated a great deal, the buck is warned of any approaching danger only through his own senses. In a group of deer, any one of the animals might sense peril, and any uneasiness in the one is quickly discerned by all. Thus, the responsibility of vigilance is spread over a number of animals and, as a result, each individual becomes a bit more relaxed in its guard.

This behavior can be observed especially in feeding animals. The lone deer, be it a buck or a doe, gives considerable time to sampling the air, listening for strange sounds, and looking about. Seldom does it feed in complete abandon for even a minute. In the group, each animal sometime or other gives way to active browsing, depending for the moment on the other deer to pick up any signals of danger.

The smart buck, during deer season, is crafty simply because he knows he is the preferred target in the hunt. Any big-racked sire today has had a few experiences in his time, and in trying to avoid these situations he naturally becomes cautious. He is known as a smart buck, but in truth, he is only smart to the way he is usually hunted.

Back some years when the forked-antler buck season was in effect in Wisconsin, old does, especially those in the backwoods, had little fear of hunters. From my stand, I used to observe several does with fawns as they fed at leisure in the swamp below me. They were not molested by the few hunters here, and they became accustomed to seeing me daily. Even the spike buck that occasionally joined them was as unruffled as a grazing cow. It was easy to conclude, under these circumstances, that these lesser animals were not as cunning as the big buck.

During the three seasons of 1949 through 1951 when the antlerless deer were legal here, it did not take long for these lesser whitetails to become as timorous as the wary, old bucks, much to the surprise of many hunters. The fact is, the sexes are born equally docile and naturally trusting of man, and it is only the hunter who causes them to behave otherwise.

16
The Rut

ITH the crisp days of early October, the buck is a picture of robust health, exuberant vitality, and lordly mien. His swollen neck adds to his pugnacious appearance, and he becomes a bit daring in his well-being, for now he steps forth from his usual obscurity and stalks in his domain with some measure of arrogance.

The manner in which the sires take part in the rut varies greatly with the individuals. Some males roam about the country without any great attachment to a particular region. These roving Romeos are often found near settlements, crossing pasturelands, and even on the outskirts of towns. That they are strangers to these grounds can be observed by the uncertain routes they make in traversing this edge country.

Other bucks prefer to set up some sort of bailiwick from which they do not stray and where they strive to keep out all intruding males. These little kingdoms are well marked, usually along runways, tote roads, or clearings, with patches of pawed ground and a scattering of buck rubs. The dirt pawings bear a little study, for they are not a mere work of exuberance without some purpose.

The sod, grass, and leaves are carefully raked to the sides, and the resultant exposed earth looks like a well-prepared flowerbed about one to two and a half feet in diameter. In the middle of this soft, earthy plot are planted one or more good imprints of the buck's hoofs. This is the trademark of the sire claiming these grounds, and it serves notice to all intruders that this area belongs to the lord whose seal is here displayed.

The beds are made with some deliberation, for the tracks are well planted in the soft earth, and seldom are there any carelessly made prints around the edge of the dirt patch. Undoubtedly, the buck also imparts some scent from his foot glands here, and he clinches his claim with a sample of his urine. Does in heat when coming across these scrapes undoubtedly also leave some of their urine to indicate their presence in the area. I have seen a dozen such markings made by the same sire in an area of less than forty acres. Each buck appears to have his own special insignia — some leave only one or two imprints, and these seem always to be of large fellows. Others might leave three or four imprints, and in some instances, especially with smaller bucks, there might be a half dozen or more tracks, some of them on the edge of the plot or else overlapping.

Some bucks are very limited in their movements, and it appears they make no great effort in the rut participation. I remember one fine specimen that used to make his evening rounds from a low, brushy flat to a farm field all through summer and into fall. Sometimes there were two other deer feeding in the field, but most often he was there alone. The rut did not disrupt his simple existence, and during the deer season one of my brothers had no difficulty in intercepting the carefree fellow.

Before the start of the active rut, the buck is as fat and sleek as he will ever be, but his condition at the tapering end of the rut in late November or early December depends on his degree of participation in the breeding of does. Some bucks come through the rut in good physical condition; others show loss of weight even during the hunting season when the rut might still be in progress. The haggard bucks enter the winter with the added handicap of lost tallow. Perhaps this is nature's way of selectively culling out the species. The old bucks have served their purpose during the breeding season, and the younger animals are given preference for survival. Much of the loss of weight in bucks during the rut is due, not so much to the animals' activity, but to the fact that the sires are more interested in the does than they are in feeding.

The whitetail buck is polygamous, but not in the same sense as applied to the bull elk with his harem. The buck will mate with one or several does, depending on the length of the mating season, and he searches out the receptive females only to breed them. Because of this, the whitetail sires are not as antagonistic toward each other as is commonly believed.

The elk herd master must prove his physical superiority to all unattached intruding bulls as well as to those aggressive monarchs who are bent on increasing the size of their harems. But the carefree whitetail buck takes his does where he finds them, one at a time, and if he is driven off by a superior suitor, he yields without hesitation and goes on his way in quest of other females. In most cases, there is no physical contact between the contenders. The larger buck moves toward the lesser male, makes a threatening charge with his head lowered, and the intruder walks away.

It is only when two well-matched bucks meet in defiance of each other that a battle is likely to ensue, and the contest continues as long as neither is overpowered. As soon as one feels he is getting the worst of the affray, he trots off in defeat, and his adversary seldom pursues the duel any further. Most of the skirmishes take place during the heat of the rut. Certainly there is little evidence of them during the deer season when the rut is tapering off in much of the deer hunting country.

In all my time in the woods, I have never seen bucks in battle, yet many times just prior to and during the early part of the rut, I have seen two bucks together or else traveling in company with several does. Only rarely have I heard of outdoorsmen who have witnessed a duel between bucks. My brother John is one who has seen such a contest.

The two challengers he encountered must have been fighting for some time before he came upon them, for the ground was already trampled and torn in a thirty-foot circle. At the time he intercepted the fracas, both mature, large-racked animals reared on their hind legs and jabbed each other with their forefeet. Then, as one lost his balance in the sparring bout and was forced to his four feet, the two continued the battle head-on with considerable clashing of antlers.

After awhile they paused for a breather as though both animals had had enough of it. Each was waiting for the other to make the next pass, but neither seemed anxious to continue. The bucks were already exhausted, and one turned to the side as though he were bored of the whole affair. The other accepted this as a sign of defeat in his adversary. The yielding buck walked off, and the victor merely held his ground.

Not only are bucks rarely seen fighting, but their battlegrounds are not commonly found even by someone prowling the deer country at this time. This all indicates that few serious contests take place among the male whitetails. Of the battlegrounds that I have seen that indicated a long struggle, only one showed evidence of blood being drawn by the contestants. The wound appeared to be only superficial, for the tracks in the early November snow showed the animals walked off after the fray, and no blood marred their separate trails. One might wonder, too, if the antlers of the contestants might have temporarily interlocked during the struggle. In such a case, it is understandable why small trees up to an inch in diameter can be trampled down to shreds in the arena of battle.

When an evenly matched duel takes place, there is a chance that the bucks may interlock antlers. The rigid beams and tines of a rack have considerable spring in their length. Since the main beams and forks bend inward, it is possible to force a slight spring in them with pressure from the front or sides. Once two sets of antlers are interlocked, no mere pulling or twisting will separate them. However, the tragedy of two prime bucks coming to a slow death because of locked antlers is not too common. Any evidence of such mishaps is more often found by hunters during the deer season. Those few that were found within a reasonable distance of my hunting grounds, and that I had made a point to see, indicated

that the buck fights had occurred a few weeks before the deer season, possibly in late October. This would place the date at the peak of the rut.

The only locked antlers I ever chanced upon were found in early spring alongside a trout stream. Fresh spring grass had not come up as yet, and the sere, old grass did not completely cover the tips of the tines. The interlocked racks were still attached to their skulls and, except for several protruding bleached tines, all else was stained by the rotting vegetation that had covered it. They had probably been lying in the mold for no more than a year and a half, and the dampness aged them rapidly.

The peak of the breeding season for whitetails of the northernmost parts of our country comes early in November, and it tends to be later and over a wider period of time in the deer's southern range. Most deer seasons include at least some of the more active rut, and this is advantageous to the hunter who, through game regulations or by choice, seeks to take a buck.

Just how much the army of hunters interferes with the normal breeding habits of whitetail deer is difficult to guess, but there seems little doubt that natural breeding habits are impeded by a concentration of hunters who keep the animals on the move. There was a time, several decades back, when a hunter might be elated at the sight of a doe running past his stand, for he could reasonably expect to see a buck in hot pursuit of the female within a matter of less than a minute. I have heard of instances where as many as three bucks, strung along at intervals, ran down the trail of a doe in heat.

I have witnessed only one case where more than a single buck followed a running doe. I was looking over some deer country the day before the opening of the season when a doe ran past me as I sat on a small knoll. A big buck with his neck outstretched and his head lowered, came bounding by about a minute later. A full two minutes afterwards, a smaller buck came running down the same route.

These were the days when it was not unusual for a bird hunter to surprise a buck completely engrossed in the pursuit of his ladylove. I have seen such animals walk by me and even stand to gaze at me while I was busy with my November trapline. Bucks were either bolder in their courting in those days, or else there were more of them in proportion to the amount of does so that competition was far keener in the wooing of the females.

Whatever it was then, the modern buck seemingly does not permit his romance to greatly interfere with any chances of losing his hide. There is the possibility that today much of the breeding takes place at night, or the rut is now spread more evenly over a longer period, so that less of it is observed even during the early bow and arrow hunting season. The whitetail is a remarkable animal for adapting itself to the encroachment of man.

The year-and-a-half-old buck, usually spiked, appears uninterested in breeding. I have seen several sets of twin spikes traveling together, and on two different occasions I have seen such twins loiter about my stand for several days with no apparent desire to participate in the rut. In the other rare extreme, an unusually old buck, a sort of retired sire, might hole up in a small area and yield the chase to the more active males. These fat and lazy recluses are not entirely useless, for often they produce venison far more tender than that from the muscled, active buck.

Does are likely to be in their second fall, or about eighteen months of age, before they attain breeding maturity, but some few, especially of the earlier born fawns, are bred the first fall of their existence. The old does are the dependable breeders, and from my experience, the barren doe is most often a year and a half old. By and large, whitetails are prolific animals; as with rabbits, their fertility is a strong factor in perpetuating the species in the face of many enemies.

Even during the hunting season, when bucks might yet be occupied with the rut, the old fellows still have some preference for country that is not especially favorable for the does and younger deer. This situation is puzzling because the old bucks seem to hang around such areas all through the fall, and the ratio of does on these grounds is very small. In fact, one of the hilly regions I hunt most every year contains very few deer, but half the animals seen there are mature bucks. Such country, so acceptable to the old sires, is generally covered with heavy timber, crossed with high ridges, and lacking considerably in low, dense shrubbery. It is most always an extensive area with few open places, and it is not generally abundant in deer food.

The low flats, dense with young popple or evergreens, are likely to contain an overwhelming proportion of does and fawns.

Such spots are often avoided by the buck hunter. I recall some of the drives we made in the popple country in times past. Nearly every effort we made would put out several deer, and only rarely would we see a buck come out of the luxuriant growth.

Since this unequal distribution of bucks among does exists even during the rut, one can only conclude that some sires are less active than others during the breeding season. It could be that some of the seasoned males prefer to take to the backwoods for their own safety rather than join the herd in the annual rutting jamboree, especially toward the end of the rut when the gun season comes around.

Wintering Whitetails

_HERE is no clear-cut pattern in the wintering habits of whitetail deer, but there is a general tendency for the animals to congregate into more limited quarters at this time. The extent of these movements varies from year to year according to the severity of the winter; and there is also considerable variation in this wintering trend in whitetails of different localities.

We can have situations where the winter deer have changed their living habits only slightly since the past fall. In the other extreme, with the animals of specific localities and during harsh winters, we can expect tight yarding. In between these extremes we have the situation that is most common these days — a general retreat from the open country with the deer forming small groupings in numerous sheltered areas.

Since not all whitetails of the snowy country respond in the same degree to the innate urge of banding together, we have a rather complex situation in our northern deer country. One can join the organized groups that make annual winter treks into established deeryards. If this is his only experience with winter deer, he gets a greatly biased picture of the general deer situation. From such limited observations came the belief, a few decades back, in the necessity every winter of regular artificial feeding stations and the present belief in the necessity of reducing the deer population whenever a severe winter causes heavy yarding. In some areas where browse is considered critically low in the yards, the population of the animals is already low despite the fact that ample food is available in the environs. In other areas the whitetail population might be much higher, but the animals fare better through the winter because they do not habitually gather in tight, congested bands. It is not so much a case of available feed as it is the strange, uncompromising habit of some whitetails to become prisoners of browse-depleted winter grounds.

Although the herding instinct of whitetails varies somewhat from winter to winter, there does seem to be a strong indication that this urge is less impelling today than it was some decades ago. During the years when brush fires ran freely every spring, most of our northern deer country was denuded of any heavy, substantial growth. There was little protection from the winter elements on the windswept barrens. As I recall, in the early 1920s every evergreen swamp of even several acres harbored the winter deer in northern Wisconsin. The brush-protected creek bottoms and those flats with heavier growth also were used by deer every winter. Seldom did one see a deer track at this time in the whitetail's summer range. Yarding was the common thing with deer regardless of winter temperature and snow depth.

Today, through strict fire control, the barrens and short-brush country have grown to young timber of such size that considerable protection from weather is afforded the whitetail throughout much of his entire range. As a consequence, we have

the tight yarding of deer only during an extremely severe winter. And here again, the tight yarding is most prevalent in specific areas long established by whitetail progenitors.

In most areas of the North, the animals gather in small numbers and in loose quarters. Only during an exceptionally harsh winter are they found in compact groups so that their grounds have anything near the semblance of a true yard. All too often, the term "deeryard" is used much too freely. In many areas, trappers and loggers who penetrate the backcountry during the winter months have never seen the yards that are so vividly described in print. Such yards are becoming the exception, but by their prominence one is led to believe all our northern whitetails are confined to such areas. In time, as our timber matures and there is equal weather protection all over the deer range, it is likely the whitetails will disperse over a wider winter range, and, perhaps, the tight yard as we still see it today will disappear.

The American elk slowly treks down the mountainsides to escape the deep snows of high altitudes. He recedes to the valleys because the lesser snowfall here makes it easier for him to feed on the exposed browse. To the whitetail, on the other hand, available browse seems only incidental in the selection of his wintering grounds. His food might or might not be abundant on the grounds he chooses, and this short-coming in the deer's otherwise strong instinct for survival puts the species in hardship during the more severe winters. But the makeup of the whitetail is such that he still prefers to tough out the extreme winters through sheer stamina. The fact that he has existed in our snowy North in the distant past and still continues to live here today indicates that this is his home, deep snows and scant diet included.

After all, was it not the environment of the North that bred the hardy, northern whitetail? When nature imposes a loss of as much as 30 percent in weight in the northern deer during the severe winter, and this loss of weight is accepted just as the shedding of buck's antlers or the changing of summer and winter pelage, is this not all a part of nature's plan? And nobody can argue with nature, for she has passed on to us myriad species of wildlife selected and developed through the ages.

Whether or not we agree with nature on the terms she lays down for the survival of her forest crea-tures seems of no consequence, for the laws of the forest persist. Nature has taken her slow time over the years to produce the adaptable whitetail, and man, by superficial regulations and misunderstanding, attempts to correct what he believes is nature's shortcomings in these modern times. We begrudge any natural loss of wildlife as though it were a complete waste. Yet, in the broad sense of conservation, is not this returning of life to the soil a true forest economy? Who is to say whether the tagged deer carted off by the hunter serves a better purpose to true conservation than the dead deer left in the woods to nourish the soil? Conservation is relatively new to man; nature has fostered it from the very beginning.

There seem to be several reasons why the whitetails of the deep snows congregate for the winter months. The apparent reason, and the one so easily acceptable, is that the animals withdraw to secluded areas for protection from severe weather. If this were entirely true, there would be little occasion for the animals to gather in one spot when there are other available areas suitable for protection from weather, and that are abandoned at this time.

It appears that the whitetails have some gregarious instinct that causes them to form large groups during a very hard winter. The threat of deep snow, prolonged cold, and difficult foraging seems to bring the animals together as though they feel a sense of well-being and security in their numbers. And those few stragglers that choose to remain to the sides of the big yard seem not to fare as well as the members of the big group.

Most of the deeryards are found in the wind-protected evergreens or in the mixture of evergreen and hardwood. These could be in the flat, low country, heavily wooded uplands, or the wet swamps on occasion. The location of protective growth rather than land formation decides where the deer set up their winter quarters. Deer ordinarily do not care for brush swamps unless there is some evergreen growth mixed in with the thickets. Yet, if the same swamp is fringed with balsams, pines, or spruce, the animals might spend the winter around the edge of the swamp without ever entering it.

Such a swamp, even if relatively dry, is not especially attractive to northern whitetails, contrary to the belief of many hunters. Deer will run to such a swamp when spooked, but they usually cling to its edges. Likewise, in winter they feed along the margins of the swamp, and one might erroneously conclude from the numerous tracks along the edge that the animals stay in the swamp. From what I have seen, the only time deer will use swamps for winter quarters, excepting the white cedar swamp, is when there is some weather protection afforded there, and there is no suitable cover elsewhere in the vicinity.

Whitetails like to winter along the evergreen-covered ridges that run alongside or between a series of swamps. They use common, well-beaten trails, usually on top of the ridges, to travel about the irregular grounds. They stray off the long, main path for short distances to browse and bed down. This is the typical winter quarters in much of northern Wisconsin's deer country.

The big white cedar swamps, more common in Michigan and Minnesota than in Wisconsin, are the natural big yards of our northern deer. These yards not only offer ideal weather protection, but the white cedar growth is the whitetail's choice winter food. Unfortunately, the cedar swamp is not common to all the northern deer country, so the animals settle for what is most available to them elsewhere.

Winter Food

Much has been written and compiled on the winter foods of our whitetails, but little of this study has been of great consequence; for if one were to make a final appraisal of the animals' diet he would find it far easier to list what they normally will not eat. Like the common range sheep, they will feed on most types of vegetation that make up our woodlands. Wintering deer, by virtue of their restricted movements, are limited to such foods as are available to them. They seem to have a preference for some browse such as white cedar, hemlock, red maple, stag horn sumac and others, but they apparently thrive as well where such foods are not available to them. It is erroneous to believe the deer's preference for certain browse is the strict criterion for measuring the importance of such browse for the animals' well-being or survival.

By its own choice, the nibbling whitetail will eat a large variety of browse, and the individual animal at times will be inclined to eat more of one than another. This desire for variety can be studied in the loosely quartered winter deer that cover a relatively large range. They might nip raspberry brier tops, twigs of aspen, white birch, hazel brush, and a host of others not usually termed ideal winter food.

The tightly yarded whitetails are limited to but a few species of browse. Even though such species may consist of what we term the deer's preference browse, the animals will not likely fare as well as those that feed on a larger variety of lesser foods. We cannot make a listing of what the winter whitetail should eat. About all we can do is compile a list of what he does eat, and such a compilation gives us little information, for he eats both what he likes and what is available to him. And sometimes he becomes a renegade to his species and goes on a strange diet.

One winter when the snow was very deep, I noticed three deer, presumably a doe with her two fawns, coming to feed nightly on a farmer's stack of alfalfa setting at the edge of a large field. The animals came from a deeryard a half-mile down the valley from the edge of the field. There were about two-dozen deer in the small yard, but only the doe and two fawns came to feed on the alfalfa. The trail trips of the raiders and the stack were no secret to the rest of the whitetails, for many animals fed on the tender, young alfalfa growth in the field when the stack was already standing. One can assume the other animals had no desire to leave the yard even down a well-beaten trail.

Even during deer seasons when food is relatively abundant, whitetails will sometimes feed on items that they should properly reject if they could read the listing of their browse preference. Speckled alders are often called the deer's starvation diet, yet several times I saw deer in swamps busily nibbling the branch tips of alders. The deer were free to travel the snowless country and avail themselves of other browse, but at this time they preferred the lowly speckled alder. One hunting season I continually flushed deer from an area of aspen slashings. The aspens were cut in late August and the dried leaves still clung to the branches of fallen trees. I had a chance to study the animals from a distance with my binoculars and learned the reason for their interest in these aspen slashings. The animals were feeding on the dried leaves.

Some years ago when the aspen growth in a particular deer country was not as tall as it is today and there was considerable smaller aspen undergrowth among the bigger trees, whitetails wintered in this area. Aspen constituted much of their diet. Today the trees are eight to twelve inches in diameter, all underbrush is choked, and the tall, barren tree trunks offer neither weather protection nor browse. Much of our northern popple country has now reached this stage and is no longer suitable for even loose winter quarters. Aspen, at one time, was definitely an important winter food for whitetails.

Travel

Normally, if the snows are very deep but powdery dry, the animals can get around surprisingly well. During February of 1962, when the snowfall in Wisconsin's Sawyer County was deeper than it had been in many years, I spent much of my time snowshoeing into winter deer areas. If I stepped off my snowshoes, I was up to my middle in the white stuff, but the deer had no trouble bounding away to the sides and they always managed to keep out of my camera range.

They could walk only along the trampled paths, for if they attempted to walk off the path they had to buck the snow like a bulldozer fighting a drift. So, otter fashion, they bounded upward on their hairspring legs to clear the depth. They landed about six feet forward and up to their shoulders in the unbroken snow. These high-clearing bounds came with surprising ease, and I noticed they used them frequently in getting around for browse.

The serious threat to wintering whitetails, whether in tight yards or in loose quarters, comes with crusted snow. The pointed, small hoofs break through with every step, and movement off the beaten trails becomes difficult. The whitetail has the grim choice of toughing it out on a scant diet where the going is good or else floundering helplessly in the deep encrusted snow in attempting to reach better browse. Fortunately, a crusted snow situation, when the winter is bitter, does not come frequently, or if it does it most likely occurs very late in winter when spring thaws can soon be expected to alleviate the condition.

There have been two or three times in my memory when we had a most adverse snow situation possible for whitetail deer. This was a firm packing of the upper several inches of the deep snow blanket, and it was caused not by unseasonable rainfall or warm temperatures but by a steady wind of gale proportions that swept over the semi-barren country. I used to skip on top of the wind-swept snow with buoyant ease when I tended my first coyote sets, but in making my rounds I had to stick to the open spaces and higher grounds where the snow was firmest. In the low spots and where brush growth hampered the packing effects of the wind, I would frequently break through. Then with some difficulty, I would have to crawl onto the firmer surface to regain my feet.

During such years there was, no doubt, some deer killing done by brush wolves. Any whitetail not yarded in wind-protected evergreen swamps was definitely at the mercy of the brush wolf that never had better going than at this time. This wind packing of snow was common in the days when brush fires kept much of the country in short, scant brush. Today, the heavier growth holds the winds in check and, except for the open fields, we have little or no wind packing of snow.

Deep snows work a hardship on winter deer even when the snow is not crusted, but this is part of the northern whitetail's habitat. In the snow belt of the upper Michigan peninsula this condition is pretty much of an accepted occurrence every winter. The inland deer areas of Minnesota, Wisconsin, and Lower Michigan have a more irregular yearly snowfall and there could be considerable variation in the snow depth in any given winter here, even from county to county. As a consequence, the plight of winter whitetails is not always the same over the entire lakes country.

When a severe winter strikes in one particular section with subsequent loss of deer, the obvious solution to the problem is to thin out the animals during the hunting seasons in order to prevent such a recurrence. On the surface, this sounds plausible, but it is a superficial antidote certainly not in accordance with nature. Even one or two animals in a yard have an equal or even greater chance of succumbing to a harsh winter than a couple dozen animals in the same yard. Just because two whitetails have a larger area to themselves does not mean they will utilize the entire yard and its browse. On the contrary, they will confine themselves to but a small portion of it.

Few deer make few trails, and in time as snow depth increases, the animals become veritable prisoners in extremely limited grounds. Where there is a larger number of whitetails, the yard is naturally expanded by the more vigorous adults, and the smaller animals can move about more freely in the broken snow. And regardless of the severity of the winter, there is a chance for some survival in the larger group.

One winter I had an excellent opportunity to study a coniferous swamp in which deer were yarded.

The main part of the swamp, of about twenty acres, contained about a dozen animals. One large arm of this coniferous jungle is practically detached from the main body. This nook of about five acres harbored a lone doe and her fawn. A small spring flows through this arm and I had a few mink traps set here, and later I put out some larger traps on trails where coyotes entered to hunt the snowshoe hare in the fringe of alders.

At first the two deer wandered over most of the little yard, even though the loose snow was about a foot and a half deep. January was a cold month and the intermittent snowfall brought the depth to over two feet. Now, as I made the rounds of my traps, the two deer could be seen frequently, for the main trail followed the flow of the spring run. February brought on more snow with continued cold weather, and when I flushed the animals they no longer had the desire to leave the short trail but merely escaped to its furthest extremity.

Late in February, an additional blanket of about a foot of snow came, and when I arrived to pull out my traps that morning after the storm, I found the deer trail half clogged with snow. The animals had passed through only once during this last snowfall. The movement of the two was now extremely limited and when

I found them they lunged off the old trail and remained there buried shoulder-deep in the snow as I passed by. Even as they rested their bodies on the soft cushion of white, they nibbled unconcernedly at browse within their reach. After I passed by, I watched them slowly struggle back to the trail.

I snowshoed along the small flow to the bigger swamp. Long before I came to the active yard, I passed over snow marked with long, irregular depressions that indicated that some time ago the deer were moving about in trails as far as this point. The yard was now confined to but less than half the swamp, but the trails were open and packed, and the animals flushed readily at my approach. In the labyrinth of trails, the deer avoided me on all sides and by the time I crossed the yard they had escaped to the other extremity of their snowy domain. I never returned to check on how these whitetails fared through the balance of the winter, but it is a good guess that the lone doe and fawn had the harder time of it.

Winter Casualties

That some deer will die from malnutrition and the effects of exhaustion, exposure, and the other ailments that accompany the severe winter is one of the conditions imposed on the northern whitetail. The individual animal is affected according to his physical condition and according to his value in the preservation of the species. Only those animals that are habitual members of a particular yard become the victims of their circumstances, and accordingly any reduction in the whitetail numbers is usually made here.

The hunter takes his game where he finds it, and if he bags an animal in the fall that might have perished in a yard the following winter, such an occurrence would be purely accidental. I have reference here to our present-day conditions where hunting pressure is such that the threat of any overabundance of whitetails is no longer the problem it was years back.

The first deer to suffer the effects of a rigorous winter are those surviving cripples carrying flesh wounds or broken legs. When the brush wolves and bobcats were more plentiful than they now are, such handicapped animals seldom lived to join in the general deer movement to winter quarters. Some decades ago, a wounded or dead deer was seldom found in the woods — only the remnants of scattered bones and torn hide indicated the spot where the brush wolves had intercepted the cripple.

There are few animal predators, except in specific areas, these days to eliminate the wounded or naturally ailing deer. As a result, such animals are often able to carry on far into the winter. When deep snows and cold bring on close yarding, these are among the first animals to succumb in the struggle for survival.

The heavy loss of whitetails due to gunshot wounds is far greater than most are willing to admit. Somehow this waste of wildlife is accepted as properly belonging to the robust sport of hunting. We are gravely impressed by the sight of emaciated or dead animals found in a deeryard, but some of this can be attributed to gunshot wounds inflicted during the past hunting season.

The severe winter when a notable number of northern whitetails might die because of cold and deep snow does not come often. Crippling losses come with every hunting season. The winter of 1961-62 was an unusually hard winter on deer in upper Wisconsin. Yet, in the two days I spent in a yard regarded as very critical for the animals' survival, I found only one small fawn that showed definite signs of weakness. Most of the animals in this yard were thin as would naturally be expected, and, undoubtedly, there were some dead animals somewhere in the yard. Yet, I made a definite search here as well as in several smaller yards and found no dead deer, and I saw only several that possibly would not survive the winter. This was in the middle of March when the snow was deepest and just before spring thaws began to relieve the situation.

That same spring, a month later, a farmer informed me he found three dead whitetails in his forty-acre brush-grown pasture. This seemed an unusually heavy loss in such a small area, so I investigated the cause of these deaths. One of the animals died of a paunch gunshot wound. It apparently died during the deer season. Another had a brisket wound and remained alone in a swampy thicket until it perished in midwinter. The third was an accidental death. The deer failed to clear the two tight strands of barbed wire stretched above a woven wire fence. Its forelegs went between the close strands, and the deer flipped over with its legs held fast in the grip of the twisted wires. This is a common experience when new fences are put up in deer country, or when a deer wanders or is driven into strange country and meets with this unfamiliar hazard.

There was no attempt made to cover this entire forty-acre plot, but even with the three dead animals found here, none of whose deaths could be connected with the harsh winter or lack of browse, there is room here for some honest thinking. If these deer had died in a small local yard, there would have been much made of the tragedy. As it is, the loss has gone by with little comment, as is the loss in countless such situations.

The fact that wounded deer are incapacitated in varying degrees and do not all succumb in one spot or at one time makes it a simple matter to regard this loss as something unimportant. If wildlife is to be preserved, steps need to be taken to curb this great waste. We have for too long used the euphemism, "unavoidable cripple losses," as a mental salve to ease our conscience of a crime. Not until man realizes the cruelty and waste of leaving an animal to perish in the woods can he consider himself a responsible hunter. Nature slowly and painfully eliminates these handicapped animals, and the final test of the deer's fitness comes with the crucial months of February and March. The careless and trigger-happy hunter is responsible for many of the casualties usually attributed to extreme winter or poor browsing conditions.

Next to feel the winter pinch are the late-born fawns. They are the misfits among our northern whitetails, and nature discourages any trend in late fawn production in the snowy country. Such small animals, even when they are legal game, often are spared by the hunter, but nature has no room for compassion. She rules with a harsh hand to eliminate the undesirables in the species. Sentimental man is inclined to kill the hale animal and spare the weakling. It is the big deer, the big goose, and the big fish that the outdoorsman wants. In this respect, he acts contrary to the laws of nature and true conservation.

The small fawns have a difficult time pulling through even a normal winter. Their short legs handicap them in getting about in snow, and their small size serves them poorly in reaching for browse. Aside from this, these youngsters do not have the stamina of the older deer. It is surprising that one occasionally sees a very small fawn emerge from its winter quarters when even the mature animals have had a hard time of it.

The mature, active bucks of the rut enter the winter in poorer physical condition than any of the other whitetails. Despite their prime in age these males have lost much and often most of their fat that would have served them in good stead during the lean months of winter. These sires have served their purpose and again nature is selective in excluding these animals from any special consideration. The sex ratio among fawns is fairly evenly split, and since one buck can serve several does the individual male of the species becomes less important to the continuation of the whitetail progeny. The prime and active buck of last fall is least favored among the adult or full-grown deer to survive the hard winter.

As seems the rule in nature, the pregnant female of any species is best fortified with the endurance necessary for survival in a crisis, and the pregnant doe fares best among the whitetails during any trying winter. The barren doe and the immature bucks seem not to have the enduring stamina of the does carrying young. This time-tested process of selectivity in survival preference belongs to the northern whitetail, and it is no mere whim of nature.

The occasional extremely heavy snowfalls are not entirely all bad for the northern whitetail. In coniferous swamps, where deer are most concentrated, the evergreen boughs are brought down by the weight of snow so that the animals have access to them. Sometimes these snow-laden branches are bent to the very ground and they do not spring into place again until the snow has melted. Balsams, with their hollow or deteriorated trunks, readily collapse with their accumulated loads of snow. These fallen trees, which crisscross the evergreen swamps to make them almost impenetrable, have served to feed the whitetails in past winters. Thus, the unsound balsam, so often condemned by the woodcutter, is not without a purpose.

Deer are not averse to following the loggers and pulpwood cutters for downed browse, even when the winter is not severe. At such a time, they are normally shy and do not feed on the tops except after daylight hours. As winter progresses and the snow becomes deeper, they become more dependent upon this convenient food, and they stay in the immediate area of the logging project. In time, the animals are less wary and they might feed during the day with disregard for the men at work. If the deer are not molested, they accept this handout with more than ordinary trust. Eventually, they might follow the progress of the sawyers, anticipate fresh available food as a tree is dropped, and move in on the treetops as soon as the workers leave the spot.

Deer will take advantage of the easy browse made by loggers, but they must first find it. If the cutting is done late in winter when the animals are well established in their winter quarters, the convenient food supply will do them no good. Deer are veritable slaves to habit in their feeding. They do not purposely make long treks in quest of better forage; they merely find it by chance. In their more unlimited movements in early winter, especially if the snow is not yet very deep, they readily find the sites of logging projects. At first their interest in the treetop browse might be no more than passive, but the deer will return from time to time to sample the tops. This habit of feeding here is formed, and as the winter becomes bitter the animals come to rely on this source of food.

Too often, when trees are purposely cut to furnish browse for hard-hit wintering deer, the cutting is started much too late. Even when the project is undertaken in the vicinity of the deeryards, the animals are reluctant to leave their fixed confinement or alter their staid habits. Any such cutting, if it is to be of much use to the deer, must be done before the animals are completely resigned to tight quarters.

The deer might be thin and haggard but their zest and capacity for eating is not greater because of this. On the contrary, their stomachs seem to become less demanding as obtaining food becomes more involved, and the loss of weight continues as the tallow under their hides and in their body cavities is being consumed. Even after a mild winter with little snow, when food is easily accessible to them over a wider range of travel, the deer are usually as gaunt as when they pull through the more trying winter. In either case, the tallow in the animals is used up during the winter. It is apparent that this excess weight of stored-up energy is not the natural year-round makeup of the northern whitetail.

The bigger modern threat to wintering deer in much of our northern whitetail country is the common domestic dog. The brush wolf for the past several decades has been the scapegoat for many killings made by roaming dog packs. Even back in the 1920s when brush wolves were far more common than they are today, I remember seeing ample evidence of dogs killing deer when the snow was deep and crusty, usually during the months of February and March.

In those days, it was generally believed that brush wolves killed deer without restraint whenever the opportunity presented itself. The craven animals were considered the gangsters of the forest, and no sympathy was shown them in any quarters. A bounty of $30 paid by the State of Wisconsin on the carcass of each mature brush wolf turned in to the county chairman attested to the feeling toward this predator. These animals were numerous in the days of the brushy stump lands, but the snowshoe hares and ruffed grouse were more than proportionately abundant.

There is no question that the whitetails crippled during the deer season were a staple diet of the winter coyotes in those days. And as deeper snows handicapped the less seriously injured animals, an occasional ailing deer was dispatched by the prowlers during late winter. These were invariably pronounced wolf kills, and they gave the brush wolf his bad reputation. This prejudice was so entrenched in the minds of most men that even today some hunters still believe the brush wolf is depriving them of a substantial portion of venison. Though it is true that in specific instances brush wolves will kill any deer they can take at an advantage, this is not a common occurrence. It usually occurs where the predators are abundant, small

game is scarce, and the deer are handicapped by deep or encrusted snow.

As I recall, hardly a winter went by without some stories being told of the ruthless deer killings made by rampaging coyotes in our own neighborhood. I know of only one instance where I had definite proof of a pair of coyotes killing an apparently healthy deer. My brother John took me on his trapline one day, and we heard the distressed bleating of a deer in a spruce swamp below us. We snowshoed to the scene of commotion and flushed out two surprised brush wolves. The small fawn was badly bitten on the lower hams, neck, and ears, so my brother finished it off with his .22 trapline pistol. He returned that evening to set traps around the carcass, but the shy killers never returned.

The similar incidents, when the killers turned out to be common dogs, were far more numerous, but even here, most people preferred to believe the deer were killed by brush wolves and later found by dogs. My brother long suspected that the neighborhood dogs were the culprits involved in most of these late winter slayings.

One evening late in February, some local loggers stopped at our house to ask my brother to set some wolf traps at the carcass of a deer near their logging camp. At daybreak that morning they had heard clamoring wolves running down a deer and they had found the dead animal, but the killers escaped. My brother agreed to investigate the scene, but he seemed not all agog for the venture. The next day was Saturday, so I was free to join him on this wolf trapping expedition. My spirits were somewhat squashed when John suggested we take only one trap. We would have only one trap to bring back, he said.

The carcass of the deer was badly chewed, but none of the flesh was eaten. "Dogs," my brother said. "A whole pack of them." He began naming some of the farm dogs in the neighborhood, and I was disturbed when he mentioned some gentle, loving collies among the possibilities.

It was a gruesome scene, more gory than anything I had seen before. We found all sizes of dog tracks, and my brother attempted to match them with the dogs of the neighborhood. After studying the maze of tracks, we left the scene of disturbance to make a large arc around it and pick up any tracks leading away from the kill. We found the trail of the animals, and it led in the general direction of the farm settlement. Now and then a track would leave the trail, and my brother named the household to

which the dog was probably returning. The final track took us to the very yard of one of the loggers, who gave us the report of the deer killing.

Dogs have a natural urge to form into roving packs during late winter, and most any of them will find themselves in a group if there is an aggressive leader in the community to promote the recruiting. As children, we often noticed a neighborhood dog in our yard, coming, as we thought, to make a social, moonlight call on our collie. After awhile the two trotted down the road to pick up additional reinforcement down the line, and in those days every householder had at least one watchdog on the premises. After a bit we could expect to see four or five animals single file past our house, going up the road in the opposite direction to muster some additional farm dogs. The pack was formed and the gentle farm dogs, bolstered by their number, became roaming marauders of the night.

There were few complaints about these killers that ran unhampered and unchecked over the wind-packed snows of lakes, streams, and barrens. The exhausted dogs would return to their respective homes before daybreak, and few of their masters would suspect their gentle dog was anything but a dedicated household guardian.

The listless dog was a model of gentle behavior during the day, but after he rested up he was ready for the nightly venture. Then he could be as ruthless and cruel as each individual composing the pack could be gentle and loving in his own yard. Some few dogs will go it alone chasing deer winter and summer, and I have taken some of these in coyote sets far from any dwelling. Not all of these were animals I could recognize as belonging to the neighborhood.

It is difficult to condemn dogs for actions that, though revolting to our refinement, come quite naturally to them. I believe these deer chasers carry a sense of guilt when they yield to their latent instincts of chasing and killing for sheer brutal satisfaction. A dog discovered in this savage behavior does not romp to his master's side to solicit affection.

We once had a small, harmless house pet, half Spitz and half poodle, which we believed never left our yard. One February evening, while driving home from town, I spotted the little white fluffy-furred fellow cross the road in company with other local dogs. I stopped the car and called to him, fully expecting the little pet to scramble into the

Model-T and save himself a three-mile walk home that, for his diminutive size, was a great distance. But the little renegade ignored me completely and slunk into the woods with his motley companions. When he came home later that night, I sensed his discomfort as he cowered to his place by the wood heater.

Most people are now aware that the harmless-looking dog can be destructive to deer if he is permitted to roam the woods at will. Even today, we hear disheartening reports of deer losses made by the domestic killers — mostly during late winter and early spring when pregnant does as well as the other deer are weakened by the siege of deep snow and cold. Today, public resentment against dogs running loose in deer country is a strong deterrent to such needless whitetail kills. In time, it is highly probable that such losses will be reduced to a negligible factor in our northern deer population. There is little to indicate such will be the case with the ever-increasing deer casualties caused by the silent, speeding cars on our highways.

Fortunately, the serious threat to deer from roving dogs occurs infrequently — a condition of unseasonable rain or thaw of such duration as to cause a glazed surface on top the snow to become firm enough to hold the weight of a dog with its sprawling toes, but not the weight of a heavier animal with sharp-pointed hooves. This is the extreme condition so unfavorable to the movement of whitetails even when they are not harassed by dogs. Prolonged warm temperatures, with or without rain, have a reverse effect on the snow, for now its entire depth settles to a consistency that is not entirely penetrated by the deer's hooves.

The more normal situation in the Northern snowbelt is continued cold weather through most of the late winter with resulting dry, light snow in the shaded winter quarters, and then a sudden break in the weather heralding the definite arrival of spring. At the start of this transition from winter to spring, the restless whitetails already expand their wanderings to a wider range. Before the snow is gone from the sun-protected winter quarters, the animals move about the brush and semi-open country, leaner and less spirited than when they had receded from it.

Spring and Summer Whitetails

EVEN as the lingering deep snow in the shade-protected backwoods is just beginning to recede, the long-confined whitetails get the strong urge to stray from their winter grounds to range over a wider area. And by the time all traces of snow are gone, the animals move about freely in their summer range, and sometimes they shift about, apparently aimlessly, as though they were not sure just where they rightfully belonged in this big, new world suddenly thrust upon them.

They roam the farmers' pastures, the outskirts of villages, and cross highways and railroads to enter the country beyond. In their newfound freedom they become nomads, and for a time seem to enjoy their unfettered movements. They may find particularly good browse in one spot and spend a day there to fill up. But tomorrow and the following days, they will be feeding elsewhere in their restless wandering.

The whitetail is not a handsome specimen at this time. Even through much of March it has been shedding its hair, and in early April its coat is shaggy. Bits of hair hang loose about its body, its neck is scrawny, and both backbone and ribs might show at close range. The mature buck, usually more haggard than the doe, has only two ragged tufts of hair to identify his noble sex. He looks more like an emaciated burro than the dashing prince of last fall.

When the whitetail's winter coat is entirely lost, the animal's lean body and scrawny neck are exposed. The new, short hair does little to conceal the ribs, backbone, and the veins along the neck. A better picture of his physical condition can be obtained by viewing the animal head-on. When seen from a distance, its body seems no broader than its head or outstretched neck. And except for its exaggerated ears, it appears as shapeless as a wooden fence post — and can often be mistaken for one. Even the doe carrying her young shows little signs of her pregnancy.

The whitetail enters the threshold of significant spring stripped of all but the bare essentials necessary for the propagation of its kind. This is the penalty the whitetail suffers when it accepts the stern habitat of deep snows and harsh winters of the northern country, and this loss of weight in deer each winter is an occurrence quite in accord with nature's plans. A plump and prime whitetail emerging from its wintering grounds would be adventitious.

Does and Fawns

By mid-spring the whitetails, considerably dispersed over their entire range, settle down in family groups to limited grounds where their daily living habits become somewhat routine. Few deer now will be seen along the roadsides, and the casual observer will wonder what has suddenly happened to the animals.

During this period of apparent inactivity, the does are heavy with young. Most of the fawns are dropped during the end of May and the early part of June. The pregnant doe leads a normal, unhampered existence until the very moment she gives birth to her young, and she seems not to anticipate the moment, for the offspring might be born most anywhere. Often they are found near a farmyard, just off a tote road, or on the angler's beaten path along a trout stream.

The youngsters are entirely helpless at birth, and their only protection comes from an innate disposition to lie down with neck outstretched and ears pinned back. Such a fawn can hug the slightest depression and escape detection even in short grass. Fawns develop the use of their leg muscles rapidly, for within an hour or two after birth, they struggle to try their long, wobbly legs; after a week or more they have sufficient strength and coordination in their legs so that they can escape most danger.

Wherever the young are born, they are soon led to the protection of dense growth not too distant from a water supply. The wilderness deer can now be seen mornings and evenings along streams, ponds, and marshes. Here, also, are available to them the succulent water plants that spring deer feed upon.

I have chanced upon many very young fawns, possibly several of which were no more than a few hours old. Of these, one was so new to the world it could not move over the ground without falling every few steps. I was fishing trout on a day when the bamboo pole was about all a lad needed for taking fish. My first impulse was to run down and pick up the struggling, leggy fellow. In the ensuing struggle, the youngster let out a feeble blat that sounded like the trembling note we children used to produce by blowing on a blade of grass held taut between our thumbs. At that instant, there came a great commotion from a nearby thicket, and the fearless doe broke out to charge directly toward me. It appeared she was not going to stop, so I took off down the creek path without my pole. When I chanced a quick glance over my shoulder to see if I had made my escape, the doe was with her young.

Sometimes young fawns will leave their beds and wander off by themselves. One of my neighbors relates a most unusual experience with a well-developed fawn that entered his farmyard. He had been busy doing chores about the premises when he noticed his small children romping about the yard with a playful fawn. The animal made no attempt to escape the tagging, screaming children, but simply cut capers about the lawn, often running far into a field only to return again to join the children. This lasted for about ten minutes, and then the spotted youngster finally dashed across the field in a straight line to enter the thicket. It was as though he felt it wise to abandon this strange venture.

One early October, while on my way home from school, I saw an unusually small fawn for so late in the season. The air was heavy with fog, and the small deer trotted toward me with its head down. First I thought this was a fox hunting mice along the weeds of the dirt road, for the animal never brought its head up all the while it ran toward me. When it trotted up to within fifty feet of me, it finally raised its head and I saw it was a very small fawn. It paused for a brief moment and then started walking toward me while I stood watching it. The fawn sniffed at me from about ten feet, bypassed me gingerly, and then continued trotting down the road. This young fawn had not yet learned to fear men.

Several times in recent years, I have seen very young fawns move unsteadily across my path along a trout stream. I tried to locate them by searching for the slightest movement of the brake ferns into which they had disappeared, but the little fellows entered the cover without disturbing a single frond. Most of the fawns escaped me completely after I spent some time searching for them foot by foot. One fawn in particular I finally discovered under the protection of a drooping brake-fern frond, and it lay flat on the ground without twitching a muscle or showing the slightest signs of breathing. I studied it for some time, regretting that I had not brought my camera.

When these youngsters are flushed from their beds, they run with their bodies close to the ground to take advantage of the grass cover, like a wily fox eluding the hunter. Not until they are mature enough to follow the mothers in their daily movements, and learn to accept the living habits of adult deer, do they bound away with high, arching leaps so characteristic of the whitetail.

The small fawns spend much of the day alone, while the does move about seemingly independent of their young. The mothers remain with their young through the night, and they are with them for brief periods during the day only to nurse them. The fawns often thought to be lost are merely at home while the mother is out browsing.

Fully mature does usually have twin fawns, and in rare cases they may have triplets. The younger females are most likely to have single fawns. The average number of offspring comes to about one and a half fawns to the pregnant doe. Their survival rate is extremely high as compared to that of most wild animals.

The whitetail has few natural enemies these days, and even the helpless young, whose only protection lies in dropping down at the slightest sign of danger, manage to escape the prowling brush wolf and the snooping fox, both of which could easily dispatch the very young fawn. It is entirely possible, as is often theorized, that the newborn fawn gives off no scent. And it is also probable that the brush wolf or red fox are unable to recognize the young animal when it lies flat and motionless; for if man, with his dulled senses, can find even an occasional fawn, the brush wolf, the fox, and perhaps the bobcat should seemingly have little trouble in filling up on tender venison at this time of the year. Whatever protection is given these young, it is something special not lavished upon rabbits, partridge, ducks, and most other wildlife.

After the doe has her young, she drops out of her family group, which normally consists of an old doe and her previous offspring, some of which could be of fawn-bearing age. Thus a new family group is started; though sometimes young twin does get together again after their fawns are several months old, and their combined families may account for a band of five or six deer. When the mother of the twin does is included in the family, we have a veritable herd of related deer with the old matriarch assuming leadership.

These deer might be scattered over a wide area at times, but they are never lost from each other for long. Even when they are dispersed by hunters, they have the tendency to rejoin within a day. The related animals have the ability to identify each other from the scent of their tracks, for when deer are spooked from an area, a particular animal might cross several deer tracks in the snow before it comes to the one it recognizes as being made by a member of its group. The inter-digital glands between the toes of the whitetail's feet give off a scent that seems recognizable to the species.

The ordinary cow, when lost, has the ability to backtrack herself, and a straggling steer can follow the tracks of the herd when it is nowhere in sight. The quickest way to locate a lost calf is by turning loose the anxious cow and letting her use her native capacities. She sniffs the ground as she moves along, and soon intercepts the trail of her calf. Deer, necessarily gifted in the use of their noses, can move about even in a very scattered formation and yet live in some contact with each other.

A large family grouping of whitetails is uncommon these days for it is unlikely the progeny could remain intact for three generations under present hunting pressure. Aside from this, it appears the deer today, especially during the hunting season, have acquired a penchant for living in small groups or even singly. It has been many years since I saw a compact band of eight or ten whitetails come out from a drive and move in close unison while making their escape.

The doe is a devoted mother in her own way, but she is not overly extravagant in the time she spends with her young. The fawns, on the other hand, demand little attention from their mothers; so little, in fact, that one might see a doe many times and never suspect she is nursing a pair of twins.

The newborn fawn is a timid creature, seemingly awed by every-thing about it. Its one strong instinct is to drop down when it is fright-ened. As a consequence, it spends its early days in concealment, and the world includes only its mother, who appears and disappears at odd moments. In time, the fawn anticipates the return of the mother, and it learns to recognize the sounds she makes when approaching.

Some fawns, only a few weeks old, start tagging along with the doe, while others are kept in hiding for several months as though the mother does not want to be burdened with the youngsters at her heels. As children, we brothers used to watch deer come to the pasture salt lick during the summer. We learned to recognize the animals as individuals, and there was one big doe, a regular caller at the salt lick, which my father always referred to as the "old dry doe." The other deer were a mixture of does with fawns, twin yearlings, and an occasional buck. The "dry" doe surprised us one evening in August when she showed up with a pair of big twins.

The young whitetails quickly acquire sharp senses of hearing, sight, and smell; yet, despite these developed senses, the inexperienced fawn has not learned what to avoid for its own safety. I have spent many hours during summer evenings watching does with their young, and it has been a fascinating pastime. The animals are easy to study with field glasses because at fawning time their reddish summer coats stand out crisply against green foliage. Once I learned where a doe frequently fed, I made it a point to arrive at the spot well in advance of the time of her usual appearance. Then, after selecting a wind vantage point, I would prop my back against a stump and comfortably seat myself while awaiting the shy performer's entrance on the stage.

Most of these studies were of backwoods deer, and the fawns had not yet experienced the sight of man. There is great advantage in having the whitetails come to you instead of attempting to approach them. The animals slowly and cautiously browse en route before they enter the opening. Sometimes I see branches moving and catch a glimpse of red far down the trail, and it may take fifteen minutes before the animals finally come into full view. Sometimes they glide through space with surprising ease and speed, then again they might dally motionless in some nook.

When I saw my first browsing deer many years ago, I remember it appeared to me very much like an overgrown summer hare — supple form, yielding legs that could lower or raise the body with ease, and the disposition to raise its front feet off the ground when feeding on overhead browse.

Once the animals edge their way onto the clearing, they feel quite secure as long as I do not move. The deer might casually glance in my general direction but they seldom notice me. After a while, if they do look directly at me, they promptly lower their heads and continue to browse. Any disruption of the whitetail's quiet browsing now would have to come from some other source, for I am now accepted as a part of the stump.

This makes an ideal setup for whitetail study because the fawn does not readily recognize danger, and the mother's attention is mostly directed toward her young. The young fawns stay near the mother, and they sometimes weave around her so closely that she is hampered in her movements. But the doe is gentle, and she turns aside rather than attempt to force her way past the youngster. If the fawn, by chance, meanders into a nearby thicket, the doe will stop eating for a moment in order to assure herself that all is well with her offspring. When she resumes eating, it is because she has seen the fawn's movement in the deep foliage.

As the young whitetails grow, they become a bit more independent in their wanderings. A doe might browse alone for a long time, but she shows concern for her little ones by periodically turning her attention in their direction. Maybe the fawns come to join the mother for a while, and then they wander away in another direction. Wherever they stray, the mother does not lose track of them.

Young whitetails imitate the moods, traits, and actions of their mother. They display ease, caution, or fear only because they have learned these responses from her. I watched a fawn when its mother was feeding with her head away from me. When I waved my hand at the fawn, it soon discovered me, but it was merely curious and, in fact, took a few steps toward me.

The little fellow kept glancing at the doe to learn her reaction to the strange object. Finally, the older deer was attracted by the young one's curiosity. Now, they both eyed me seriously. The big doe raised her head, snorted, and stamped her forefoot, and the fawn did a good imitation of the same gesture. When the old whitetail whirled around and trotted away, the fawn followed her precise movements. From that moment on, the young deer would respond with fear to a similar situation.

When the family is together, the young and mother often exchange glances, and if the doe raises her head to stare at some distant object, the fawn seems to sense the apprehension in her eyes. The little one freezes in position, looks in the same direction, and then glances back at its mother. If the doe forgets her concern and starts to feed again, the offspring, likewise, becomes relaxed.

When danger is imminent, the mother dives into the brush with a warning snort. She crashes through the thicket noisily, circles about, pauses to snort and thrash around, and after a few minutes her brood is gathered to join her in flight. But even as the deer family is now far in the woods, the old doe continues to snort, and the young by this time have become thoroughly impressed that they are in danger.

Fawns are inquisitive, always nuzzling and sniffing objects in their path. They start to forage when they are a few weeks old, although they depend largely on their mother's milk for the first few months of their existence. In their dainty eating, they sample the most tender foliage, as though they were nibbling merely for want of something else to do.

Their time is not fully occupied in browsing during midsummer when they are only two or three months old. Consequently, when the doe is feeding, the fawns will drop down to rest periodically. They do this quickly, as though the decision were made on the spur of the moment. The mother, meanwhile, seems to know exactly where they are, for she does not stray far from the spot.

The young whitetails sometimes frolic about in a clearing while the mother watches with passive interest. The playful mood apparently does not come often, for I have seen only several instances where the young frisked about in a frivolous vein. Once I saw one fawn chase another in a small circle, much as puppies do in play. They would stop to rest up for a moment, then if one of them wanted to continue the chase, it would sprawl forward with its forelegs and neck outstretched on the ground and its head cocked upward and to the side as though it were challenging its playmate to a game of tag. The game was over when one of them walked away to nose about for a bit of browse.

Even the older fawns might be disposed to a bit of sport when the mood suits them. I was amused one evening at the antics of two yearlings, apparently twins, jabbing each other with their front hoofs, as they stood erect on hind legs. The sparring lasted a minute or two, and in all this time, the contestants remained erect on their hind legs while they moved about like two boxers. They both dropped to the ground simultaneously, rested a bit, and then proceeded to graze at the edge of the field.

The whitetail, compared to most animals, is relatively mute, and its young seldom gives voice to complaint. On the rare occasions I have observed, a fawn would let out a soft bleat while with its mother, as though the young merely wanted to make its presence known. The doe, in recognition, simply glanced at her young. There are times, too, when the fawn will emit a cry of distress, although I have witnessed only one such situation.

A hunting partner of mine, who is both experienced and reliable, tells me he had seen a troubled, bleating fawn run past him during a hunting season. The fawn was very small even at this late date, and it let out tremulous bleats at frequent intervals as it trotted through the woods. Apparently, the late-born youngster was searching for its mother from whom it was separated.

The white spots on a fawn are most pronounced at birth; as the animal grows in size, the markings become less noticeable. By mid-August the fawn, when seen from a distance, is not easily distinguished from the adult deer. During September, when fall pelage gradually replaces the summer's red coat, the fawn takes on the appearance of the adult except for size, and even here a large fawn might easily be mistaken for a yearling.

Coloring in the coat of a deer of either sex can vary a bit from one animal to the next. In a group of deer on a field, one can often pick out one pelage that differs slightly from the normal. Often a deer with an unusually dark back, especially a buck, can be readily recognized when it is in company of normally colored animals. All whitetails do not shed their winter and summer coats at precisely the same time, and during these two periods of the year there is a marked variation in the pelage of the whitetails.

The extremes of albinism and melanism, white and very dark coats, are too rare for the ordinary hunter to hope to see in his limited observations of whitetails. Over the years I have seen a few white deer that I had recognized as albinos. And I have also seen some white and part white deer that I assumed were albino or part albino.

During the summer of 1963 my attention was called to the existence of a white deer about ten miles from my home. This deer and its normal twin were usually confined to an area of about forty acres. I failed to get any photographs of this deer, although I had caught glimpses of it several times that year. However, I did succeed in getting some pictures of this handsome white buck during the summer of 1964 and again during 1965. Not until 1965 did I get close enough to the animal to observe its coat had a slight tinge of yellow, and its eyes and muzzle were of normal color, not pink as in the case of a true albino.

This buck was a mutant. The deer of this particular country apparently still carry the genes of ancient white ancestors, and undoubtedly the white and part-white deer I had seen previously in this area were also mutants.

My brother Tom had seen a similar deer with a slight yellowish tinge during the spring of 1964 at a point fully five miles from where the mutant buck was commonly seen. This animal, he said, appeared to be a large doe, and he was able to study it from a distance of about a hundred feet as it grazed on short clover in a hay field. He noted that the tarsal glands on this deer appeared normal in color and, hence, stood out prominently. No white deer has been sighted in this particular area since, and it is possible that the two animals were one and the same, though it seems improbable that the one so commonly seen should stray so far from its established home.

Tom, who takes more than a passive interest in the ways of whitetails, used to watch a mottled deer a few years ago grazing in a field near his home. The coloring of the animal was a strange mixture of white and normal. Its front quarters were of normal pelage, but the hind half of the animal was blotched with large patches of pure white. Its odd appearance seemed not to handicap the animal in its association with the other deer feeding in the field.

Summer Foods

All through July and August, the whitetails do considerable grazing, for like sheep, they are equally grazers and browsers. They seek fields, roadsides, and forest openings for grasses. This is the time they find food in sufficiency, and their one purpose is to take advantage of summer's lush living. But even through July and August, the whitetail, with its summer pelage, appears lean despite its constant feeding.

During September, aided by the change to winter's heavier coat, the deer becomes more pleasing to the eye. Ripe grasses, concentrated in food value, rapidly build up fat on the animal. Like the bear in fall, fattening up for winter's hibernation, the whitetail starts laying up tallow to carry it through the months of deep snow when food becomes less available.

For once the whitetails can afford to be selective in their eating, and they will travel considerable distances to fill up on choice foods. The adaptable deer learn to acquire a taste for farm crops whenever they are available to them. Soybeans and rye are especially attractive to deer in the fall, and great numbers of the animals forsake their natural foods for these farm crops. The succulent, but tart, cranberry, whether wild or cultivated, is also eaten. Apples, too, are relished by some deer, but the desire for the orchard seems not as strong as the soybean and rye fields.

Some mature deer, especially bucks, will feed on ripening field corn. The taste for field corn is not easily acquired among whitetails, or else the taste for foods varies in different animals and in different years. I remember a cornfield that, in six years, attracted a few adult deer only one fall. Yet during this one fall, the animals fed in the field regularly.

Acorns are a natural fattening food for whitetails, and the backwoods animals start moving toward the oak growth in late September and October if the trees are bearing fruit. The seeds of perennials are relished, also, especially the tiny nutlets found in goldenrods. The entire downy tops are eaten for the nourishing seeds they contain. The whitetail now becomes a veritable gourmet, and individual tastes at this time can be satisfied with a wide assortment of foods.

19

Deer Guns and Sights

*T*HE whitetail in his wide range is a deer that clings closely to the cover available to him. His habitat includes such cover as the various thickets of the East, the swampy growth of the South, the woods of the North, and the scattered vegetation of the arid states, and he is hunted in all these diversified areas. The gun that most fits this all-round requirement is a light gun of fast action using a heavy, blunt bullet traveling at moderate speed with sufficient power to bring down a deer under present-day hunting conditions.

Rifles

Such a rifle would include calibers like the .308, the .30/06, and the .270. Certainly, any hunter purchasing a new deer rifle today would want something in this class. There was a time when the .30/30 was considered a caliber that would fit all whitetail-hunting requirements, but it must be remembered that the hunters and hunting conditions of today are not quite the same as in the heyday of the .30/30 some decades ago.

Under present hunting pressures, the whitetail is a mighty nervous and flighty animal. Not all hunters are marksmen, and there is nothing as discouraging to a new hunter as knocking down a deer only to have it struggle to its feet and escape. It is far better for such a man to use a heavier-calibered rifle than anything in the .30/30 class. And disappointing, too, is the situation in a heavily hunted area when your deer runs a considerable distance after being well hit with a lesser-powered rifle. Better by far to use something like the .308 and its 180-grain bullet with a good possibility of putting the deer down on the spot.

In the more open whitetail range, there is a trend toward the lighter calibers. These rifles, with their flat trajectory and high velocity, are deadly and accurate for ranges up to 200 yards. Such guns include the .243 and 6-mm calibers. They are, however, not recommended for brush shooting.

Hunters are independent thinkers who make individual decisions about deer rifles through their own experiences or those of other hunters whose opinion they respect. Fortunately, we have a fine array of suitable guns so that no hunter need be forced into the role of a conformist.

The autoloader, though somewhat temperamental if not kept clean, especially in extreme cold and sleet conditions, is the fastest of the several actions. It could very well be the choice of the man who has had experience with such an action in a rifle while in military service. It is made today in the Browning .270, .308, .243 Win., and the .30/06; Winchester in the .284, .243, and .308,; Harrington & Richardson in the .243 and .308; Remington in the .243, 6-mm Rem., .280 Rem., .308 Win., and the .30/06; and the Ruger in the .44 Magnum.

The pump action is available in the Remington .243, .270, .308 Win., and the .30/06; and in the Universal .44 Magnum. The pump, or slide action, is fast, and with a little experience the gun can be held pretty well on target while it is being cocked for the next shot.

The lever actions made today are the Marlin .30/30, .35 Rem., and the .444 Magnum; Savage in the .300 Sav., .243, .284, .358, and the .308 Win.; Winchester in the .243, .284, .308, .30/30, .32 Spec., and .44 Magnum; Sears in the .30/30; and Western Field in the .30/30. To many, the lever action does not repeat as quickly and as easily as the pump action, but others after being accustomed to it find it highly satisfactory. This is often a matter of personal preference.

The bolt action, though less popular for whitetail hunting, and slower in reloading than the others, is a very reliable gun and considered the most accurate of the actions. Whether its degree of extreme accuracy and positive operation offsets its slower action is for the hunter to decide. Many target shooters are attached to the bolt action and find it very satisfactory for deer hunting. Because of its appeal to many target shooters, it comes in a wide variety of makes and calibers.

Some of the common makes in the bolt action are the Browning, Harrington & Richardson,

Remington, Mossberg, Savage, Weatherby, Western Field, Sears, and Winchester. The hunter desiring the accurate bolt action will not suffer for lack of choice.

Aside from these makes and calibers suitable for the whitetail, there are many discontinued models, quite appropriate for taking this game animal, still being used today. A hunter can become attached to his rifle because it has served him well, he has learned to use it efficiently, or has been lucky with it. A man does best with the gun he has complete confidence in, and I find it tactful never to slight another man's gun. It is like slighting the hunter himself.

Some bullets will deflect considerably from their intended target if they hit even some minor obstruction such as a twig. This tendency for deflection or glancing in a bullet is caused mainly by the bullet's shape, its weight, construction, velocity, and its spin. The bullet best fitted for passing through brush without excessive deflection from its course is the heavier, blunt bullet of not too high velocity, and with not too much spin. These requirements are found in varying degrees in any acceptable whitetail rifle with its proper loads.

There was a day when the Model 95 Winchester and the Marlin carbine with the .30/30 cartridges were considered ample for the needs of any whitetail hunter. The 170-grain softpoint bullet has a flat enough trajectory, and if properly placed, enough killing power for deer at a range of at least 150 yards, and this will include most shots taken at whitetails. These guns have had a long continued appeal as a result of their reliable fast lever actions, their light weights, and the fact they can be held securely in one hand at balance point. They are quite sufficient for taking the whitetail when in the hands of a good marksman hunting under ideal conditions.

Conditions are not ideal, however, when a concentration of hunters causes your game to be edgy and flighty. Nor are all the men afield today the good hunters who can approach a deer for the well-placed shot required for the .30/30 and other comparable calibers. The anxious weekend hunter, who in all probability will not see too many deer in his short outing, will want to make the most of his chances. For him the higher-powered gun is best.

In my usually consistent hunting group of three brothers, we have a .308 Remington semi-automatic, a .35 Marlin lever action, and a .30/30 Winchester lever action. There is no clash here, whatever. Each of us is quite content with his rifle, and I must admit my attachment to the .30/30 is not without some sentiment. The gun is the right weight for me, especially for still-hunting, and I am aware of, and willing to accept, its limitations.

A main point to remember is that the hunter should understand his gun. He should be familiar with its trajectory, have it sighted in for his probable shooting range, and know its killing effectiveness for any range he will shoot. If he is well aware of these and uses his gun accordingly, the two will be in harmony for practical and enjoyable hunting.

Shotguns

In recent years the shotgun has become a popular weapon for taking the whitetail because of necessary hunting regulations. Due to the animal's penchant for invading any area where food is abundant and there is at least some cover available, there are good deer concentrations in areas of dense human populations. Plainly, the deer rifle with its long range is quite unsuited here.

The rifle slug used in a shotgun is simply a method of converting your shotgun into a crude deer rifle. It has good brush penetration and yet is not so long-ranged as to gravely endanger other hunters in the area. There is a rather wide variation in the range and accuracy claimed by users of the shotgun slug, but most will agree its rapid deceleration and rainbow-like trajectory makes it only slightly longer-ranged than buckshot. Any shotgun used at all should have at least some rudimentary rear sight so the barrel can be lined up with the target for a quick shot.

The rising trend in this type of shooting has resulted in a demand for special shotguns made to accommodate rifled slugs. These guns improve the placement of the slug, so that shots of up to 100 yards can be effectively made on deer, and here good iron sights or a low-powered scope fitted on your shotgun is a necessity. It is most probable that the development and use of the shotgun for slugs will continue as does the trend for whitetails to establish themselves in the populated areas of the United States.

The shotgun with buckshot is also used for deer hunting in some states and areas. The 12-gauge shotgun used with No. 00 buckshot is deadly up to about 50 yards, and with No. 0 shot it is effective up to about thirty-five yards. The only deer I killed with buckshot, at about forty yards, dropped on the spot.

Yet, I would not recommend shots at over fifty yards. The proper use of a shotgun with buckshot is best achieved by the man who can accurately estimate range on his hunting grounds and is fully aware of the performance of his gun. One might underestimate his target by fifty yards with a deer rifle with no apparent ill effect, but a mere fifteen-yard error with a shotgun could result in an ineffectual hit or complete miss.

The one advantage in using buckshot in dense cover is the probability of getting close to your quarry for a quick shot. If the range is short, as it must be, the shot need not be made with the accuracy of a rifle. In the South the shotgun for deer has long been used because of the close but quick shots available to the hunter here in the whitetail's habitat of dense growth and swamp.

Telescope Sights

In this day of progress and rapid change, the telescope sight has ushered in an entirely new conception of what a gun sight should be. It is a safe bet than anyone, especially the young hunter, who once uses a scope and gets thoroughly accustomed to it, will never fall back to iron sights. The choice of a scope, like the choice of a gun, must be made to fit one's particular hunting needs. The whitetail throughout his range holds close to cover, and because of this it is most probable that the 2 ½X or 3X is preferable for most situations. Such a scope has a wide field of view, is easy to place on target, and gathers ample light so that even the man whose eyesight is on the decline will find it a boon to his hunting. There is, I think, a tendency for some hunters to use a scope too high-powered for their hunting requirements.

The two-power scope on my rifle is ideal for putting on the target immediately. Since the scope is set ahead of the receiver, and my eye naturally comes to within about seven and a half inches of the eyepiece, I find the target as easy as with my old iron sights.

As the scope is so far ahead, I also have considerable vision around its thin rim, and this helps me in spotting the game if I am not on target. For this same reason, this particular scope is also good for running shots.

The variable scope now in prominence has some merit over the fixed-power scope if it is set for low power and turned up only to identify a distant object. Seldom will anyone have occasion to use anything more than a 3X magnification for actual shooting of the whitetail in his normal habitat.

In those states and areas where bucks only are legal game, the variable scope can be turned up for high magnification so that an animal seen in the open can be studied for any forked antlers or mere spikes. The hunter is ready to squeeze off the shot as soon as identification is made. There is a safety factor here, too. A man using his scope to study game at a great distance or in a thicket will never make the grave error of shooting at anything but his intended quarry. Normally, though, the hunter will get better service from his variable scope when hunting whitetails by keeping its magnification down to its most practical setting of 2 ½X or 3X.

The common, good reticules in a scope are the crosswires, the dot, and the flattop post. Choice is largely a matter of preference, and often reflects a hunter's past experience with gun sights. The dot does suggest a peep sight and the post appears as a knife sight perched on the front of a rifle barrel. Either of these are good once the user becomes accustomed to them. The minute dots and minute spacers on scopes for range finding are useful

in the open spaces of some parts of the West and Southwest, but they are of little avail in most of the whitetail's brushy habitat.

The hunter must consider his scope as a part of his gun and not as a worthy addition to it, and he must be able to swing his weapon on target in one smooth sweep. This takes practice æ considerably more than with iron sights. I find it worthwhile to do some target practice on a range in order to familiarize myself with my scope and learn what to expect of it. Now my scope is naturally on target when I bring the gun to my shoulder.

Unlike the sturdy iron sights, a scope can be jarred out of alignment with a solid jolt as in a fall, and it is well to check on the gun's bullet placement again when his happens. I find it very reassuring to check the gun's shooting accuracy immediately before the deer season and at least once or twice during the hunt. There is nothing like the complete confidence one has in knowing that when he eases off his shot the bullet will hit exactly where he held his gun. The gun, of course, should be sighted in to accommodate the range that will include the most likely shots.

During snow or rain, if the precipitation appears of short duration, I merely protect my scope by shielding it under my arm when walking, or else I put on the protective caps over the glasses if I am sitting on a stand. If the precipitation continues for any length of time, I remove my scope and keep it under cover, and flip up the peep sight or else use the knife sight that is a part of the scope base.

Iron Sights

Despite the wide acclaim accorded telescope sights, iron sights on the deer rifle have not as yet been relegated to the museum or gun collector. These sights have some virtues that might keep them around for some time. They are rugged, simple, inexpensive, and accurate at moderate range on large targets. Because of this, most beginners start off with iron sights.

In the past many hunters failed to realize that a good sight was one that offered the least obstruction to viewing the target. The very deeply notched rear sights and the buckhorn type were used by many hunters because they appeared accurate. The drawback here is that they are quite ineffective for spotting game quickly because so much of the target is shielded by them. The shallow "V" is much preferable for a rear sight since it gives less obstruction to the shooter's vision. The eye easily picks up the front sight along the shallow groove.

The peep, or aperture, sight never had the acceptance in the past it rightfully deserved. It is so utterly simple to place the front sight on your target with little attention required to center the target picture through the aperture. Such simplicity was not too impressive when I first became acquainted with this sight, but I soon realized it was accurate for me at least up to 100 yards, and it was much easier to use for spotting and following game, especially through the larger aperture that I much prefer. Besides, there is not the blurring of the sight image on dull days. The hunter whose eyes are not as keen as they might be finds the aperture sight easier to use than open sights. The scope sight, however, would undoubtedly be his better choice.

Gun Care

There are some simple precautions to observe in caring for your gun during the hunting season. Many hunters bring their cold rifles into a warm room after the hunt. This causes condensation, and if the gun is in a well-insulated case it might not dry out thoroughly overnight. Then it could freeze when taken out for the hunt. Or a careless hunter might leave his wet gun in the car to freeze.

A good practice is to leave your cold, dry gun and cartridges locked in the trunk of your car, or else to keep them in a cold room overnight. Only when your gun is wet with rain or snow should it be brought in and thoroughly dried inside and out. It should then be wiped with an oil-dampened cloth. Care should be taken not to get any oil on the scope lenses as this could cause permanent damage to them. Fouling of the mechanism in deer rifles in the field is due mostly to improper attention to the guns after the hunt the evening before.

There is much to be gained by thoroughly acquainting yourself with your gun. The short experience you have with your rifle during the deer season hardly suffices to make you completely confident in your weapon. Any interest in your deer rifle during the off season, such as occasional target practice, merely bringing your gun up to your shoulder, or reading up on your gun's possibilities keeps you close to your firearm, and all this will add much to the pleasure and success of your next hunt.

The story of whitetail hunting is also a story of the deer rifle, and much gun history has been made

during this century. It would appear that some of the guns existing early in the century were there solely for the purpose of creating variety, for they could hardly be called effective deer rifles by today's standards.

Those were the days when every man could be identified by the weapon he carried, for the strange rifles were as individualistic as were the men who toted them. The hunter who had more than usual interest in firearms could recognize and trace the ownership of a gun even after it had been traded off or sold several times, so long as it still remained in the general neighborhood. Each gun had its peculiar history, and each owner imparted to it some color and personality. The fortunate man with a new deer rifle had a superior firearm giving off a lingering odor of factory bluing. This automatically gave the possessor an enviable status in the neighborhood hunts.

I have a small collection of some of the cartridges used in the northern Wisconsin deer country from about 1915 to about 1940. From this date on, the old guns were being rapidly replaced by more modern deer rifles. We boys inadvertently gathered these shells through the years when any gun was considered a suitable deer rifle. Since I was sandwiched in between four other brothers, two older and two younger than myself, our interest in shell collecting spanned a considerable period.

When my father purchased his .41 Swiss in 1917, this army rifle, to my knowledge, was the only such musket in our county, and at the time, we thought it had about everything a deer hunter needed. The bolt-action rifle held two handfuls of cartridges, had an attached cleaning rod, and a small compartment in its stock for carrying cleaning patches. It was such a massive, heavy weapon that by the time my older brothers were big enough to raise it to their shoulders, they had come upon something much lighter, though probably of equal antiquity.

There was a .43 Egyptian going the rounds of the settlement, and I recall a single shot .45/70 trapdoor Springfield used in the area. The Winchester lever action was by all odds the most commonly used deer rifle seen in the woods. Our shell collection indicated the use of such caliber rifles as the .30/30, .35, .38/40, .30/40, .44/40, .45/90, .40/82, .33, .38/55, .38/56, .45/70, .40/60, .32/40, .38/72, .32/20, .405, .25/35, .25/36, .303, .300, .25/20, .41, .43, .351, .250/3000, .25, .30, .32, and .32 Special.

Although the .30/30 was the most common caliber of the Winchesters used at this time, there were sufficient other calibers and odd rifles about to make shell collecting an engrossing hobby. My older brother got a .35 auto loading Remington in 1920. This deer rifle was considered quite above and apart from the commonly used guns of the time, and its status as such remained through the decade in our area. It is still a good gun for deer hunting in timbered country. Since deer hunting was largely a means for replenishing the household meat supply among the local folk, the trend toward the modern sporting rifle for more enjoyable hunting was slow in coming.

The tendency in the whitetail hunter today is to own a scoped rifle that is large enough for any North American big-game animal. The heyday of the deer hunter whose gun marked him somewhat of an individualist is fading into the past.

Many of the old firearms, though still serviceable, are being retired to gun cabinets or given respectable display in the den. And many a seasoned hunter in whitetail country has at least one of these guns, and I know of some, hardly considered collectors, who have a dozen or more of these odd-calibered guns that are so woven with stories and personalities of earlier American hunters.

20
Clothing and Equipment

$\mathcal{T}$HE comfortably attired hunter is the eager and efficient hunter, and if he can be properly dressed for the entire day he will be alert and contented while afield. The man who wears the same hunting clothes all day and every day regardless of weather during the entire hunting season is certainly not going to keep his morale on a happy plane.

What one wears on a frosty morning is not likely to be suitable for the warmer afternoon. There can be downright cold temperatures or unseasonable warm spells, gentle rains or veritable snowstorms all in the same deer hunting season on one's particular hunting grounds. With a little thought to proper attire, one can make his outing quite pleasant even with adverse and varying weather conditions.

The hunter's dress dictates the kind of hunting he will do. If he is underdressed for the weather, he will naturally move quickly and cover much ground in an effort to keep warm. And he could become a careless, noisy hunter. If he is over-dressed, he will perspire and become uncomfortably warm to the point where he loses zest for the hunt. And if he becomes wet from deep, thawing snow or precipitation, he will likely call it a bad day and head for his comfortable quarters.

Outerwear

Today, practical clothing is available to every outdoorsman. It is now merely a matter of preference or experience for the hunter in selecting his gear for the field, and some knowledge here is helpful. It amounts to a bit more than merely purchasing a red "uniform" that automatically dubs its owner a deer hunter. Most of the serious and experienced hunters I know seldom wear a complete hunting ensemble for the simple reason that weather conditions do not warrant it. In the belt of the northern whitetail, temperatures during the deer season can vary from 15 degrees below zero to 60 degrees above. The novice will, perhaps, be a slave to his new hunting outfit and think himself not properly attired without it regardless of the weather. Hunting to him, then, can become something less than a happy experience.

Despite the many synthetic fabrics on the market, and some are quite remarkable, I have yet to find anything the equal of good wool to serve the varying needs of the hunter. The very comforting softness and practicability of woolen clothing, be it in underwear, socks, trousers, coat, gloves, or cap, simply cannot be matched in any other fabric. Wool is light, warm, makes for almost noiseless hunting, is comfortable in damp weather, and is even tolerable when wet. It will serve you well in wear for many seasons.

Even with wool the hunter should have some variety in his gear to compensate for the extremes in weather. Light- and medium-weight trousers would be ideal, as would a light and medium shirt. A light and a medium woolen jacket is a luxury for a quick change during a sudden rise

or fall in temperature. Any other clothing adjustments can be made with light or medium underwear.

Underwear

There is other good underwear besides wool. Cotton thermal underwear is not bulky and will keep you warm, and it can be obtained in several weights. Insulated underwear might be good for ice fishing but it can be quite bulky and warm for the hunter on the move or if the temperature rises. Yet, insulated underwear is good for trail watching on a frosty morning. In fact, it can be snug during milder weather if one remains on the stand all day.

Seldom is the day such that the hunter can stay comfortable all through his hunt with the clothing he put on for the brisk morning. This could be due to temperature rise, warmth acquired in walking, or a change in hunting method. An extra shirt and jacket of a lighter weight plus a pair of socks and gloves kept in your car can give you some clothing change that will be truly appreciated many times.

One of the most practical garments for the upper body is a down-filled vest. It weighs but a few ounces, it is extremely warm when fully zipped, and does not hamper arm or shoulder movement as does a jacket. Yet, if the body, especially the back, is kept warm, the entire body is not likely to suffer from cold. As the temperature of the body rises, one merely opens the zipper a bit to allow cooler air to circulate about the body. With the zipper fully unfastened, the down-filled vest hangs loosely with air circulating about freely. This light garment can give you comfort over a wide range of temperatures. It is not, however, practical for rainy or snowy days.

Footgear

Footgear is all-important, and here there seems to be considerable preference and tolerance among individuals. For me, I find nothing better than a light pair of woolen socks in ten-inch felt shoes worn with ten-inch, light dress overshoes. This combination is very light, extremely warm, and keeps the feet comfortable over varying weather conditions from bitter cold and deep snow to an unseasonable warm rain. It is most ideal for trail watching where cold feet can become a problem. Felt absorbs considerable moisture before any foot discomfort is experienced. Since felt shoes dry readily overnight,

one can start the next day's hunt with a fresh change of socks and be all set for another day of foot comfort.

When there is no snow and the ground is dry, leather hunting boots make a welcome change for the hunter. In fact, it is well to slip into different footgear on occasion if for no other reason than to give your tiring feet a change of pace. Nothing refreshes your feet and prepares them for the next day's jaunt better than bathing them in cool water at the end of the day.

Some men are perfectly comfortable in rubber pacs with leather uppers, and some hunters apparently find all-rubber footwear practical, especially the rubber-insulated boot. The thorough drying of insoles for each day's hunt is certainly recommended with rubber gear.

Anything that hampers circulation about the arms or legs makes for cold hands or feet. Some hunters stuff their trouser legs into their boot tops. When the boots are laced there is a certain amount of restriction to blood circulation here, and on a cold day this could cause cold feet. I prefer to have my trousers hang loose over the boot tops. This also keeps moisture from entering the boot.

Sagging socks that slide down into your boots can cause you no end of annoyance. When this happens to me, I fasten the sock top to my underwear with a safety pin. The pressure caused by wearing a garter is sufficient to restrict blood circulation and results in cold feet.

Comfortable feet are absolutely necessary for an enjoyable hunt, and the secret to this well-being in the field is to keep one's feet dry. If necessary and practical it is well to bathe the feet during midday, or even to change to more appropriate footwear if weather conditions call for it. One hunts well only if he is free from any slight source of physical distress, and cold, damp or sore feet rob a man of the full pleasure of a hunt.

Gloves

An extra pair of red, light gloves can be really appreciated after a few hours of hunting in wet snow or moisture-laden brush. I prefer to wear buckskin choppers with woolen liners on frosty mornings or bitter cold days. If they are loose fitting, one can easily whip them off to free the bare hand for a quick shot.

Headgear

For any hunter, and especially the still-hunter or the man on the stand,

any excess or bulky clothing about the neck or head proves a great handicap. A parka, turn-up collar, or earflaps rob the hunter of some vision, hearing, or both. A parka, especially, greatly reduces the efficiency of a hunter. It cuts the scope of vision to a narrow sector, it shuts off sounds, and it creates considerable distracting noises inside the hood as one moves his head about. I know of several instances in my own hunting group when a member missed out on an easy shot because his parka did not allow him enough vision to the side. There is a tendency for the man wearing a parka to refrain from turning his head from side to side because of the noise this creates in his ears.

If my ears become cold, I merely pull my cap over the upper part of them. This pins the tops of my ears to my head and keeps the entire ear warm without shutting off my ears to any sounds.

To sum up, one should avoid any harsh clothing about the neck or face that might produce any annoying sounds in his ears. These noises come louder than the sounds made by moving deer. To the still-hunter and trail watcher, the world of sounds is most important.

When your outer clothing does not properly meet the color requirements for safety in the woods, one can always wear a light, properly colored vest as an outer garment. Again, wool is preferable here because of its softness and quietness. The vest should be large enough to wear over a variety of hunting shirts and jackets. Where deer hunting tags must be displayed on one's back, the tag can be attached to the light vest and worn every day.

Equipment

Any equipment one carries on the hunt should certainly be limited to what is actually needed. Much, of course, depends on the type of hunting one will do. Personally, if I am on the move I want to be streamlined for the hunt, and that means no bulging pockets containing a hand warmer, thermos of hot coffee, cushion to sit on, or binoculars unless I plan to trail watch. These items had best be left in the car to be called for if really needed. One can become so burdened with gadgets that might come in handy that he becomes a veritable slave to these accouterments and his hunt suffers because of it.

The very small hunting knife is to be preferred to the cumbersome, foot-long weapon commonly seen dangling from the belts of so many exuberant youngsters. I use an ordinary jackknife and it has served me very well over the years. A small precision compass is necessary and the hunter should know how to use it. The mass of redcoats who hunt the roadsides hardly need a map as long as they have compasses. Anyone planning a considerable hunt into the hinterlands should have a map. If he orients the map with his compass and then locates himself on the map, he will have a clear picture of the area he is hunting and the direction he will be traveling. It is entirely possible to successfully hunt strange deer country with the aid of a map and compass.

The members of my small group each carry an empty cartridge shell for use in signaling each other during the hunt. This proves most effective for keeping our party operating as a unit. Signaling blasts from a cartridge shell is much better than straining one's voice to round up a strayed member of the party or to assemble the group after the drive.

I used to carry binoculars, especially if I intended to spend considerable time on stands. My rifle scope now eliminates the use of this extra burden. A small nylon cord (for dragging a deer), matches, and a red handkerchief should complete the necessary hunting items to be carried on one's person. Some carry an extra box of cartridges, but I find four rounds plus the filled magazine have always sufficed.

If I plan on an extended hunt far off a road I pack a sandwich in my pocket — and maybe a candy bar or two. It is surprising how this little snack will do for the day if you become engrossed in the chase. On many occasions I finish off my lunch en route home from the hunt, and my supper is not slighted because of it. Only the lukewarm hunter needs to surround himself with many things in order to keep himself amused and occupied while in the field.

21
The Trend

*N*O OTHER large game animal in the United States is as adaptable as the whitetail in coping with the ever-changing environment. Moose, caribou, wild sheep, and mountain goats are restricted to a narrow environment peculiar to the species. Once these ancestral homes are altered, the well-being of the animals is affected. Much of our wildlife in the northern states, including the timber wolf, Canada lynx, and the fisher, is either extinct or on the way out because its wilderness environment is no longer conducive to the species.

But the whitetail deer, opportune nomad that it is, moves about a varied environment ranging from the big-timbered wilderness to the open farmlands. Like the cottontail rabbit invading the city lawns, the whitetail is lured to the succulent growth of the more open country wherever it may be in its normal range. It is its stomach rather than the safety of its hide that largely determines where its numbers are concentrated. In its search for sustenance, it has gradually extended its domain far to the south once more to reclaim the country where its numbers were so mercilessly reduced to the point of extinction about a century ago.

Where once the entire North country was a veritable garden of lush deer browse, it is now entering the period of a developing new forest with a resultant dearth of shrubby growth. The whitetail picture in the North, whether we like it or not, is changing, and the once familiar cry of encouragement "to hunt back in" for better deer hunting is now accepted with considerable reservation in many areas. There is some backwoods country that has long passed the peak of ideal whitetail habitat, though its reputation for good hunting still lingers, at least in the memory of some men. And these hunters, either because of their sheer love for their backwoods hunting grounds, or because of unwillingness to accept the trend of the whitetail movement, are finding themselves out of step in the modern army of hunters.

Not all the wooded country in the North has outgrown its use for good whitetail habitat, though it seems apparent that the continued forest growth will result in less browse in the years to come and, consequently, less deer in the once popular cut-over lands. We are now in a period where much of our young hardwood growth is not yet mature enough for logging, but the stand is so dense as to starve out all undergrowth.

There are some extreme examples of this predicament where soils are most favorable for tree growth. Some thirty miles northwest of Marquette, Michigan, not far inland from Lake Superior, I have seen young hardwoods grow so dense as to make walking through the young forest very difficult. Hardly a ray of the summer's sun penetrates the overhead foliage to cast a fleck of light to the somber ground. The small but towering tree trunks bristling with withered branchlets far above my reach attest to the lack of sunshine reaching the ground of this jungle. Neither blade of grass nor leaf of shrubbery find encouragement in this element. The lush foliage of this young forest, as seen from the roadside, presents an overall picture of nature's abundance, yet this is actually a forest desert quite unsuited to the needs of our deer, winter or summer. This forest growth is the big threat to the once broad range of our whitetail in the North.

There is also much wilderness land, formerly good deer country, now overgrown with mature, unhealthy poplar and mixed hardwood stands of little commercial worth. These trees promise no value as a forest in the foreseeable future, yet the stand is rapidly outgrowing its use for the whitetail.

Farmland clearings are not reclaimed by new growth as quickly as burnt or logged land. The thin soil of relinquished farmlands yields stubbornly to the encroaching of the surrounding forest, and as the growth slowly engulfs the openings, young trees and shrubbery, the vanguard of the forest invasion, will continue to supply deer food for many years. Farmlands evacuated several decades ago are still a big factor in maintaining the animal population, and this trend of abandoning the marginal farmlands in the North will help serve the deer of the future.

Today, those men who, by habit or preference, hunt the backcountry, keep themselves informed on hardwood logging operations in their hunting area. Deer move in on such grounds even when the cutting is in progress, and after feeding there for a winter they never quite abandon it; and as the succulent second growth comes up even during the next year, the animals become established in the new home. It continues to be good white-tail habitat for the next several years, and the jungle of dead treetops serves as good cover in the meantime. Unfortunately, unless there is considerable cutting of standing timber, the small openings in the forest close rapidly and conditions revert to the former state of scant underbrush.

Bolt cutting, especially in the vast poplar expanses, is a big factor in encouraging a continuous sprouting of both browse and cover. My best hunting grounds have been kept attractive to deer over the past decades because of the consistent logging operations on these grounds. There is always a variation of tree growth here from mere shoots to maturing trees, and as a result, the suitability of this poplar country for whitetails has wavered but little during the many years I have hunted this area. It will continue to produce good hunting so long as new browse is encouraged.

A heavy stand of mature poplar trees can be nearly as effective as a hardwood or evergreen stand in shutting off sunlight to the forest floor to repress new growth. It is apparent over the years that these species, including the American aspen, the large toothed aspen, and the balsam poplar, once so common throughout much of the North, are slowly yielding to the hardwoods. Yet, these mature trees of the willow family still cover much of our deer country and, except for the choice of conveniently located stands, pulpwood cutting is lagging far behind the available supply of these fast-growing trees. It is this acreage that, at present, holds little for the whitetail.

There was a time when every household, whether in the country or in the towns, depended on firewood as a fuel for heating. This was no small factor for creating needed cut browse for wintering deer and encouraging the rise of new growth. Today, the use of oil and gas for heating and cooking, even in the backwoods, is just another modern trend not in harmony with the white-tail's well being.

There have been many changes from the days when deer hunting meant packing off to the woods for a full season's stay in the old hunter's shack. The call of the North woods was once answered only by the hardy souls to whom the ruggedness of camping in the rough was accepted as a necessary part of the hunt. Though the chase of the whitetail continues, many of the sturdy qualities of the erstwhile Nimrod are no longer with us, nor are they entirely essential these days.

The practical deer hunters, and especially the newcomers, come to hunt the game animal where it is most plentiful, and many a bag is filled without the hunter straying a quarter of a mile from his parked car, a farm field, or a side road. The task of dragging in a deer killed even a mile back in from any road is becoming the exception today. Because of this easy hunting, our hunting force is inflated with many soft-handed members who make the outing not so much for their sheer love of hunting but for the ease with which they can assume the stature of a hunter.

With the change in its habitat, the conforming whitetail has learned to live in a world in which it cannot escape the presence of man. In turn, it can be wary or trusting, according to its mood at the moment, or how it interprets a situation. Yet, it has no choice but to tolerate man, the strange creature who is sometimes a harmless intruder and sometimes the arch enemy.

In this precarious existence that faces it today, the whitetail progeny has developed defensive traits that were not observed in deer of four decades ago. The animals at that time, according to my knowledge of them, had a natural fear of man throughout the year, undoubtedly due to the fact that hunting then was not strictly confined to the legal season only. Deer fed in the old logging-camp clearings and the settlers' rutabaga patches, usually during the night, and most probably during the moonless, rainy, dark nights if they were commonly hunted throughout the summer. The salt-hungry animals seldom ventured to the salt licks before twilight or after dawn except on rainy days. The sight of a feeding whitetail in broad daylight during the summer months was certainly not as common as it is today.

Over the years, as off-season hunting has virtually ceased, the deer relaxed their guard for the most part of the year, only to take it up again during the hunting season; and now it seems that all their reserve energy is expended in artful efforts to elude the hunter.

The modern whitetail has learned it invites more risk by running the gantlet of many hunters when it travels a great distance in its escape from one man, so it now seeks to evade its enemy rather than flee him. It feels a measure of security in remaining in its bed as long as it can hear the hunters stirring about to its sides. Only when the threat of danger comes directly and determinedly toward him does it become uneasy and willing to leave its cover. And when it does leave, it does so with a deliberate and calm attempt to evade the danger at hand and keep its enemy at a safe distance to its side from where its ears follow the progress of the passing hunter. Because of its reluctance to run any great distance in a direction directly away from the point where it is started, driving is becoming less effective in the heavily hunted areas; and trail watching meets with little success when the whitetail knows the danger of following trails with hunters everywhere about it.

Where there are deer and sufficient hunters moving about, as is the situation in the semi-agricultural country of which I am speaking, there is normally a heavy kill of animals during the initial few days of the season. And too often the game is not bagged by the stealth of the hunter nor by the carefully laid plans of an organized hunting group. The men attracted to roadside and fieldside hunting are not the serious, dedicated hunters of the past or, for that matter, are not the same as those who still prefer to camp back away from the mass of hunters.

It must be admitted that much of the increase in our hunting force in the past decade is due to the white-tails concentrating in localities that permit ease and convenience in big-game hunting. Here, with men milling about in a limited territory, one man has as good a chance as the next of seeing a deer. No one need be a hunter of great caliber, and the prime requisite is nothing more than to be able to shoot reasonably well. This type of hunting does not appeal to all men, yet it must be acknowledged that the most deer are taken with the least physical effort in this modern hunting trend.

Where once the hunter made a preseason excursion into his favorite hunting grounds deep in the woods, he now likely drives his car down the highways and side roads to learn which fields and roadsides attract the largest number of animals. He might see many deer in the fields at sundown and after, and his car's headlight might pick up the eyes of deer feeding alongside the road. The leisured, roadside reconnaissance is encouraging, and the prospective hunter has his spot selected. But when he returns for the hunt, he finds the animals are not nearly as plentiful as his survey revealed, and he wonders what has happened to them.

The truth is that the whitetails come to feed in fields from a considerable distance, and even should this distance be a mile in all directions from the feeding grounds, this could include a happy number of animals in the field on a favorable night. Yet, when the deer are dispersed over the four sections of country, which this circumference would approximately encompass, a hunter might spend a day in this seemingly veritable deer country without seeing a single animal. Other areas far removed from a field, but still favorable for whitetails, might contain more of the animals, but the road-cruising, deer-country prospector is influenced by what he sees. And there is no easier way to see whitetails than by driving by hay fields or grassy roadsides in deer country on a quiet October evening.

With the labyrinth of roads opened up throughout deer country,

most of today's hunters can put up at hotels or resorts and be at their hunting grounds within a matter of minutes. And the residents of towns and cities need drive only an hour or two in order to reach the heart of the deer country. Such convenience has produced the part-time or weekend hunter.

Today's sportsman is so pampered with such an array of gadgets and attire for ease and comfort that deer hunting is no longer a privilege of the hardy outdoor clan. The golfer, bowler, or the spectator sports fan now takes to the field to participate in a venture that once belonged to a rugged outdoor group.

The gun with its telescope sights has greatly lessened the requirements demanded of the hunter. A gunsmith sighting in a scoped rifle can make the novice a dead shot on a standing target. The automobile, the scoped gun, the warm, comfortable attire, and the ease of today's hunting tend to make one man equal to the next in securing venison. The hunter, as we once knew him, is being rapidly replaced by the modern sportsman who needs be less encumbered with woods lore or any great love for the outdoors.

Convenience is the public cry in hunting or fishing. We prefer our trout at the bridge sides and our whitetails along the roadsides; and if the game is far back in, we clamor for and get a road to the most remote wilderness stronghold. In short, we want our wildlife brought to our backyard.

I know of a comfortable hunting cottage that was built adjacent to a good deer runway. The site of the cottage is in a narrow neck of land between two large swamps, and the runway passing through served as a funnel for the animal traffic of the deer country to either side. A bulldozed road leads to this dream cottage into the heart of this hunter's paradise, but, alas, the road has brought in a host of hunters, and the deer no longer use the runway. This is the story of much of our wilderness development. We do not develop wildlife itself, but rather create an access for exploiting it.

With the constant building and improvement of our roads to accommodate an ever-increasing number of fast, silent cars, we have brought on a grave threat to all our wildlife. The highway killing of both animals and birds mounts yearly, not because of a general abundance of wildlife, but because of the increase in fast traffic through areas where woodland creatures are concentrated. These magnificent thorough-

fares with their broad, landscaped roadsides lure the woodland denizens to an oasis of better living. Few species of animals or birds thrive in the dense forest where both browse and insect life is scant. The roadside's tender growth attracts not only deer and small bird life; but also such animals as mice, cottontail rabbits, and game birds.

The road opening is also favorable for insect life, and the warmth of the pavement is sought by the lesser crawling creatures. During their breeding period, turtles idle along the highways as though they had discovered a new acceptable environment. Snakes emerge from the cool grasses to absorb the warmth of the blacktop, and frogs on occasions gather on the blacktop as though they had taken a holiday from their world of grasses. Even the lumbering porcupine, the spring migrating muskrat, and the occasional mink are not averse to using man's thoroughfare in their travels.

Songbirds and some animals are attracted here by the abundant insects, and the meat eaters find fare in the birds and rodents. Partridge seek the gravel on the road shoulders, and the application of salt on the winter highways accumulates in sufficient quantities just off the edge of the pavement to satisfy the whitetail's needs. Hawks, owls, and ravens come to the highways to feed on the slaughter left in the wake of automobile traffic. We build these roads to take us into the wilderness country, but in so doing, we are destroying that which we come to seek. All this we meekly accept in the name of progress and modern development.

Deer losses caused by highway vehicles are reaching high proportions and will continue to increase under present conditions. Figures of an estimated yearly kill in any state will never be determined with any degree of accuracy, for, like the unrecovered gunshot deer left to die unrecorded, so the animal injured only slightly by the moving car most probably ambles off to the thickets to die. The whitetail, though endowed with great stamina, has small and brittle bones, and its delicate body structure cannot take the impact of a seemingly slight blow of a solid force without causing serious injury to the animal. I have had occasion to help prepare a venison supper from the carcasses of several deer purchased from Wisconsin's Conservation Department. The animals, victims of automobile traffic, were undoubtedly the lesser damaged of the state's numerous highway casualties, yet not much

usable venison could be salvaged from the bruised carcasses.

The whitetail does not fear the automobile nor its occupants, and in some strange manner, it accepts the two as belonging to each other. This harmless combination moves quietly along the road, much as a hawk glides silently overhead, and the presence of the automobile has become part of the whitetails' environment as has the paved road, the farmer's field, the sounds of an outboard motor or chain saw. The mind of the deer seems unable to cope with an object it cannot recognize as an enemy.

The midsummer doe and her young are especially susceptible to the danger of the speeding automobile, and the peril to the family group is augmented by the season's heavy traffic. As the doe and her young feed in loose formation, they often find themselves separated by a road, and when the animals are spooked, it is very probable that one of them will cross the road to join the others in the escape. The driver might be fully aware of the deer standing off the roadside in plain view, but he might not see the partly obscured deer on the other side of the road. It is the deer that jumps onto the highway from nowhere that takes the driver by complete surprise.

In times past, when night traffic was not as great as it is today, the headlight was more certain to capture the eye of the whitetail and hold it for a prolonged period. Today, the beam of a light does not hold the same fascination to these animals, and, frequently, they do not bother to face the light. The driver has little warning when he does not see the glow of eyes of the animal standing in the road ditch ready to make a crossing. And when the deer leaps across in front of the vehicle, the glare of headlights blinds the animal into helpless confusion.

During the fall rut, the buck preoccupied with the mating urge becomes a helpless victim of the automobile. Any experience the whitetail might get that would impress upon it the danger in a moving vehicle is likely to end in a fatality, and so the animal remains exposed to a danger it has not learned to avoid. The active buck, moving in a larger range now crosses roads without restraint, and his travels bring him into country where he otherwise seldom ventures.

In the fall of 1962, for a two-week period beginning October 10, I noted three mature bucks killed by cars close to the village of Birchwood, Wisconsin, in an area that can be encompassed by a circle one and a half miles in diameter. Two of the bucks were killed within a half mile of the village limits, and all were killed in places where deer are not normally seen during other times of the year. It is obvious that, at least during the rut, deer can be killed by highway traffic in areas where the animals are not plentiful.

The whitetail is selective in its eating if it has a choice, and with a tall, young forest asserting itself at the sacrifice to lesser growth, it will naturally take advantage of the better foraging alongside the highways. Road kills will increase as the automobile traffic increases and as deer will be continually lured to the summer's lush growth along the roadsides. When it becomes apparent that, in time, the automobile will play a major role in keeping our whitetail population in check, we will have to face some unpleasant decisions. At present, the public is not concerned enough to accept drastic measures that would be needed to stop this extravagant waste of our wildlife.

22
The Future

T IS easy enough to get along with the whitetail deer. No other big-game animal of North America thrives so well in its association with civilization. It lives in a wide latitude of country from the primitive forest to farmlands, though it seems more properly to belong to brushy or semi-open country. The whitetail feeds on almost any kind of vegetation available to it. It is extremely prolific, is relatively free of diseases, and it is not demanding in its simple wants. All it asks is reasonable protection in its diverse environments.

No other animal clings so tenaciously to its natural range, though there have been great changes in the ancestral home of the northern species during the past hundred years. And no other large game animal has been so relentlessly persecuted over these years only to persist with meek endurance in a hostile world. The whitetail is truly a boon to the modern hunter. While other game species are succumbing to man's aggression, it appears the conforming whitetail is with us to stay.

We are favored with a good whitetail population today with, perhaps, more of these big-game animals than at any time in the past. There is, however, one harsh fact we must bear in mind. The carrying range of our deer is being pretty well utilized, and we can at best expect no increase in the animal's population. Yet, our hunting force increases yearly and, whether we like to believe it or not, hunting pressure of today is the big controlling factor in our whitetail population.

Legally and illegally killed deer now account for the largest share of deer mortality. Next in line comes the crippling of the animals by gunshot or arrow, much of which is needless, and here the loss is appalling. Automobile casualties are assuming a bigger percentage of the annual kill each year, and in some of our populated states it represents an alarming portion of the total kill of whitetails. It is in these three areas where deer kills can be reduced if their number is to be preserved for continued good hunting in the future.

The day of the hardened game poacher is largely in the past, and the threat to the whitetail here is becoming a negligible factor. The danger of heavy winter concentrations of deer and the resulting complications will be with us as long as there is a whitetail foraging in the deep snows. We can reduce this loss numerically by reducing the deer population, and we can stop it entirely only by exterminating the whitetail here.

A whitetail, whether legally or illegally taken, killed by an automobile, dead of gunshot wounds, or succumbed to a severe winter, is a dead animal. We have some control over all but the last of these, and even here we might feed the animals to alleviate their plight. If we are to conserve the whitetail we will have to do it where we can.

The American public, on the whole, has not attained the stable maturity necessary for evaluating our generous heritage and its proper place in an economy-minded nation. We are still a frontier people seeking new lakes and better hunting grounds, but we find there are none. We will have to do with what we have, but we will have to do it more wisely.

We strongly need to cultivate an aesthetic appreciation of our remaining wilderness — the deep, shaded forest, sedge-filled marshlands, sphagnum moss-carpeted cold bogs, wooded hills, the mountains and the deserts.

Man, pressed on all sides in this world of regimentation, never so needed the tonic of an undisciplined outdoors where the tinkle of a waterfall, the bloom of a desert plant, or the hooting of an owl ease the mind of nagging cares. If we are to rely on fish and game alone to lure us to the wilderness, in time we might become mere highway tourists stopping to make showcase observations of such points of interest efficiently laid out for us. The smell of dew-drenched vegetation, the cheery warmth of the rising sun over an October lake, or the lonely desolateness of a late fall or winter woods will no longer be part of our experiences.

We have now arrived at the point where deer hunting as a sport has come of age, and the filling of the bag becomes not nearly as important as the enjoyable and safe hunt in our great outdoors.

The Hunter's Library

25 Years of Deer & Deer Hunting
The Original Stump Sitters Magazine
edited by Daniel E. Schmidt
For the first time ever, *Deer & Deer Hunting* magazine opens its vaults and presents a comprehensive look at the articles, photographs, and personalities that built North America's first and favorite white-tailed deer hunting magazine. Heart-warming tributes are given to the magazine's founders, and never-before-published articles provide valuable whitetail insights that cannot be found elsewhere.
Hardcover • 8-1/4 x 10-7/8 • 208 pages
10 b&w photos • 150 color photos
Item# DDH25 • $29.95

Quality Deer Management
The Basics and Beyond
by Charles J. Alsheimer
Raise quality deer herds with bigger bucks and larger antlers through quality deer management (QDM). Learn how you can participate through land development, proper harvesting, maintaining good doe-to-buck ratios, and establishing nutritious food sources. Contains tips on land management, good forestry practices, controlling antlerless deer herds, and how to sell QDM to neighboring landowners. Even landowners of small plots can participate.
Hardcover • 8-1/4 x 10-7/8 • 208 pages
200+ color photos
Item# QDMGT • $39.95

Bowhunters' Digest
Advanced Tactics, 5th Edition
edited by Kevin Michalowski
Learn advanced bowhunting tactics from more than twenty top bowhunters including Greg Miller, Bryce Towsley, M.D. Johnson, and Gary Clancy. They'll teach you how to hone your hunting and shooting skills to increase your success. Become familiar with the latest equipment and accessories and find out how to contact archery manufacturers, dealers, and other resources with the state-by-state list.
Softcover • 8-1/2 x 11 • 256 pages
300 b&w photos
Item# BOW5 • $22.95

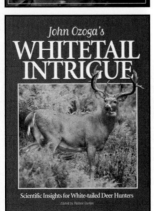

John Ozoga's Whitetail Intrigue
Scientific Insights for White-tailed Deer Hunters
by John Ozoga
Edited by Patrick Durkin
Renowned deer researcher John Ozoga shares his insights into the continent's most popular, adaptive and majestic species of wildlife. Drawing from his popular articles in the science-based *Deer & Deer Hunting* magazine, Ozoga takes deer hunters into the whitetail's society, discussing its social communication, survival in the herd, and the whitetail's future. Illustrated with vivid full-color wildlife photography to help explain the author's fascinating insights.
Hardcover • 8-1/2 x 11 • 208 pages
100 color photos
Item# OZOGA • $34.95

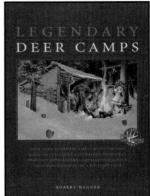

Legendary Deer Camps
by Robert Wegner
Travel back in time to experience deer camps of famous Americans such as William Faulkner, Aldo Leopold and Oliver Hazard Perry. Rediscover classic hunting traditions such as freedom, solitude, camaraderie, rites of initiation, storytelling and venison cuisine through a series of famous deer camp biographies and rare historical paintings and photographs. This is the second book in the *Deer and Deer Hunting Classics Series*.
Hardcover • 8-1/4 x 10-7/8 • 208 pages
125 b&w photos • 75 color photos
Item# DERCP • $34.95

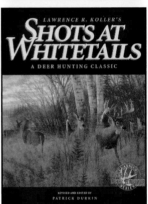

Shots at Whitetails
A Deer Hunting Classic
by Lawrence R. Koller
Revised and Edited by Patrick Durkin
Deer & Deer Hunting reintroduces the hunting classic Shots at Whitetails by legendary Adirondacks deer hunter Larry Koller. While guns and bows have changed since Shots at Whitetails was written in 1948, the deer remains the same elusive, majestic animal, thus keeping this oft-quoted book keenly relevant for today's deer hunters.
Hardcover • 8-1/4 x 10-7/8
314 pages
20 illustrations • 30 color photos
Item# SWTT • $29.95

Whitetail Tracks
by Valerius Geist
Photographs by Michael H. Francis
This fascinating historical perspective on whitetails helps hunters and non hunters alike understand the effect humans have on the evolution of North America's number one big-game animal. You'll understand why hunting is a positive cultural force in shaping whitetail deer management today. Enjoy the stunning whitetail photos of Michael H. Francis while learning why whitetails continue to thrive.
Hardcover • 8-1/4 x 10-7/8 • 176 pages
150 color photos
Item# WHTPF • $34.95

Whitetail Behavior
Through the Seasons
by Charles J. Alsheimer
More than 160 striking action shots reveal a rarely seen side of North America's most impressive game animal. In-the-field observations will help you better understand all aspects of the whitetail deer, from breeding to bedding. Nature lovers and hunters will love this stunning book.
Hardcover • 9 x 11-1/2 • 208 pages
166 color photos
Item# WHIT • $34.95

To order call **800-258-0929** Offer OTB2
M-F 7am - 8pm • Sat 8am - 2pm, CST

Krause Publications, Offer OTB2
P.O. Box 5009, Iola WI 54945-5009 • www.krausebooks.com

Shipping & Handling: $4.00 first book, $2.25 each additional. Non-US addresses $20.95 first book, $5.95 each additional.
Sales Tax: CA, IA, IL, NJ, PA, TN, VA, WI residents please add appropriate sales tax.
Satisfaction Guarantee: If for any reason you are not completely satisfied with your purchase, simply return it within 14 days of receipt and receive a full refund, less shipping charges.

Tips And Tactics From The Experts

Aggressive Whitetail Hunting
by Greg Miller
Answers any hunter's questions on how to hunt trophy bucks in public forests and farmlands, as well as in exclusive hunting lands. It's the perfect approach for gun and bow hunters who don't have the time or finances to hunt exotic locales.
Softcover • 6 x 9 • 208 pages
80 b&w photos
Item# AWH01 • $14.95

Whitetail The Ultimate Challenge
by Charles J. Alsheimer
Here's the key to unlocking deer hunting's most intriguing secrets. Find insights on where and how to hunt whitetails across North America. Plus, Charlie Alsheimer helps you become a better outdoor photographer.
Softcover • 6 x 9 • 223 pages
150 b&w photos
Item# WUC01 • $14.95

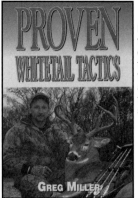

Proven Whitetail Tactics
by Greg Miller
Both entertaining and educational, this volume, from one of America's premier deer hunters, explains effective strategies for scouting, calling and stalking whitetailed deer in the close-to-home locales available to most hunters. Packed with tips and tactics that spell deer hunting success.
Softcover • 6 x 9 • 224 pages
100 b&w photos
Item# AWH02 • $19.95

Rattling, Calling & Decoying Whitetails
How to Consistently Coax Big Bucks into Range
by Gary Clancy
Edited by Patrick Durkin
Deer hunting veteran Gary Clancy explains how deer hunters can coax whitetailed bucks into heart-pounding range with calls, decoys and rattling horns. This book is crammed with anecdotes, diagrams and photos to teach you time-tested decoy techniques to lure bucks out of hiding. Also included is a look at the whitetail's many vocalizations and how you can talk the deer's language. Whether you're a novice or seasoned hunter, you'll quickly grasp Clancy's easy-to-understand hunting techniques.
Softcover • 6 x 9 • 208 pages
100 b&w photos
Item# RCDW • $19.95

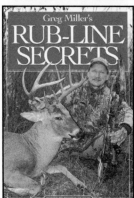

Rub-Line Secrets
by Greg Miller
Edited by Patrick Durkin
In *Rub-Line Secrets*, Greg Miller takes deer hunters to the graduate level in teaching them proven tactics for finding, analyzing and hunting a big buck's rub-line. No one has enjoyed more rub-line success than Miller. His straightforward approach to hunting rub-lines is based on more than 30 years of intense hunting and scouting. The book is illustrated with photos and diagrams that help Miller explain his proven rub-line tactics.
Softcover • 6 x 9 • 208 pages
100 b&w photos
Item# HURU • $19.95

Modern Muzzleloading for Today's Whitetails
by Ian McMurchy
Edited by Patrick Durkin
Muzzleloading expert Ian McMurchy reveals what hunters should seek when buying an in-line rifle, and then offers insights on their use from the shooting range to the deer woods. In-line rifles revolutionized muzzleloader deer hunting in much the same way the compound bow propelled bowhunting into a pastime for the hunting masses. McMurchy also offers detailed advice on developing straight-shooting, hard-hitting loads for deer hunting, and how to discover each gun's long-range
Hardcover • 8-1/4 x 10-7/8 • 208 pages
100 color photos
Item# MODMZ • $34.95

Greg Miller's Greatest Whitetail Adventures
The Stories Behind His Most Memorable Hunts
by Greg Miller
Remember your greatest deer hunt? How about your worst? Join *Deer & Deer Hunting's* Greg Miller as he relives his most memorable white-tailed deer hunting experiences. He'll have you reminiscing about opening morning excitement, buck fever, and other highs and lows you've endured in search of "the big one." Learn great hunting insights and tactics from a veteran hunter as he relates his own experiences.
Softcover • 6 x 9 • 208 pages
100 b&w photos
Item# CLSBH • $19.95

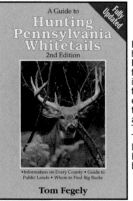

A Guide to Hunting Pennsylvania Whitetails
2nd Edition
by Tom Fegely
If you are one of the 1.2 million deer hunters taking to the woods every fall in Pennsylvania, this fully updated guide is for you. Tom Fegely provides the latest information on a county-by-county basis for every region of the state. Since the first edition appeared in 1994 there have been tremendous changes in deer management and herd dynamics in the Keystone State. This is your chance to stay up-to-date. The book also includes maps showing locations of all state game and forest lands and tips on where to look for the biggest bucks.
Softcover • 6 x 9 • 304 pages
200 b&w photos
Item# PAWT2 • $16.95